The Just
Family

SUNY Series in Social and Political Thought

Kenneth Baynes, Editor

The Just Family

RICHARD DIEN WINFIELD

The State University of New York Press

Published by
State University of New York Press

© 1998 State University of New Y ork

Printed in the United States of America

For information, address the State University of New York Press,
State University Plaza, Albany, NY 12246

Marketing by Fran Keneston
Production by Bernadine Dawes

Library of Congress Cataloging-in-Publication Data

Winfield, Richard Dien, 1950–
       The just family / Richard Dien Winfield.
            p.   cm. — (SUNY series in social and political thought)
       Includes bibliographical references (p.   ) and index.
       ISBN 0-7914-3997-6 (alk. paper). — ISBN 0-7914-3998-4 (pbk. :
alk. paper)
       1. Family. 2. Family—Moral and ethical aspects. 3. Social
values. 4. Social ethics. I. Title. II. Series.
HQ518.W47   1998
306.85—dc21   98-20728
                                                                   CIP

1   2   3   4   5   6   7   8   9   10

For my in-laws,

Kusum and Suresh Gupta

Contents

Preface

The Just Family presents a further step in the reconstruction of ethics whose broad outlines I have developed in *Reason and Justice* (Albany: State University of New York Press, 1988) and the second parts of *Overcoming Foundations: Studies in Systematic Philosophy* (New York: Columbia University Press, 1989) and *Freedom and Modernity* (Albany: State University of New York Press, 1991). *The Just Family* has its immediate sequel in *The Just Economy* (New York: Routledge, 1988) and *Law in Civil Society* (Lawrence: University Press of Kansas, 1995), whose elaborations of the structure of civil society have their own successor in the forthcoming *The Just State*.

Portions of chapters 4 and 5 were written with the support of a Senior Faculty Research Grant from the University of Georgia Research Foundation.

My essay, "Ethical Community Without Communitarianism", which appeared in *Philosophy Today* 40, no. 2 (summer 1996): 94–104, is incorporated with some alterations in chapter 1. Material from my article, "Friendship, Family and Ethical Community," published in *The Philosophical Forum* 28, no. 4/29, no. 1 (fall 1997/winter 1998): 1–20, is incorporated in modified and expanded form in the introduction and chapters 1 through 3.

The Perplexities of Conceiving the Family as a Normative Institution

Hardly any ethical question cuts so near and dear as how the family should be ordered. In times of international and domestic peace, social and political affairs readily hover above daily life as a remote public world where personal involvement has little impact and from which personal destiny can escape unscathed. Yet controversy over family values directly strikes home, invading the private sphere from which no haven can be found.

Far from being an eternal predicament, this accentuated prominence of family matters reflects the ongoing upheavals of modernity. With the accelerating destruction of traditions privileging birth right, gender, race, and other natural[1] distinctions at the expense of self-determination, with the accompanying demarcation of social and political domains,[2] and with the extrication of both civil society and state from kinship relations, the household has won a disengaged existence in which family values can figure as autonomous issues and individuals can enjoy a private sphere that only family affairs immediately address.

Nevertheless, as much as the liberation of economic and political power from household bonds has transformed the family

1

into an association with concerns radically its own, the possibility of rationally judging between competing ideals of household life has remained mired in dispute.

Obstacles to an Independent Family Ethics

The road to an independent family ethics seems barred by the intractable resistance of household relations to any ethical reconstruction. Unlike society or state, the family appears to be directly rooted in biological requirements of sexuality, procreation, and upbringing, making household association a sphere of natural necessity from which the freedom constitutive of ethics seems excluded.[3] For if the family comprises an organ of species being, structured in function of sexual difference, reproduction, and nurturing, family members can hardly be responsible for the fundamental shape of household community. Life in the family becomes an anthropological fate, whose flourishing may be judged in physiological terms of health and disease or by evolutionary criteria of fitness for survival, but not by ethical standards of right and wrong.[4]

The banishing of the family beyond good and evil seems equally inescapable on the rampant psychological view that the household is a crucible of personality formation within which psyches receive their emotive identity and experience either emotional fulfillment or distress. The psychological privileging of the family in personality development may reflect the disengagement of the household from society and state and the resulting isolation of young children from anyone but immediate family members.[5] And granted that this disengagement has some normative privilege, one might surmise that the family can be examined in its own right as the institution where psychic structure figures most decisively.[6] Nevertheless, these moves still leave the family a playing field of psychological mechanisms, in which autonomy figures only as the outcome of proper personality development. Once more, talk of rights and duties fades before issues of health, where now what matters are the therapeutic questions of whether family members adequately promote one another's mental well-being.

Admittedly, the presence of biological and psychological dimensions in family life need not exclude an ethics of the household so long as what distinguish family association are not merely physiological and psychological processes. After all, neither reproductive biology nor personality formation automatically dictate how family members define their interrelations, especially when spouses can forge a domestic life for themselves without indulging in child rearing. Yet granted that household association does not reduce itself to producing and rearing offspring, where might the element lie by which the family warrants norms of its own?

Love seems to be the likely candidate, informing household bonds with a felt unity of adoration and devotion that sets them apart as much from biological and psychological compulsions as from the impersonal ties of other normative spheres. Yet how can love, imbued with feeling and subjective attraction, be a pillar of family right and duty? With all its arbitrariness and transience, can love be a basis for distinguishing an ethical household from romantic attachments, where lovers may be subject to the moral imperatives of intimate friendship, but otherwise escape the rights and duties of belonging to a common home? Love, like physiology and psychology, may well be one element in family life, but can it mandate the norms governing control of family property, provision of care, child rearing, or any other constitutive activity of family affairs?[7] Whether Platonic, romantic, or simply erotic in character, love can hardly define family association if love relations can occur independently of household membership. Indeed, under the banner of freedom of the heart, love can be the ground for abandoning children to public institutions[8] and ignoring every marriage commitment. Like any other factor that can be differentiated from the family, love cannot serve to determine household norms when it leaves unspecified its own relation to the family.

A similar dilemma undermines any attempt to ground a family ethic in functional terms. Determining principles of household conduct by how they serve independently given aims always leaves unanswerable why families should be retained in the first place, as well as what shape the family ought to have. Since the ends for whose sake the family is to be fashioned are defined apart from family association, their fulfillment is always possible by other means, including alternate household arrangements. Moreover, with family organization subjected to external provisos, the norms of family conduct lose their specificity, merging with every other recipe that falls within the general technique of choosing means to achieve the privileged goals to which private life is subordinated. The application of choice theory to the family brings these difficulties to an absurd extreme, where household ties are measured by their maximization of an atomistically defined desire satisfaction. Such a strategy may attract Nobel prizes in economics,[9] but it turns a blind eye to the unity of a shared private domain that comprises the starting and end point of distinctly familial relations.

The Incongruence of Family Ethics with Property Right, Morality, and Politics

No solution is provided by turning to the standard alternatives to functional accounts of conduct: namely, the relations of property right, comprising the sphere of ownership and contract, and those of moral accountability.

The appeal to property right seems attractive, both because modern marriage has come to rest upon the consent of the marriage partners and because notions of fair contract seem to offer standards for reforming family relations in line with prized aspirations of freedom and equality.[10] Might marriage be merely a civil contract since spouses more and more commonly marry by mutual consent? And if so, might background conditions of unequal opportunity for men and women have to be altered in order to allow the formal liberty of mutual consent to be a truly evenhanded agreement, with no one-sided compulsions compromising the free consent of the weaker party?

The example of Kant highlights the anomalies inherent in taking the first step toward reducing family ethics to property right. To fit marriage into the mold of contract, Kant is compelled to argue that spouses mutually consent to the exclusive reciprocal use of one another's body, entering a relation in which persons figure as factors of property, subjecting themselves to treatment as things.[11] Kant intends that individuals thereby limit the use of their sexuality by another through the mutuality of right, so that each party regains its autonomy by appropriating the other who has appropriated it.[12] Nonetheless, these provisions verge upon a mutual enslavement undermining the autonomy necessary for entering into contract since the appropriation of each party's body has no limitation that would leave room for any independent manifestation of the individual's will.[13] Kant cannot refrain from postulating these all-encompassing appropriations since any more restricted contractual language would reduce marriage to a limited enterprise indistinguishable from a mere exchange of particular services. Kant here runs up against the fundamental stumbling block of any attempt to conceive family ethics in terms of property right: the juridical independence underlying contractual relations is precisely what the unity of the family submerges by constituting a common private sphere to which one must first belong in order to enjoy the rights and duties differentiating domestic life from relations among outsiders. To the degree that spouses join into a single unified person, interacting without any intervening terms, the conjugal relation cannot be reduced to the abstract right of contract, which constitutively concerns interaction through disposition over property, that is, factors *external* to persons.[14] Accordingly, when Kant attempts to subsume marriage under contract, he must reduce the relation of spouses to a relation of their external facticity, that is, their bodies. Given the substantial unity of conjugal ties, the contractual relation turns into a total appropriation of each spouse's body by the other party, undermining the juridical independence of the contracting individuals and thereby subverting the entire marriage contract itself.[15]

The hedges of prenuptial agreements and the wrangling over property in divorce proceedings do not contravene this submersion of contractual independence in conjugal union. For if property right enters into household relations at all, it is only in regard to the prospective or ensuing dissolution of the family through divorce or death.[16]

Consequently, when feminists such as Susan Moller Okin[17] prescribe how relations within and without the family should be reformed to enable spouses to marry in genuine conformity with right, they appeal to norms of contractual liberty that cannot lay hold of what is distinctive in family ties.

Any attempt to derive family norms from liberal notions of distributive justice falls into the same dilemma. Distributive justice might seem to have ample scope in family relations, given the incidence of dowries, gifts to kin, inheritance, alimony, and other provisions of mutual aid.[18] Nonetheless, because the procedural justice of social contract thought always privileges the individual liberty and separate self-selected interests of persons,[19] liberal theory cannot coherently acknowledge how membership in a family could confer rights and duties that are irreducible to calculations of self-interest, property entitlements, or applications of a categorical imperative.[20] Indeed, within the family, the very circumstances of justice, as construed by liberal theory, have been supplanted.[21] As Hume and Rousseau already recognized, with "all distinction of property . . . in a great measure lost and confounded"[22] in the trust, affection, and unity of ends distinguishing family association, the independence and opposition of individual interests is already preempted without the intervention of social contract and civil government.[23] Yet although liberal thinkers like Hume and Rousseau may conclude that the family makes standards of civil justice irrelevant by already realizing the harmony of aims, they ignore how the family involves interests and goods qualitatively distinct from those that can enter into the atomistic considerations of any utilitarian calculus or social contract.

Admittedly, family members remain discrete persons with distinct goals and ambitions that may well conflict. Yet, this does not reduce their mutual rights and duties to those that apply between members of society who do not belong to the same family.[24] The love and intimacy of family relations are not liable to redistribution on the same terms as property or any other "primary goods" that provide the resources for realizing any permissible choice. What removes family ties from common disposal is that they rest upon a unity of obligatory favoritism drawing a sharp divide between family members and outsiders.[25] For this reason, it makes little sense to adopt the program suggested by Okin of conceiving the just family by determining what persons under a veil of ignorance would agree to concerning domestic organization.[26] The embrace of liberty and rational self-interest underlying procedural justice simply provides no compelling rationale for instituting families in the first place, especially when family ties introduce parochial attachments undermining any patterned distribution to individuals.[27] And if this whole issue be dodged by embracing "reflective equilibrium," which restricts ethics to providing a coherent apology for our given moral intuitions and practices, one can always question why these dogmas and conventions should be sanctified, particularly when reflective equilibrium can never justify any exclusive claim upon reason, given its own capitulation to prevailing belief.[28]

Nor can the framework of distributive justice be applied to the household by treating the family as though it could be reduced to a mini-welfare state, following Walzer's errant suggestion.[29] Far from guaranteeing one another the external resources for equal economic opportunity as separate players in the market, family members rather are obliged to ensure one another's well-being as sharers in the exclusive privacy of the household.[30] Therefore, it is hardly surprising that liberal theorists like John Rawls[31] and James Fishkin[32] suspect that the family poses an insurmountable impediment to distributive justice, engendering an insoluble trilemma where fair competition and equal opportunity cannot be upheld if the autonomy of the family is simultaneously respected.[33]

To the degree that family members have special ties to one another, morality[34] is no more amenable a resource than contract for providing ethical sanction to distinctively domestic relations. Because moral subjects hold one another responsible exclusively for those aspects of their deeds prefigured by their personal choice of conscientious purpose and intention, the rights and duties of moral accountability extend to all agents, irrespective of their membership in any existing associations. Whether moral agents embrace a utilitarian concern for the equal considerability of the welfare of everyone or a deontological concern for the lawfulness of intentions, conscience extends across every institutional boundary, laying hold of individuals simply in their capacity as agents responsible for acting with the right purpose and intention. Accordingly, morality is blind to kinship distinctions, obliging agents to attend just as dutifully to the right and welfare of strangers as to that of fellow family members. From an exclusively moral point of view, a family ethic is just as unimaginable as a political ethic that differentiates between what rights and duties citizens share and what rights and duties apply between citizens and noncitizens.[35]

Yet if the particular boundary of the family makes its ethical standing problematic for those who model normativity after property right and morality, a parallel dilemma faces those who conceive of a good life as coextensive with the political life of the citizen in the best state. For, as Plato recognized, if conduct has its exclusive worth in contributing to the common good enshrined in the body politic, then families are dispensable evils in virtue of the divisive, parochial loyalties they foster. This dispensability of the family holds even if politics is modeled after household relations of paternalism.[36] Then the very identification of family and state raises the issue of why paternalistic rulers need maintain particular families among their subjects.

Similar difficulties arise if the alleged dichotomy between public and private realms is denied with the claim that the personal *is* political. Some feminists have argued that political norms should be applied to the family since 1) power is central in family life, 2) political decisions determine the very boundaries of the domestic sphere, 3) the family is where individuals become gendered, with vital implications for political involvement, and 4) the division of labor within gender-structured families prevents women from fully participating in the public sphere.[37] All these points have their truth, yet none call into question the divide between domestic and political spheres, nor render family relations political in character. Power, in the abstract, enters into any structure of interaction in which roles are differentiated, yet power is distinctly political only when it determines the entire structure of the body politic and engages in governing, as opposed to managing households or enterprises.[38] For this very reason, every nonpolitical institution has its boundary confirmed by political decision. Yet this does not mean that property relations, the family, the economy, or court systems are themselves political institutions engaging in the ruling activity that orders its own sphere of politics while presiding over prepolitical domains. Conversely, that different arrangements of the family, as well as other prepolitical institutions, can affect the political opportunities of individuals does not mean that these institutions are themselves organs of political activity. Rather, it reflects how prepolitical institutions serve as preconditions of political community. Accordingly, the interrelation of prepolitical and political spheres only confirms the distinction between them, a distinction that nevertheless indicates how they are not indifferent toward one another.

Treating the family in terms of a private/public dichotomy obscures this interrelationship by reverting to the paradigm of ancient Greek thought, which tends to ignore the social sphere by absorbing economic activity into the household and distinguishing the family solely from the political arena of the polis, to which the public domain is reduced. This reduction takes its extreme form when the family is identified with personal privacy, as if the household left individuals captive in the singularity of their own experience, something Hannah Arendt suggests in claiming that mass society leaves everyone in the isolation of being members of one family.[39] The dichotomy of private and public would better be reconceived as a trichotomy of family, society, and state, both to correspond to the modern conditions that feminism critiques and to keep straight the different forms of community.

The Specter of Relativism and Nihilism Haunting Family Ethics

Whether privileging property right, morality, "economic rationality," or politics, prevailing ethical theories leave no room for conferring any independent worth upon the family. Either ethical conduct is incongruent with the particular, substantial ties of domestic life or it enters into family affairs only in those recesses that involve norms given independently of household bonds. In the latter case, where, for instance, property relations intervene or the domestic servitude of some family members enables privileged others to participate in public affairs,[40] the possibility of a distinct family ethic remains in doubt.

This lingering theoretical uncertainty might seem to fly against modern developments that have disengaged the family from economic and political affairs by replacing household autarchy and hereditary occupations with market relations operating independently of kinship, by instituting social welfare institutions diminishing the role of household care and inheritance as bulwarks of livelihood, and by erecting states in which political power is shielded from birthright and nepotism. No longer can marriage retain its laurels as a political alliance or economic transaction, nor can family life figure as an essential fixture of rule or production.

Yet these same modern developments have been accompanied by other transformations of family organization that have called into question what if any norms pertain to relations between spouses and between parents and children. With the increasing prevalence of no-fault divorce on demand, the spread of prenuptial agreements limiting common household property, and the growing legal recognition of unwed couples of any gender and sexual orientation, the very significance of marriage has been cast in doubt. Similarly, the resulting increase in single parent households, in public day care of children of all ages, in premarital sexual activity, and in the intervention of courts and welfare bureaucracies on upbringing, have all raised questions about what parent-child relations should be. And the very rationale for the family has become clouded with the growing proliferation of single persons, be they adult children living on their own, women postponing or avoiding marriage and child rearing to pursue educational and career opportunities, self-sufficient widowed "senior citizens," or any others for whom available housing, economic independence, and social welfare guarantees make life without kinship a secure and untarnished option.[41]

In face of this shifting ground, can a family ethic be redeemed by following recent communitarian gropings toward identifying some independent human good that household community realizes in distinction both from political virtue and from the claims of unencumbered autonomous selves? If this good is defined, following Aristotle, by appeal to human nature, skepticism can always challenge both what content such an essence contains, as well as why a given nature from which convention can deviate should dictate how conduct and institutions ought to be determined. Aristotle's own attempt to define the relevant human nature in terms of reason and rational willing only returns us to the starting point of ethics, which, after all, employs reason to determine what conduct and institutions are rationally justified. The outcome is no better if the content of the particular good that family life realizes is culled from some historical tradition, for doubt can always be raised as to why that or any tradition should be entrusted to dictate how the family ought to be structured.[42]

If the natural and psychological dimensions of the family resist ethical incorporation, if the most popular ethical theories find no place for family values, if appeals to human nature and tradition are suspect, and if the boundaries of the modern family themselves appear in flux, can a family ethic be established at all?

Are norms of family organization merely cultural conventions, defying rational justification and undeserving of any hegemonic ranking and regulation? Certainly the diversity of the historical record and the annals of modern anthropology testify to the absence of any natural convergence in the relations among spouses or those between parents and children. Yet does the fact of a cornucopia of alternate household conventions deprive reason of the ability to mandate universally valid norms of family conduct? Must we admit that no particular family arrangement is "theoretically required or even generally preferable,"[43] as thinkers such as Michael Walzer would have us believe? Are family values to succumb to the juggernaut of nihilism?

Multiculturalism and Family Values

The multicultural bandwagon might appear to support an unconstrained pluralism in family practices, especially if toleration of cultural diversity gets tied to the postmodern dogma that reason and conduct are always hostage to historically given practices, so that any attempt at justifying knowledge claims and ethical norms must always appeal to privileged concepts and vocabularies reflecting interests, power formations, or other pragmatic concerns. Why not accept the coexistence of alternate family regimes, each representing the values of a particular culture or subculture, each obtaining legal sanction with a separate family law having exclusive jurisdiction for members of its group? As long as members of each community abide by the consensus distinguishing their particular culture, conflict need not arise, at least until families themselves become multicultural cauldrons, with intermarriage between communities. And in such cases, could not spouses agree among themselves to accept one or the other family system and put an end to an otherwise unresolvable dispute?[44]

Yet can multiculturalism signify a blanket toleration of all cultural practices, including all family forms? The postmodern argument for multicultural pluralism tends to vitiate itself. Because too few cultures practice toleration, any implementation of multiculturalism becomes a contradictory enterprise, where respecting unreconstructed, intolerant cultures entails the oppression of their counterparts. Further, when postmodernism makes global claims about the foundation-ridden character of discourse and conduct, it relies upon reason to discredit rational justification, subverting the authority of its own diagnosis.

If multiculturalism is to have any coherent justification or implementation, it must instead signify a modern, rather than postmodern toleration. Although modern times have witnessed a continuing contest between traditional, modern, and postmodern movements, modernity distinguishes itself from all premodern, let alone postmodern civilization by recognizing that autonomy should reign supreme in theory and practice, that all custom and tradition must conform to reason if they are to have binding authority, and that the rationality of conduct and institutions resides in the realization of self-determination. Whereas premodern civilization accepts the authority of given tradition independently of reason and autonomy, postmodernity presumes that thought and conduct can never attain genuine independence, that both are conditioned by given conventions, and that all knowledge claims and values are relative to the historically contingent cognitive and practical foundations on which they rest. Although the closet liberals of postmodernity wish that democracy and toleration follow from the perspectival, conditional status they ascribe to all norms,[45] the postmodernist deconstruction of knowing and conduct fosters the opposite extreme of affirming a will to power, in which the universal claims of truth and value are unmasked as hegemonic assertions of irreducibly particular interests that might as well be advanced for what they are. For if the norms of all theory and practice are exposed as expressions of unjustifiable particular standpoints, democracy and toleration are themselves vehicles by which one standpoint achieves supremacy under the veil of universal right.

A more consistent path lies in openly imposing one's values as nothing but a power play for subjecting others to one's own wholly particular standards. Yet, whether ushering in democratic toleration or fascist tyranny, postmodern thought's acceptance of the conditioned character of reason and action renders inexplicable the authority of its own position, leaving the project of modernity ultimately untarnished.[46] That project departs from premodern tradition and postmodern irony alike by allowing for toleration in conformity with self-determination, a conformity requiring that property relations, moral accountability, household affairs, society, and the state all be liberated from bondage to cultural differences, so that ethnic, linguistic, and religious identity have no more role in restricting the opportunities of individuals in their family, social, or political involvements than birth, race, gender, or sexual orientation. If multiculturalism signifies this liberation of all spheres of life from discrimination that privileges factors given independently of freedom, then the toleration of cultural difference extends only so far as those cultural conventions abide by the rights of individuals. With respect to the family, cultural diversity would then permissibly extend only to practices that do not conflict with the rights and duties specific to the household.

Upholding this modern agenda requires, first, justifying the exclusive normativity of self-determination, and then, second, establishing what the family must be to comprise an institution of freedom, congruent with the other spheres of right.

The travails of liberal theory exhibit the difficulties of achieving either task. Justifying the legitimacy of freedom remains a futile endeavor as long as appeal is made to prior factors, such as the internal collapse of teleological ethics, facts of nature or self-interest. Hobbes may well have been correct in denying the possibility of identifying a highest good as the ultimate arbiter of conduct, yet reason's inability to prescribe an immediately binding end just as readily allows for a nihilism that grants liberty no more privilege than bondage to any arbitrary norm. Anthropological facts of relative human equality are as devoid of immediate prescriptive authority as any calculations of self-interest, for in each case, the exclusive warrant of these factors is itself in need of justification.

All such attempts to ground freedom run up against the dilemma undermining foundational argument in general: by distinguishing what confers legitimacy from what possesses legitimacy, foundationalism ensures that the factor begetting validity can never exhibit what counts as validity. The moment something is privileged as the prior condition determining what counts as valid, that legitimating factor fails to meet its own standard of legitimation. By being a foundation from which normativity issues, the privileged factor has a content given prior to the derivation of valid knowledge or conduct. Hence, the privileged factor cannot derive its own content from the derivation by which validity is established. To achieve the needed identity between legitimating factor and legitimated content, the foundation would have to determine itself. Yet, in so doing, it would cease to be a prior ground of derivative terms. Instead, the foundation would eliminate itself as such, giving way to something self-determined. In other words, once foundationalism becomes self-critical and attempts to be internally consistent, it collapses into freedom, which allows for no distinction between legitimating factor and legitimated content.

Freedom and Family Ethics

Freedom is immune to foundationalism's insoluble problem of justification because self-determination comprises something that cannot owe its character to anything but itself. Escaping all juridical dependence[47] upon antecedent givens, self-determination can command an unparalleled legitimacy residing in the two complementary sides of its freedom from foundations: on the one hand, the negative liberation from the given, whereby what is specific to freedom is undetermined by any prior factors, and, on the other hand, the positive autonomy wherein self-determination gives itself its own character precisely by being what it determines itself to be. Unlike any foundationally justified practice, self-determination is therefore, normatively speaking, presuppositionless and self-grounding, eliminating the gap between justifying factor and justified conduct.

Accordingly, if self-determination is to be properly conceived, it cannot be thought in liberal fashion as a given principle determining something other than itself, where the form of autonomy is given either by nature as the capacity of choice underlying all conduct or by abstraction as a privileged choice procedure from which legitimate institutions are derived. In both cases, freedom's own character would be defined antecedently to all acts of will, whereas whatever conduct its principle would sanction would equally owe its determination to a privileged factor. Hence, neither freedom as principle nor its derivative domain of conduct would be self-determined. In order for self-determination to give itself its own character, the very agency of freedom must issue from its willing just as much as the content of what it wills. Then, the form and content of autonomous agency will be products of free willing, engendering an artificial agency enabling conduct to figure as the self-determination of self-determined agency.

For conduct to succeed in defining its own agency and thereby achieve genuine self-determination, individuals must act in regard to the volition of one another, engaging in conventional practices within which they can first exercise types of freedom comprising those enabling practices themselves. By willing one's relation to others so as to allow them to will their relation to other agents as well, one can individuate one's own agency through one's willing, as one among other self-determined individuals.

Such artificial agency is at work in every exercise of rights, since rights, in contrast to privileges, can only be enjoyed by participating in a framework within which all other participants in principle respect each other's entitled freedoms by willing in conformity with one another. In such a context of interrelated conduct, individuals are able to determine themselves as holders of the rights involved, for example, as property owners, moral subjects, market agents, legal subjects, or citizens, by observing the rights and duties whose performance comprises the enabling context in question.

If one instead restricts oneself to acting upon external things or one's own body, one can never generate an artificial agency individuated through the will's own activity. Technical or monological action always remains within the orbit of the formal, natural liberty that employs a capacity of choice presupposed but never determined by the individual's isolated volition. The isolated agent may indeed exercise a "second order desire," capable of deciding among desires given to the individual. Yet this power of choice neither determines the content of the ends among which the agent is at liberty to choose, nor the formal capacity it itself exercises. In both respects such monological willing remains bound to givens—the given contents of desire and the given form of the capacity to choose. The monological, technical capacity of choice can thereby rightly be called the natural will since its form is not artificial, issuing from acts of volition, but rather the given precondition of them all. Yet it would be a mistake, both theoretically and practically, to accept the liberal credo, underlying so much contemporary philosophy of action,[48] that freedom is defined by the natural will.

For when individuals interact in respect of one another's willing, they are able to occupy a nonnatural, conventional role exercising an intersubjectively recognized freedom defined by the reciprocally connected volitions that build their conventional practice and individuate them as participants. Although each participant is able to exercise the artificial agency at play thanks to the correlative participation of others, this dependence is a constituent of, rather than a restriction upon, the realization of the specific freedom each agent exercises in their interaction. If instead one participant dominated another, the agents could not individuate themselves as particular exemplars of a freedom brought into being in their interaction. The dominating agent would fall back into the unilateral volition characteristic of the technical domination of things, whose form always precedes its exercise.

Far from being a natural given or a function of the self, self-determination must thus consist in modes of interaction where each participant's exercise of freedom involves respecting the like exercise of freedom by others, who equally determine themselves in recognition of the congruent autonomy of their peers. In the ensuing web of right and duty, freedom will not stand apart from institutions of justice as their prior principle. Rather, self-determination will itself comprise a system of institutions of freedom whose artificial agencies will inhabit different spheres of right, each involving its own distinctive entitled prerogatives, yet integrating with one another into a single self-ordered whole. The very normativity of freedom requires such an integration, for otherwise different freedoms would limit one another for the sake of some ground external to self-determination and the spheres of right would find themselves connected by an order imposed upon them all, rendering them dependent rather than free.

If the family can be structured as one such integrated sphere of right, wherein individuals exercise rights and duties as autonomous family members that are nowhere else available, the possibility of a discrete family ethic will be secured. This ethic will consist in realizing those entitled freedoms by which spouses, parents, and children engage in household roles affording them a mode of self-determination otherwise unattainable. Only then will a domain of family values be established free of the pitfalls of foundationalism that have subverted other strategies for upholding the normativity of household relations.

Yet, how must ties between spouses, parents and children, siblings or other kin be configured for the family to comprise an institution of freedom with its own nonarbitrary rights and duties? Although property entitlements and moral accountability may consist in forms of interaction where individuals determine themselves as owners and conscientious agents, neither provide modes of self-determination encompassing anything resembling the particular unity of the household. As liberal theory's difficulty treating the family reflects, the inclusive partiality of family ties escapes the externality of property relations and the universality of moral concern.

If the normativity of the family is to be secured by conceiving a distinct sphere of household freedom, the frameworks of property and moral relations must be left behind, together with the ethical theories that have privileged them. Instead a structure of freedom must be found that can accommodate a mode of self-determination in which agents determine themselves as members of a joint private domain with its own characteristic good and corresponding rights and duties. The prime resource for providing such a framework is ethical community, which has increasingly become a focus of attention more for accommodating social and political freedom than for encompassing family self-determination. Yet ethical community cannot be immediately appropriated for developing the normativity of the household. Current conceptions of ethical community are so plagued by distortions and incoherences that these missteps must first be exposed to clear the terrain for rethinking family values.

The following work endeavors to determine what the family should be by rehabilitating the concept of ethical community as the proper framework for systematically conceiving family ethics. Although justice has been given many senses in the tradition, the normativity of self-determination signifies that giving individuals their due amounts to realizing their rights in all the spheres of freedom. Conceiving the just family will accordingly involve establishing that normatively valid family relations consist in a distinct mode of self-determination, whose autonomy serves as a precondition for social and political freedom, while requiring a free society and a democratic government to maintain itself. The resulting concept of the just family will provide the standard by which all debate over family values should be decided.

CHAPTER I

Ethical Community as the Framework for Family Ethics

The Rationale for the Renewed Turn to Ethical Community

In both theory and practice, controversy over framing conduct and institutions has increasingly revolved around the idea of ethical community. Advanced more and more frequently under the banner of "communitarianism," this idea has cast an alluring spell. However vaguely it be drawn, ethical community is widely entertained as a practical panacea to the alienations and anomies of modern life, where instrumental rationality and atomistic self-interest have allegedly supplanted tradition without supplying any new bonds of intrinsic worth. And just as commonly, the concept of ethical community is appealed to as a remedy to the complementary dilemmas of the two leading competitors in contemporary ethical theory, teleological and procedural ethics. On both fronts, a turn to ethical community has taken center stage. If this turn sometimes has a nostalgic air, yearning for the faded spirit of ancient assemblies, town meetings, and village commons, it equally reflects the perennial character of the underlying issues, as much in dispute when Plato and Aristotle argued for the polis in opposition to the natural ties of tribal association and the instrumental association of social contract, as when Hegel defended the ethical life of family, civil society, and state against the advocates of restoration and the contractarians of his day. Although we can take advantage of the experience of past ages that have grappled with ethical community in theory and practice, the worth of their achievements can only be known by first certifying the valid content of ethical community and the place it should command in the conception and reality of conduct. If instead particular forms or general ideals of ethical community are examined solely in respect to their internal coherence or historical success, the de jure question of what normativity ethical community possesses will remain unanswered.

The current rehabilitation of ethical community, comprising the communitarian turn in ethics, has its own lessons for reconstructing theory and practice provided one rethinks its formulations with the same critical autonomy that needs to be applied to every earlier experience. Above all, what the communitarian turn uncovers of the inherent logic of ethical community must be distinguished from what it ignores and perverts.

To its credit, the communitarian appeal to ethical community is grounded in an understanding of the complementary limitations of teleological and procedural ethics. Admittedly, teleological ethics adopts a plausible strategy by seeking the legitimacy of conduct in the given nature of its ends, transforming ethics into a science of a highest good. Since all conduct is purposive, assessing the value of actions and institutions readily seems to depend upon ranking the worth of their ends and overcoming a paralyzing disunity of aims by locating one goal to which all others are subordinate. Every candidate for a highest good, however, ultimately succumbs to the skeptical doubt that its particular content is devoid of universal validity: Since any putative ultimate end, be it happiness or human perfection, cannot retain its normative primacy if any other factor grounds its archimedean role, its authority must reside in its own immediate givenness. Yet every particular content can be ascribed an immediate givenness, especially when no higher tribunal can be relied upon without undermining the primacy of the end it is intended to sanction. Indirect proof offers no salvation, since any attempt to show that no other ends can possess value without contributing to the putative highest good still leaves open the possibility that the ends of action are not what make conduct and institutions valid. Hence, teleological ethics remains caught in the bind of rooting conduct in a particular content, whose universality remains doubtful.

By contrast, procedural ethics falls into precisely the inverse dilemma. Abandoning any attempt to found normativity in privileged ends, procedural ethics instead appeals to a privileged form of willing, involving a principle that determines conduct independently of any particular end.[1] Right hereby precedes the good, insofar as what makes conduct valid is conformity to an antecedently prescribed formal requirement that first allows an end to qualify as good. Yet, because the privileged form of willing is prior to all particular ends and actual conduct requires that something particular be willed, this content must derive from some other source. But no further law can mandate how to decide which extraneous end should be chosen as the goal of action in conformity with the privileged procedure since the procedure has exclusive normative primacy. Whatever end is willed thus enters in arbitrarily as far as the privileged procedure is concerned. For just this reason, procedural ethics is haunted by the specter of formalism, according to which its formal principle of willing cannot mandate any particular end and determine actual conduct unless some privileged good is surreptitiously introduced. As a consequence, no achieved goal can be certifiably right, as such, leaving the ethical an unrealizable ought to be and the agent trapped in an interminable struggle to act in independence of given ends without benefit of any unequivocally sanctioned alternative. Hence, whereas teleological ethics stamps conduct with a particularity lacking universality, procedural ethics leaves conduct governed by a universal law devoid of any intrinsic particular content.

On both sides, the root of failure has a common logical form: an inability to unite the particular and universal dimensions of conduct. Accordingly, overcoming the limits of each side involves a common solution: somehow arriving at a form of willing whose universality is concrete, possessing a lawfulness that specifies particular ends of its own, or, to put it inversely, involving action in pursuit of particular ends that intrinsically enjoy a common legitimacy.

It is just such a solution that the communitarian turn purports to find in its idea of ethical community. Defined in function of the remedy it is to provide, ethical community is here conceived as an association in recognition and pursuit of shared values, where membership involves fulfilling a role carrying with it the obligation of consciously reproducing the bonds of community that comprise the very association in which that role can alone be performed. On this basis, each member is able to pursue particular aims that are automatically shared in common by all other individuals who duly fulfill the roles defined by their membership in the community. Alternately, what is recognized by all individuals as a condition for belonging to and participating in the community is a common good that contains within itself the activities that realize it. That is, the structure of the community is itself what all participants realize in reaching the aim of their role, just as their activity is nothing but a constituent element of the association they perennially seek to sustain in fulfilling their station.

This intrinsic connection between the agency of membership and the unity of the community overcomes the one-sidedness of teleological ethics insofar as the particular ends that are sought in occupying one's station are inherently universal with respect to the community. Indeed, their conformity with the ends of every other member consists in nothing other than the reproduction of the unity of the community, which exists in nothing but their congruent activity.

On the other hand, the limits of procedural ethics are equally overcome in that the universality of conduct consists in acting in conformity to actual roles that presuppose and reproduce the very good that they seek to realize. What ought to be is no longer an unreachable beyond, but rather a form of community that must already be at hand in order to make possible engagement in the very roles that aim at its reproduction. Accordingly, agents are no longer caught in the dilemma of choosing between arbitrary goals and conformity to an empty lawfulness, where morality is an endless striving, always falling short of the fulfillment of duty. Instead, members of the community actually achieve ethical virtue by fulfilling their role, whose fulfillment is the very life of the community to which they belong.

The Fatal Limits of the Communitarian Turn

From F. H. Bradley through such current figures as Alasdair MacIntyre, Michael Sandel, Charles Taylor, and Michael Walzer,[2] the proponents of the communitarian turn have left the idea of ethical community with little further content, with the result that they have committed themselves to two fateful qualifications that ultimately undermine the solution they seek: 1) that ethical community is the exclusive structure of normative conduct, and 2) that the concept of ethical community does not itself mandate the particular content of the roles, ends, and association that it may take.

These qualifications of the idea of ethical community reflect an embrace of the type of thinking underlying Wittgenstein's private language argument.[3] That argument took the inability to find resources in the structure of consciousness for distinguishing between certainty and truth, or between subjective stipulation and objective validity, as indicative of how objectivity must be sought in given intersubjective conventions whose shared practices provide standards of justification that can be distinguished from merely subjective belief. Such conventions, however, cannot themselves be susceptible of any justification, since that would require appeal to some other measure of "objectivity," which is impossible if shared practices are the exclusive source of normativity. Accordingly, the intersubjective conventions that provide nonsubjective meanings and knowledge are themselves contingent, ungrounded practices, with the same arbitrary lawfulness as games.[4] Similarly seeking to overcome the limits of appealing to "the given" or to the form of individual willing as sources of normativity, communitarians have turned to ethical community as a historically contingent structure of shared practices with the same arbitrary content and the same exclusive norm-sustaining role as the language games to which Wittgensteinians turn as the locus of meaning and truth.

Thereby, on the one hand, communitarians absolutize ethical community, identifying all normative conduct with the activities ingredient in ethical community. Rendering the domain of ethics coextensive with the roles animating ethical association, this absolutization excludes any morality without community as well as any property entitlements that might be given independently of the distributive prerogatives enjoyed through membership in such putative ethical institutions as the family, the market, and the state. Such denial of any normative action existing apart from ethical community rests upon the assumption that the only alternative is an atomistic ethic, grounding conduct in the acts of the self upon itself or upon external things and succumbing to the same pitfalls that undermine teleological and procedural theories. That there might be other forms of interaction involving rights and duties given independently of membership in some existing community is simply not considered.

Complementing this absolutization is a commitment to the formality of the concept of ethical community. At the same time that ethical community is advanced as the exclusive framework of normative conduct, the idea of that framework is held to leave undetermined what particular institutional configurations and correlative roles and aims it may involve. Since these details are not contained in the concept of ethical community, they are beyond a priori prescription. Instead, they must be left to the grasp of a historical understanding that describes the contingent conventions of history that alone provide content to the otherwise empty scaffold of the idea of ethical community.

This formality is of crucial significance for it directly resurrects the very same problems that the appeal to ethical community is designed to overcome. Just as teleological ethics can not demonstrate the universality of its particular candidate for the good, so communitarianism here renders the content enshrined in ethical community an arbitrary and transient phantom of history. And just as procedural ethics cannot tie the universal form of willing that it privileged to any particular ends without falling back upon teleological appeals, so communitarianism has ended up leaving the universal idea of ethical community powerless to specify any particular institutions to concretize its unity. Although each putative ethical community may well comprise an institutional system reproduced by the roles its members constitutively perform, the historical contingency of its content renders its universality something wholly relative to the particular conditions of its existence. Far from being genuinely universal, the specific content of institutions and agency is only common to a particular, contingently given community, whose own existence is devoid of any further justification. Hence, it makes no sense to judge one community by the values of another. Moreover, the legitimacy of no community can be upheld from within, for all that any can lay claim to is the accidental fact of its own existence. Any successful transformation of one regime into another institutional order will thus have no more and no less rationale than the preservation of the status quo. Whatever community results will possess the same purely internal validity, whose fortuitous foundation makes its authority an arbitrary fate, which its members have no more reason to flee than to embrace. Although the roles they assume carry with them duties tied to the reproduction of the community to which they belong, once that membership be questioned, no ethical imperative remains. In effect, the communitarian turn offers little more than an injunction to occupy one's station. This might satisfy an Eichmann, but it otherwise reflects a formality in the idea of ethical community that rivals that of any categorical imperative.

No remedy is to be found by appealing to historical necessity and claiming that, although no ethical community is universal, each particular shape arises in a necessary sequence, leaving it the exclusive ethical option for its time. This gambit, offered by F. H. Bradley[5] and commonly misattributed to Hegel,[6] only further weakens the ethical claims of communitarianism. To begin with, upholding the claim of any necessity in historical development is problematic enough. No empirical study of history can establish necessity, since not only is the accuracy, representative character, and trustworthiness of all historical testimony subject to doubt, but all any study of historical fact can confirm are particular patterns of association in what happened to have been observed. Alternately, any attempt to conceive a priori some necessary development in history is at pains to maintain the difference between history and nature upon which reference to anything historical depends. Once the willful caprice of convention drops out of consideration, cultural development hardly becomes distinguishable from a natural evolution. Yet even if historical necessity be granted, it can provide no remedy to the formalism afflicting the communitarian turn. For if the content of every ethical community is not only particular to a historical period, but a necessary product of historical development, how can the activities of its members possess the basic autonomy on which ethical responsibility depends? Far from being a regime in which duties and virtues have their life, ethical community would become a prisoner of necessity, resembling more the instinctual society of social insects than an association in recognition of any good. Instead of obtaining normative validity, a historically necessitated ethical community would be removed from the sphere of ethics and take its place as one more background condition beyond which the domain of right and wrong begins.

Liberating Ethical Community from Its Communitarian Deformation

If the concept of ethical community is to provide a solution to the dilemmas plaguing contemporary ethics and serve as a guide to reconstructing modern institutions including the family, the two defining dogmas of the communitarian turn must be supplanted. For this to be achieved, the concept of ethical community must undergo a dual transformation.

On the one hand, ethical community can no longer be conceived as a formal framework, whose content is relegated to historical accident. Instead, ethical community must obtain a universally valid content, bringing necessary concreteness to its concept. As the experience of teleological and procedural ethics testifies, such normative content cannot be supplied by appeal to privileged givens masquerading as highest goods or by recourse to privileged forms of willing posing as archimedean procedures of ethical construction. In both cases, factors are immediately advanced as sources of normativity that cannot be legitimated in accord with the very standard of legitimacy that they impose. So long as what is justified is different from what supplies justification, the justifying element cannot possess the character of being justified that it confers upon what derives justification from it. Whether the legitimating standard be a privileged given content or a privileged determiner of sanctioned ends and institutions, the abiding distinction between legitimated conduct and legitimating factor, a distinction generic to foundational justification, introduces this debilitating incoherence.

What alone eliminates the distinction and the foundational dilemma it reflects is the identification of normativity with the reality of self-determination. This identification is implicit in the internal dilemma of foundationalism in that what confers legitimacy can possess legitimacy only if it loses its distinction from what it legitimates and serves as its own standard. In that case, what is justified and what justifies become one and the same, enabling the erstwhile foundation to meet its own normative requirements by grounding itself and thereby ceasing to be the determiner of something other than itself, of something determined from without. By finally satisfying its own standard of normativity, the foundation cancels itself as a foundation, rendering self-determined bestower and bearer of validity alike. Through this self-elimination of foundationalism, freedom emerges as the very being of normativity. No other alternative is possible, for what is not self-determined is determined by something else, reinstating the situation of foundationalism, whose own internal demands can only be met by removing the ground-grounded distinction and reverting to self-determination.

Far from being relative to the historical contingencies of Western culture, self-determination commands an unqualified validity. Unlike any other shape of conduct, self-determination owes its measure to nothing but itself, overcoming the gap between legitimating factor and legitimated conduct that fatally haunts foundational justification, to which postmodernism dogmatically limits rationality and ethics.[7] Because reason and action need not be conditioned by foundations, we are not condemned to exercises of ideology critique or reflective equilibrium, unmasking the privileged vocabularies allegedly underlying our values and becoming self-conscious of how we can accommodate our given historical conventions in a consistent manner. The autonomy of reason and action provides the remedy to these misadventures in pragmatism: because self-determination alone escapes dependence upon extrinsic foundations, it enjoys the self-grounding, presuppositionless character that normativity ultimately requires.[8]

If ethical community is to escape the relativity of an externally conditioned content and take its place as a genuinely ethical structure, it must therefore be reconceived as an association of freedom, whose agencies, ends, and institutions are defined by nothing other than their role as constituents in the reality of self-determination.

This does not signify that a normatively valid ethical community must somehow escape having natural preconditions altogether. Like any form of conduct and association, ethical community must share the natural features that underlie the existence of a plurality of agents. Yet these prerequisites, comprising the physical, astronomical, chemical, biological, and psychological conditions without which rational agents cannot interact at all, do not thereby prescribe what shape ethical community should have. Precisely because these natural conditions are the enabling prerequisites of all conduct, they cannot serve as principles for differentiating between the good and bad conduct that they equally make possible. Hence, the presence of such enabling factors in no way undercuts the *normative* independence of a community whose bonds consist in modes of freedom.

By contrast, any community whose roles, ends, and institutions are instead allowed to be prescribed by factors given independently of freedom will at best comprise a "natural" ethical community, with a tainted validity. Although the members of such a community, like the ancient polis or the patriarchal household, perform roles in recognition of a common good that they reproduce as the existing framework of their activity, their stations reflect structures of domination, where hereditary rank, gender, race, cultural traditions, and other heteronomous factors constrict autonomy. This is the terrain of tragedy, for the given particularity of natural ethical community precludes any preestablished harmony between the competing obligations of other associations within the same body politic or between the aims of different "naturally" defined nations. Chance may provide a fleeting respite of compatible norms, but the fate of historical convention may just as readily impose conflicting duties for which no peaceful resolution is possible, except for the capitulation of one side.

Insofar as the communitarian turn leaves ethical community determined by historical accident, it effectively reduces ethical association to a sphere of such "natural" determination, where legitimacy is invested in given conventions devoid of any unconditioned validity, save for the purely contingent circumstance that history gives rise to institutions of freedom. In that case, which modern times have partially witnessed, normativity resides in the self-determined character of the conventions, rather than in their shared acceptance by those who practice them.[9]

Reconstructing ethical community as an association of freedom might well appear to be at one with the task of determining self-determination that has preoccupied ethics and convulsed modernity ever since the claims of liberty supplanted the teleological appeal to a highest good. The great difficulty that stymies traditional attempts to conceive freedom has been their inability to conceive the free will such that both the form and content of its agency, that is, both who and what are willed, are determined by its volition. Lacking this double reflexivity, the will remains defined by factors it has not imposed upon itself, reducing its freedom to a merely formal capacity of choice, choosing among independently given alternatives with a faculty it has not chosen. So long as the free will is conceived as a function of the self, it cannot help but suffer this dual limitation and have a given, natural form of agency that is the perennial precondition, rather than the product of its willing. In this respect, liberty, the faculty of choice, is a natural will, whose capacity to decide among given ends is indeed the presupposition of any act of volition.

Although the ubiquity of the natural will might persuade one to reduce all volition to its liberty, in the nonnatural, historically emergent context of ethical community, individuals can very palpably exercise an artificial agency whose own character and ends are determined by the very willing that reproduces the association within which it alone can be exercised. For instance, individuals can exercise the specific political freedoms defining the agency of free citizen, but only as a member of a democratic state, whose institutions themselves consist in nothing but the political self-determination of its members. Hence, the character of their agency is itself the product of the institutional freedom they engage in, allowing them to exercise a mode of willing that is genuinely self-determining. One might therefore be tempted to consider normatively valid ethical community as identical with the reality of self-determination. Given the identity of freedom and normativity, one would then end up confirming the second dogma of communitarianism, which absolutizes ethical community as the exclusive framework of legitimate conduct.

Yet the rehabilitation of ethical community cannot take this route and simply eliminate the formalist assumptions of communitarianism and supplant natural determination with the artificial freedoms of ethical association. The second communitarian dogma absolutizing ethical association as the exclusive mode of normativity must also be overturned. For, far from being coextensive with the reality of freedom, ethical community cannot coherently comprise a structure of self-determination at all unless two other modes of freedom are admitted whose autonomous agencies are not defined by membership in an existing community. These two types of freedom without community are the self-determinations constitutive of property ownership and moral accountability. Ethical community cannot enjoy normativity without recognition of their independent being because both property relations and morality are necessary preconditions for exercising any freedom as member of an existing association.[10]

Property and Morality as Preconditions of Ethical Community

Contrary to communitarian dogma, the two freedoms without community are not atomistic in character. Determining oneself as a property owner and as a moral subject both involve interacting with and in respect to other agents who do the same. To exercise the agency of a person, that is, to count as a free individual recognized to have entitled possession, one must objectify one's will in some factor in a manner recognizable to and recognized by another person, whose own will enjoys the same recognized status. Otherwise, one simply has intercourse with what gets treated as things, exercising a technical mastery in which no question of entitlement can enter. Similarly, to act morally, one must will and be held accountable for willing in respect to the right and welfare of other morally accountable agents. Otherwise, one's deeds have no moral dimension.[11] In each case, the freedom at issue involves an exercise of right tied to a corresponding duty to respect the correlative freedom of those who are bound to respect one's own like freedom. As such, the freedoms of persons and moral subjects irreducibly involve relations of plurality in which the exercise of right has an objectively recognized existence.

Yet, in engaging in these interactions, property owners and moral subjects still do not respect each other's entitlement on the basis of being members of any preexisting community. The rights and duties of personhood and moral accountability extend beyond the reaches of every particular institutional framework. It matters not whether one belongs to the same family, participates in the same society, or is the fellow citizen of another person and moral subject. In each and every institutional context, one remains bound to respect the due property entitlements and moral accountability of others and have one's own autonomy as person and moral subject respected. These rights are unavoidably basic because no valid institution, that is, no institution of freedom, can ignore them without undermining itself.

This is most apparent with respect to the right of persons to be respected as an owner. Exercising this right always involves being recognized as inalienable proprietor of one's own body, since otherwise one is liable to being owned by another like any other rightless factor.[12] Consequently, whenever respect for the right of persons is not incorporated in existing conventions, individuals are in the position of slaves, for whom no act is recognized as juridically their own. In such a situation, the individual can no more be held morally accountable than occupy any institutional role, such as family member, economic agent, legal subject, or citizen, to which rights and duties apply. Accordingly, no ethical community can give its members an autonomous agency, be it as codetermining spouse and parent, autonomous member of society, or self-governing citizen, unless they be recognized as persons owning at least their own body.[13]

The recognition of moral accountability is equally indispensable. If individuals are not entitled to be held responsible for acting with both the right purposes and intentions and an understanding of what is good, how can they fulfill any roles as members of a community whose bonds consist in modes of freedom? The determinations of conscience may well conflict with the demands of rectitude required, for example, by citizenship, but if moral autonomy is totally ignored, rather than partially restrained, the possibility of ethical rectitude is itself undercut. Agents can hardly enjoy the rights and observe the duties of self-determined family membership, social responsibility, and citizenship if they are not held accountable for conscientiously acting with the right purposes and intentions. When moral autonomy is ignored, agents cannot determine the scope of their own deeds. Their purposes, intentions, and conscience no longer have any bearing upon what they are held responsible for and how they in turn judge others. Such a situation is commonplace under conditions of "natural" ethical community, where slavery goes hand in hand with the submission of conscience to the external authority of given tradition, be it secular or sacred. Truncating the autonomy that can be exercised in community, this predicament deprives all roles of any moral dimension, while leaving action at the margin of community, where one's station no longer dictates what is to be done, determined by factors other than freedom.

Ethical Community as the Obligatory Complement of Property Right and Morality

Whereas ethical community can neither be nor be conceived without incorporating the independently determined freedoms of property and morality, these freedoms without community can be exercised prior to as well as spatially removed from ethical institutions. Nevertheless, property relations are no more able than moral strivings to guarantee the realization of their own freedoms by themselves. Neither one can unequivocally determine nor securely uphold its own rights and duties in each and every case. If owners are left to their own devices, as defined by the constituents of property relations, nothing can prevent the outbreak of malicious and nonmalicious violations of property entitlements for which no satisfactory solution is available. Whereas owners can always disagree in good faith in their interpretations of property boundaries and terms of contract, property relations contain no universally recognized authority to provide a binding adjudication of such disputes and award due compensation. Victims of accidental harm to their person and property face an analogous predicament. Those whose own person or property is allegedly responsible for such accidental harm may well dispute their liability as well as the magnitude of damages. In either type of nonmalicious wrong, good faith disagreements or unintended torts, unless owners come to settle their dispute, the violation of right will persist. Similarly, the same absence of some higher respected power leaves malicious wrongs bereft of any authoritative charge, adjudication, or punishment, leaving victims no other recourse than revenge, which risks being interpreted as a wrong of its own.

These limits to the security of person and property call for some remedy and, in the absence of an institutional solution, personal initiative is the only immediate option, an option characteristic of the moral situation, where the individual must independently determine the particular content of the good and bring it into existence through personal effort. Yet recourse to moral agency only adds problems of its own.

The engagement in moral conduct does indeed actualize freedom to the degree that the limits of responsible action are recognized to be determined by the knowing and willing of the agent, in that moral subjects hold one another accountable only for that part of their deed and its consequences that are prefigured in their purposes, intentions, and conscience. Yet paying heed to the moral prerogative of subjectively determining the realization of right generates a dilemma brought to a head in each agent's effort to act on conscience. Here what purposes and intentions count as good is left to the independent determination of the agent, whose initiative is required to bring right into being. Yet, if others are to recognize the right of the moral agent to act on conscience, they are liable to fall into contradiction with the edicts of their own conscience. What one moral agent knows to be good based on conscience need not conform to what any others hold good. Since the good is not a merely private matter, but something objectively and universally valid, one cannot respect the conflicting conscience of another without denying the claims of one's own. The only escape from this dilemma on the basis of moral accountability is the fortuitous happenstance that one's conscience has spoken in unison with every other. Yet since such harmony depends upon purely external circumstance, it hardly upholds the autonomy of moral action.

The requirements for overcoming the limits of property relations and morality are therefore twofold. To overcome the limits of property, the reality of right must not consist simply in an external factor, outside of which willing occurs. Rather, the reality of right must incorporate the activity of willing that brings it into being. Then freedom will have an existence that sustains itself. Alternately, to overcome the limits of morality, the subjective determination of the good must be such that what each agent independently aims at is inherently in consonance with the aims of others. Then, the actions realizing right will have a coherent unity.

Ethical community, reconstructed as an institutional system of freedom, provides a solution on two levels.

On the one hand, since ethical freedoms have as their own prerequisite constituents the respected autonomy of person and moral subject, ethical community provides an existing institutional order in which property relations and moral accountability are objectively observed in conformity with the other community freedoms they make possible. Without incorporation within ethical community, property and morality either remain prey to incipient conflicts they cannot themselves resolve or get propped up by some convention given independently of freedom, thereby compromising their own validity. By contrast, within ethical community, the freedoms of owners and moral subjects get sustained on the basis of ethical self-determination. This does not involve a limitation upon ethical freedom, undermining its own autonomy. Because property and morality are themselves prerequisite ingredients in ethical freedom, upholding their self-determinations is part and parcel of ethical community's own reproduction.

On the other hand, ethical community overcomes the limits of property and moral self-determination by constituting a mode of freedom uniting their complementary dimensions. In ethical community, the good at which conduct aims contains the activity of its realization insofar as membership involves knowing and willing goals whose achievement reproduces the whole, thereby securing the unity of each member's volition with the performances of the rest. Consequently, the boundaries of the objectification of willing have a common and commonly recognized existence in the unity of the community, removing all incipient conflicts and equivocations so long as members uphold their roles. Moreover, since ethical institutions reproduce themselves in face of possible failures of rectitude, their constitutive activities must also involve overcoming deviations in conduct. In these ways, ethical community provides the objectively recognized realization of right that property relations fail to secure, as well as the universal conformity of subjective initiative that morality is ever seeking.

Hegel and the Rehabilitation of Ethical Community

With ethical freedom presupposing property and morality, and property and morality requiring incorporation in ethical community, the false dichotomy of atomism and ethical community must be supplanted by the threefold differentiation of property right, morality, and ethical community. Only then are the constitutive preconditions at hand for conceiving as well as realizing the institutions of freedom that comprise the complete system of ethical community.

The basic conceptual framework of this threefold differentiation has, of course, been pioneered by Hegel in his *Philosophy of Right*. By conceiving right as the reality of freedom, thereby identifying normativity with self-determination, and by then distinguishing the three fundamental modes of freedom as Abstract Right, Morality, and Ethical Community, Hegel provides the basic framework for prescribing the different institutions of ethical association without succumbing to the dual dogmas by which communitarianism deforms and delegitimizes ethical community.[14]

Yet when Hegel advances to differentiate ethical community as a politically self-regulated system of family, civil society, and the state, he partially capitulates to the communitarian agenda, allowing all three ethical spheres to be branded by natural distinctions. Bending to the history of his and, alas, our own day, Hegel ties the family to a heterosexual monogamous union,[15] where roles are defined by gender, dictating for the husband a privilege to represent the family in society and state and for the wife a bondage to domestic affairs.[16] These measures permit factors given independently of the self-determination at issue to restrict the freedom of competent individuals to marry whom they choose and to codetermine their household affairs. Moreover, these curtailments of family freedom limit social and political freedom by gender, restricting wives' access to civil society and the state. Hegel makes both public spheres further hostage to natural privileges by giving monarchy and estates decisive roles in civil society and the state. Instead of enforcing equal economic opportunity among classes defined by different forms of market earning, Hegel retains estates, whose feudal distinctions define membership partially by hereditary rank and combine corporate and political privileges, undercutting the demarcation between civil society and state.[17] By next making the head of state a hereditary monarch instructing an estate assembly,[18] Hegel allows birth right to curtail the equal political freedoms of representative democracy.

The Place of the Family in the Division of Ethical Community

Despite these major lapses, Hegel still provides a basic conceptual anatomy of family, social, and political association that permits differentiating the modes of ethical freedom independently of extraneous factors. Hegel maintains that the family, civil society, and the state are ethical communities whose unity can be distinguished as immediate, mediated, and both immediate and mediated, respectively.[19] This categorization parallels the threefold division of determinacy into given, determined, and self-determined determinacy that Hegel develops in his *Science of Logic*. Hegel's theory of determinacy there appropriately begins with an account of im-

mediacy, the so-called "Logic of Being," since any putative com-
mencement with mediated or self-mediated determinacy would
already presuppose given determinacy as a constituent, either of
the ground of what is mediated or of the content that ends up
being determined by itself. The sphere of determined or mediated
determinacy comes next in the "Logic of Essence," insofar as determined determinacy incorporates determinacy as such (further
qualifying it as mediated by a determiner), whereas self-determined
determinacy incorporates determined determinacy (since what is
self-determined involves determined determinacy, with the qualification that what determines is identical with what gets determined). Logical determinacy accordingly exhausts itself in the
"Logic of The Concept" with an account of self-determined determinacy, where what is mediated and what mediates are one and
the same. To the degree that determinacy can be given, determined,
or self-determined, the differentiation of immediate, mediated, and
self-mediated ethical community could be said to exhaust the logical possibilities.[20]

In line with this division, domestic community can be understood as an immediate ethical association in that its unity is based
on the shared feeling of its adult members to bond together into a
joint private sphere for whose consolidated, but particular right
and welfare they are mutually responsible. The shared feeling on
which spouses base their ethical commitment to one another is immediate in that no further factors provide necessary conditions for
its presence. Individuals are not compelled to marry owing to any
qualities they possess or any relations they incur; they must feel like
marrying one another and although this immediate resolve may be
accompanied by any number of other considerations, none independently mandate that marriage must ensue, let alone who must marry
whom. Indeed, it is the very givenness of feeling that permits it to
be the vehicle of the immediacy of the marriage commitment.

Similarly, the union of spouses into a joint household is immediate in that the connection of their welfare and interests is the
given basis of their family roles, rather than the product of any
mediating term, such as some separate commitment or initiative,
as in commercial partnerships or political alliances. Precisely because spouses thereby form one united person, with no third terms
intervening, their relationship within marriage cannot be formulated in contractual terms, which always concern possession or
disposition of some factor external to persons.[21]

Admittedly, the element of feeling in family association introduces a form of passive receptivity in which individuals unite in

virtue of an inner modification that they have not chosen or concluded, but immediately experience. Accordingly, Hegel characterizes feeling as something in which the agent is unfree, that is, naturally bound.[22] Yet Hegel goes beyond acknowledging this passive receptivity in feeling to tie the immediacy of family association to further natural givens, restricting marriage to a heterosexual union in which biological sexual differences mandate different family roles for wife and husband. This definition of household unity by natural features, however, undermines the family's status as an institution of freedom, capable of commanding normativity. Not only does it introduce a relation of subordination between spouses, but it ascribes different family roles to adult members independently of their willing. Moreover, it adds factors extraneous to how family association, civil society, and the state differentiate themselves as immediate, mediated, and self-mediated ethical communities.

Comparisons between family and civil and political community make this clear, if only by way of anticipation. In distinction from the immediate ethical community putatively characterizing the normatively valid family, civil society, whose basic structure is the market, associates individuals through the mediation of the pursuit of satisfying self-selected needs for what others have to offer as means of their own self-seeking. Thus, in the network of commodity exchange, individuals satisfy their complementary market needs by obtaining goods from others in return for providing what the latter want. By contrast, individuals belong to their family immediately, as members of a joint private domain in which what each owns belongs directly to the other members of the family[23] and where the right of each member to have his or her welfare upheld is immediately connected to the duty to contribute to the welfare of all. In both cases no other factors intervene as mediating terms of their relation. For example, spouses are responsible for one another's welfare just as are parents for their children's well-being simply by being members of the same family and not because of any particular agreements made among them.

The same absence of mediating conditions applies to the role of feeling and intimacy in family ties. The sentiment underlying marriage and the resolve to preserve the marriage union exhibit immediacy to the degree that nothing but a mutual desire to marry provides necessary or sufficient grounds for marriage between any eligible prospective spouses. Although different individuals might be classed as right for one another by possessing certain general qualifications, no assortment of objective properties can dictate entry into marriage without the mutual feeling to take the nuptial vow. If any general external grounds sufficed to make individuals spouses, the autonomy of marriage would be undercut. This is especially true since the marriage bond involves specific individuals to the exclusion of all others, rather than the general relations exhibited by law in civil society and political activity, which constitutively aims at governing the whole body politic. Since the individual is an object of feeling, whereas the universal is an object of thought and law, letting other considerations dictate marriage independently of sentiment would subject spouses to an extraneous imposition.

Similarly, the direct unity in the private affairs of family members places individuals in a situation where nothing stands as a barrier to the most personal of ties. Social and political involvements may set individuals in relations of vital importance, but none involve the complete melding of private domains by which family relations take on a personal character, where the feeling to make common cause is a sentiment for removing all juridical distance from the other person, save for ownership of each member's own body.[24]

Significantly, none of these dimensions of immediacy involve reference to gender differences, sexual orientation, or any other natural distinction. If they did, characterizing the family as immediate ethical community would disqualify the household both as a mode of self-determination and as a form of genuine ethical community.

Not surprisingly, the mediated character of civil society can equally be specified apart from any reference to gender, sexual orientation, or any other factor that might have a putatively natural definition. Civil society can comprise a mediated ethical association insofar as its unity reproduces itself through the reciprocal pursuit of self-selected needs for what others have to offer as the instrument for achieving their own particular interests. In this respect, the commodity relations building the basic structure of civil society are not an exercise in a natural, atomistic self-seeking, as much modern economic theory would have one believe. Commodity relations rather comprise a mode of conduct in which market participants exercise economic freedoms that can only be enjoyed within the context of an existing market where economic need and earning inherently involve relations between agents in recognition of their commodity ownership and complementary social interests. What their natural differences may be are otherwise matters of indifference for their participation in this interaction.

Unlike domestic community, the ensuing social community is universal in scope, spinning its web of economic freedom beyond household and national boundaries alike, fostering a world market even though the ends its members aim at always remain particular in content. For this reason, civil society's global community of interest functions as the *ground* of interdependence whose *appearance* is the pursuit of personally selected interests constitutively tied to the satisfaction of the interests of others.[25]

Free political association, for its part, can easily be seen to have neither a simply immediate nor mediated unity. Its members are citizens not because of some shared feeling, nor through the mediation of aiming at particular ends distinct from political union. Rather, citizens exercise their constitutive political freedom by consciously willing the form of the whole body politic to which they belong. Thereby engaging in acts of self-government whose aims are universal, citizens reproduce the political institutions that preside over particular households and national civil society, allowing the totality of ethical life to form a self-ordered whole, resting on its own freedom. The body politic thus has immediacy by not having its unity determined by some external condition and simultaneously has a mediated character by consisting in a self-rule that continually aims at reproducing the constitutional framework within which its political freedom can alone be exercised. Achieving this self-determined unity, where what is mediated and what mediates are one and the same, normative political community unites the immediacy and mediation characterizing household and social community.

The necessity of the division of ethical community into distinct spheres of family, civil society, and state can be corroborated by supplementing Hegel's differentiation by immediacy and mediation with an architectonic reflecting the scope of each association and the character of its defining ends. Reconstituted as an ethical community of self-determination, the family comprises an association *particular in scope* and *particular in aim*. The household extends only so far as a particular private domain and its members perform their household roles aiming at sustaining the particular welfare of their family. By contrast, in civil society the association is *universal in scope* but *particular in aim*. Although members of civil society interact in pursuit of self-selected interests, they do so through a network of market relations, civil law, and public welfare institutions capable of extending beyond household and national borders, as world markets and international agreements can attest. Even when civilians make common cause in trade unions, professional associations, employer federations, consumer organizations, tenant leagues, and other social interest groups, their shared interests are still particular, distinguishable from those of other groups, whereas their membership in the social interest group is predicated upon that group's interaction within civil society, to whose universal system of interdependence it must relate in order to achieve its aims. By contrast, in politics the association is *universal in scope*[26] and *universal in aim* when a state stands by itself and politics focuses on domestic self-government. Then citizens act politically by seeking to determine the order of the whole to which they belong, a whole that extends as far as domestic affairs. Finally, the association is *particular in scope* and *universal in aim* when one state interacts with others within the sphere of international relations. In that case, the body politic still aims at governing the entirety of its own order, but does so as a particular regime among others. Thereby politics exhausts the logical possibilities of organizing ethical community according to the particularity and universality of its scope and aims, suggesting once more the completeness of the basic division of family, civil society, and state.[27]

With the conceptual resources underlying these rudimentary divisions, the system of ethical community may be duly reconstructed, purging all residue of illegitimate natural determination and developing the complete reality of the freedoms that should define membership in the household, society, and the state.[28] Rescuing ethical community from the communitarian turn, this reconstruction deserves to be the central agenda of ethics today, as much in theory as in practice.

In respect to family ethics, this challenge plausibly involves conceiving the just family as an ethical community whose unity is immediate, with a scope and aim that are equally particular. Indeed, the rational reconstruction of ethical community first must address the family. Whereas the family does not incorporate civil or political association, civil society absorbs families within its market, legal, and welfare institutions, whereas the state presides over both household and civil society. Accordingly, the family is the most elementary ethical community, presupposed by civil society and state. Any theory of civil society or of the state that fails to take into account the family and how it relates to social and political freedom therefore condemns itself to blind incompleteness.

Conceiving the just family as a form of ethical community, of course, does not simply depend on whether either of the above logical schemes certify the completeness of the differentiation of ethical community and the place of the family within the division. What directly matters is whether a family order can be determined that comprises a structure of freedom sui generis and whether the integration of this family regime with the other institutions of freedom can be made intelligible and coherent. If these dual questions can be affirmatively answered, then a mode of family life will be established enjoying the foundation-free normative validity that self-determination uniquely commands.

To help focus how the family can figure as a valid form of ethical community, several preliminary issues warrant exploration. First, how can the family avoid being determined by natural and psychological exigencies compromising its normativity? Secondly, how can family ties be distinguished from friendship without appealing to natural considerations? The answer to the first question will remove lingering obstacles to recasting the family as an institution of freedom, whereas the answer to the second will save family association from reduction to property or moral relations.

CHAPTER II

Nature, Psychology, and the Normativity of the Family

The Role of Nature in the Family

Not surprisingly, the family has been traditionally acknowledged to be the institution most rooted in nature. Insofar as the household unites individuals immediately into a joint private domain, family relations seem to be where nature comes to the fore, where domestic intimacy puts bodies into touch, where sexual interaction and reproduction have their obvious home, and where individuals first depend upon one another for biological and psychological survival, whether as nurtured child, sibling, or spouse.

Yet if domestic intimacy leaves the door open for physical relations, are these defining elements of family life, reducing household community to a sphere of necessity beyond good and evil? Alternately, do these natural aspects of family relations function prescriptively, determining the obligatory character of any or all family roles, or are they optional accompaniments of household relations from which family rights and duties cannot be derived? And if the joint privacy of the home makes the family the natural locus of reproduction and child rearing, do the biological dimensions of childbearing and nurturing render the family a normatively neutral arena of parental instinct? Alternately, do these dimensions independently prescribe any norms of family conduct or is their role in the household ethically optional and subject to ethical regulation only in function of the requirements of self-determination? By the same token, does the family's role in personality formation render family community a sphere of psychological compulsion, in which therapeutic concerns alone apply and beyond which autonomy lies?

The answers to these questions depend first upon determining what natural conditions necessarily underlie family community. Thinkers who favor a natural determination of the family commonly appeal to five factors, often assumed to go hand in hand: the species being of humans, sexual differentiation into male and female genders, bisexual reproduction, the process of physical and psychological maturation, and the metabolism with nature of rational agents. If a family ethic is to be possible, these factors must not reduce all household relations to functions of biological or psychological compulsion, in which the freedom of normative conduct is absent. On the other hand, if all or any of these factors are to determine how the family ought to ordered, they must be noncontingent elements of household organization that family ethics must accommodate or optional aspects required for family self-determination.

The Contingency of Sexual Differentiation and Bisexual Reproduction in the Family

The starting point in most arguments defining the family in natural terms is the assumption of two features whose necessity is far from self-evident: the sexual differentiation of spouses and a corresponding bisexual reproduction. On this basis, the argument goes, male and female will unite as spouses in fulfillment of their sexual urges and the requirements of species propagation, generating parent-child relations following the biological imperative of nurturing dependent offspring.

Families historically may well have predominantly had spouses of different sexes. Yet this fact guarantees neither that such an arrangement must always obtain, nor that it should exclusively prevail. And if it is merely one possibility among others, its historical prevalence is no more an argument for its normative validity than the long tradition of slavery and other forms of bondage is grounds for their legitimacy. What prevails may have might on its side, but the existence of a practice is hardly identical with conformity to right.

This untenability of might makes right may seem at odds with the unity of ought and is achieved by ethical community. Yet, even though ethical community obliges its members to abide by norms already embodied in the institutions required for exercising their roles, this unity of ought and is is not natural; it must rather be enacted through the historical foundation of specifically ethical institutions, whose internal norms owe their legitimacy not to their observance, but to their identity with principles of self-determination. The mere existence of particular conventions with internal norms of their own thus does not guarantee that they unite ought and is as do ethical institutions of freedom. What counts is whether they comprise structures of self-determination.

Nonetheless, even if the prevalence of heterosexual male and female spouses confers neither necessity nor normativity, the sexual differentiation of spouses might still appear dictated by the commonly presumed necessity of reproduction within the family and of the bisexual character of human propagation. Yet both assumptions can be questioned.

First of all, spouses can conceivably forge a common household without producing children within it, either by choice or due to physical or psychological inability, or because they produce children with individuals other than their spouse. Each of these alternatives could be embodied by one, some, or all couples, even if the option of universal Shakerism, infertility, or impotence leads to extinction.

Moreover, whether spouses produce children together or with others or refrain from reproducing, the nurturing of children can occur outside the family under other auspices. Alternately, spouses could follow the pattern of many animal species by indulging their sexual urges and performing their reproductive function, but then separating without ever establishing a family. Needless to say, if nurturing occurs outside the family, the family loses its position as the locus of psychological development, granted that early childhood experience plays a privileged role in personality formation. Consequently, even if individuals were sexually differentiated and necessarily bound by heterosexual urges to engage in sexual reproduction, family relations would still be undetermined by these compulsions, allowing household community to operate on terms amenable to ethics.

Besides, the reproduction of rational agents capable of participating in family relations need not occur bisexually. First of all, the biological equipment of bisexual reproduction is contingent even among humans. Although the differentiation of male and female is generally taken for granted, people are actually distinguished sexually along a much more gradated continuum, centered in the bisexuality of hermaphrodites and extending through individuals possessing both male and female sexual organs in differing degrees of development to those more common extremes where one variety exclusively predominates. The possibilities of human propagation are thus far from fixed, especially with genetic engineering conceivably enabling human intervention to remove the burden of childbirth from one gender.[1]

Secondly, family ethics, like any other ethics, applies to finite rational agents in general, insofar as finite rational agents alone are capable of exercising rights and observing duties to others. What qualifies rational agency as human are contingent features of species being that have no exclusive claim upon the possible extension of ethical relations. Even if we have yet to encounter nonhuman rational agents, ethically privileging the distinguishing features of homo sapiens would involve the same mistake as limiting rights by race, gender, sexual orientation or any other factor irrelevant to their exercise. As for the possibilities of other forms of rational agency, the diversity of life on earth already suggests that individuals capable of associating in families could conceivably reproduce asexually or not reproduce at all, be it as the result of terrestrial or extraterrestrial evolutionary developments.

Thirdly, it is far from self-evident that spouses need be sexually attracted, be it on the basis of bisexual reproduction (the common precondition for bisexuality, heterosexuality, and homosexuality) or asexual reproduction. Whether marriages be arranged by outsiders or entered consensually, spouses may well never experience or lose sexual passion for one another. Moreover, even if sexual attraction does occur, that fact hardly guarantees that sexual relations transpire in the private life of spouses. Individuals may be unwilling or psychologically and/or physically unable to act upon their desires, and even when that is not the case, their sexual desires may be frustrated by the disinterest or disability of their spouse.

Consequently, bisexual reproduction and sexual attraction are merely contingent factors in family relations, even if the family is a more compatible site for them among humans than the impersonal interactions of property relations, morality, civil society, and the state. On this score as well, family organization is free from reduction to natural functions.

The Contingency of Parenting in the Family

The biological underpinnings of parenting might also seem questionable, not only because nurturing can occur outside the family, but because neotony (the incomplete biological development of individuals at birth)[2] may well be another contingent peculiarity of human species being that need not apply to all other possible rational agents. Certainly, the variety of life on earth testifies to how the extended dependency of human infants is by no means shared by all creatures. One can well imagine rational beings arising, either on earth or extraterrestrially, who could be biologically independent moments after birth, eliminating the physical necessity for nurturing.

Moreover, the mammalian configuration of birth and nurturing, where pregnancy, delivery, and lactation all place special biological demands upon the woman, neither mandates other gender-defined family roles, nor automatically applies to all possible rational agents capable of conjugal relations. Pregnancy, childbirth, and breast-feeding may well curtail the activity of the mother, but only during these events or their aftermath, and only then when the biological burdens have not been reduced or eliminated by technologies as speculative as extrauterine embryo incubation or as familiar as baby formulas. And even if the human biology of pregnancy, childbirth, and lactation may have hormonal and psychological consequences for the mother predisposing her to be attached to her offspring, these ramifications neither guarantee that the mother will choose to nurture her child nor preclude that other persons, be they male, female, or something in between, may exercise the role of nurturer just as conscientiously and caringly.[3] Consequently, the mother-child unit need not be a universal feature of mammalian family life, even if only the female gives birth and lactates.[4] Nor can empirical theories, such as Gilligan's study of moral development in women,[5] provide support for defining family roles by gender, both because observed differences in moral thinking between genders and sexual orientations have neither descriptive necessity nor prescriptive authority, and because raising children in a homophobic gender-structured society already injects conventional differentiations, putting any results at one remove from what is allegedly given by sexual nature.[6]

Nonetheless, the biology of mammalian reproduction might appear to have important consequences for family organization given the paternity ramifications of how the child can be seen emerging from the womb of a specific woman, whereas evidence of fatherhood is less readily available. Both maternity and paternity have two distinct levels: the biological and the conventional.[7] The conventionally recognized father and mother of children may or may not converge with their biological parents. Without genetic testing or its equivalent, conventional paternity will often be recognized without any knowledge of who the biological father may be, whereas the identity of the biological mother will rarely be a mystery except in cases of untraced orphans.[8] Indeed, under these conditions, a society in which promiscuity reigns makes both levels of paternity unclear and leaves kinship resting with the female.[9] Since inheritance and any social or political arrangements that privilege family ties make kinship of fundamental importance for individuals, the difference in the identifiability of maternity and paternity can have crucial consequences.[10] These consequences apply both to how households are governed and, in particular, to how the promiscuity of husband and wife are differently weighted, especially when patrilineal succession seeks to preempt its matrilineal counterpart.[11] Yet this predicament depends upon four circumstances: that family members reproduce along mammalian lines, that genetic testing or its equivalent is not available to conclusively identify biological parents of either sex, that reproduction and upbringing occur within the family, and that institutions outside the household permit kinship relations to confer advantages and disadvantages within their spheres.[12] Not only are these circumstances all contingent, but the last, allowing kinship to privilege individuals in social and political life, is at odds with the equal opportunity mandated by social and political freedom.[13] Consequently, however much historical significance the biological disparity in paternity and maternity may have, this disparity has no independent ethical significance.

Of course, the necessity of parenting is not reducible to biological nurturing. It equally involves educating the child in all the theoretical and practical disciplines needed to participate in the institutions of freedom as an autonomous agent. Since these institutions are not natural, facility with their modalities cannot be something individuals possess at birth, in the manner of social insects. Moreover, since the conventions of the spheres of right involve positive, discretionary determinations beyond the limits of purely rational prescription, individuals could not rely upon their own reasoning to arrive at the practical knowledge they need to exercise their rights and fulfill their obligations. Some tutelage will always be required to acquaint individuals with a working knowledge of the property relations, moral engagements, household order, civil society, and constitutional regime into which they have been born.

Because such tutelage will invariably be a precondition for the exercise of full rights by individuals, the family might appear necessarily to involve parenting, minimally consisting in training the young to become competent participants in the institutions of freedom. Yet, even this mandate is conditional upon upbringing occurring within the family rather than in some other arena.[14] Nothing about the nature of tutelage in the institutions of right ties it indissolubly to household parenting, unless the psychological prerequisites for autonomy can only be provided by kinship relations.[15] Because right involves respecting the autonomy of others and being recognized as autonomous in turn, one is tempted to argue that experiencing the unconditioned love and care of family intimacy is a prerequisite for both honoring the rights of others and possessing self-respect. Yet every sphere of right involves becoming recognized as an autonomous agent whose self-determination is tied to observing the entitlements of others. If child rearing does occur within the family, then individuals will first encounter the reciprocal recognition of right in the home. This temporal priority, however, does not guarantee that engaging in relations of right is impossible without the antecedent immersion in family relations. Nor does it entail that personality ceases to develop after early childhood.[16]

Of course, the overwhelming majority of modern psychological theories treat the family as the framework most vital to the development of an autonomous personality. And many social theorists, like Max Horkheimer, are prepared to single out the family as an all-important educational agent in the reproduction of human character required by social life.[17] Yet, the family's centrality in personality formation may itself be a contingent circumstance tied to the modern development of the disengaged family. Under these relatively recent historical circumstances early childhood is spent in the nuclear home, a private world separated from workplace, assembly, and extended kin in which isolated intimacy reigns between parent and child.[18] This contingency of the family's primacy in childhood development would still hold even if psychoanalytic theory were reformed to free the development of personality from the assumption of gendered parenting in a society that privileges males and prohibits same-sex marriage.[19] For then it could still be questioned whether the family must figure as the primary factor in personality formation and socialization.

Nonetheless, the historical contingency of the disengaged family and the personality formation it fosters[20] need not undercut the psychological requirement for parenting if 1) the realization of freedom requires separate spheres of family, social, and political right, and 2) the separation of these spheres places upbringing within the family, unless parental abuse, incapacity, or death and an unavailability of adopting parents requires social welfare institutions to provide a surrogate home. Yet even if these conditions hold, parenting will still not be a universal feature of the household since spouses may simply not have children. At most, parenting will be an option, whose particular norms may or may not involve reference to biological maturation, depending upon the degree of neotony of the young.[21]

Furthermore, even when parenting occurs, the mere biological and psychological requirements of upbringing will still leave undetermined all other norms of family life that go beyond these imperatives. Hence, no historical family regime is legitimated by the fact that children are born into a world to which they must become acculturated, since all recorded family structures go well beyond the bare necessities for meeting these needs.[22] This irreducibility of family structure to an instrument of reproduction and nurture is, of course, guaranteed by how the same function can be served by arrangements outside the household. That circumstance alone signals that what distinguishes family life and its specific norms lies elsewhere.

The Family and the Human Metabolism with Nature

Appealing to anthropological necessities of human metabolism with nature provides no better tool for rooting family norms in natural relations. The example of Engels's *The Origin of The Family, Private Property and The State* is instructive. Although Engels there wishes to provide an account of the historical formation of the family, from which a critique of the modern household can be drawn, he identifies the determining factor in history as the suprahistorical, anthropologically mandated twofold production and reproduction of immediate human life. Consisting in the furnishing of the means of existence (of food, clothing, and shelter, and of the tools for their production) and in the propagation of the species, this dual process supposedly governs the evolution of the family, as if undeveloped labor productivity dictated domination of society by kinship and advances in productivity subordinated kinship groups to the property regime of civil society over which a central state presides.[23] The market of civil society may well comprise an economic order in which continual revolutions in productivity become a matter of survival for competing firms and where production has disengaged itself from household and state. Yet productivity can increase apart from market institutions and without freeing society and state from family ties. As with any functional account, Engels's conception privileges ends that have no inherent connection to what they allegedly determine. He assumes that the imperatives of subsistence production and species propagation regulate the shape of the family and its relation to other institutions, when reference to those imperatives leaves completely undetermined what type of institutions are to be subordinated to such ends in the first place. Just as base/superstructure schemes posit a relation without specifying the content of the related terms,[24] so Engels's privileging of production and propagation leaves entirely up for grabs whether families need exist at all and if so, what structure they must have. Moreover, because he roots family organization, like production, in anthropological conditions, the family joins the economy as a realm of necessity beyond which the domain of freedom and genuine ethical concerns first begins. This relegation to necessity makes any *normative* critique of the modern family, such as Engels endeavors, a nonsensical enterprise.

The Family and Evolution

The family may avert reduction to an instrument of production or propagation, yet can family organization escape the imperatives of successful adaptation that evolution mandates? Natural selection within a species seemingly cannot operate with much resilience under conditions of consistent inbreeding, since then similar alternatives represent the only genetic choices, save for rare mutations that intermittently appear. By contrast, if outbreeding is pursued, a greater variety of genetic options are provided from which natural selection can favor the superior adaptabilities most fit for survival. Accordingly, individuals who reproduce through inbreeding will be less likely to prosper than those who systematically practice outbreeding, through such devices as incest taboos and extra-tribal matrimony.[25]

Such an argument would seem to support the notion that evolution will mandate family organizations that incorporate incest restrictions and promote the widest possible selection of spouses.[26]

Yet any appeal to evolutionary dynamics assumes that the conditions of natural selection have not been overturned by the emergence of rational agents and their communities. That would be the case only if the interactions of agents mercilessly obeyed the principle of the survival of the fittest, instead of setting barriers to the war of all against all and extending care to weaker individuals. Yet the family is precisely one institution among others that interrupts evolutionary pressures by supplanting struggles for survival among individuals with a united effort to uphold the common good of the household and all its members. Even if the joint efforts of family members could not shield them from competition with more able family units, any number of social arrangements, from corporate organizations to social welfare agencies, could ameliorate this problem and free family organization from evolutionary constraints. For this reason, incest taboos and extratribal matrimony are not necessary outcomes of the struggle to survive, but require other groundings. Once more, the dynamics of nature leave the family free to erect a second nature of its own convention.

The Family and the Birth of Culture

Some, such as Freud and Lévi-Strauss, have suggested that the establishment of incest taboos and exogamous marriage first engenders the morality and culture distinguishing humanity from other species.[27] Allegedly, the prohibition of marriage among family members creates society by compelling individuals to marry members of other households, bringing families into relation with one another, creating the social arena in which markets can bloom, politics can be fostered, and art, religion, and philosophy can gain a public audience.[28]

The fundamental civilizing importance here ascribed to incest taboos is undercut not so much by the recognition that many other species avoid incest[29] as by the possibility of other grounds for engaging in social relations. These possibilities have been acknowledged throughout the tradition of ethics. Anticipating the political economists, Plato and Aristotle both suggest that individuals are capable of forming organic societies (Plato's City of Pigs and Aristotle's village association) simply to satisfy their complementary needs, whereas the whole liberal tradition never tires of claiming that individuals' mere capacity of choice gives them reason to institute a civil society apart from any family membership and incest taboos. These genetic accounts cannot provide justifications of the institutions at which they arrive, for this would render justice normatively dependent upon antecedent processes, introducing the foundationalism fatal to normative argumentation. Nonetheless, they point to how the requirement of "civilization" does not impose exogamy upon the family. Yet again, the design of family community is left open to prescription by norms sui generis to the household.

Traditional Kinship and Family Ethics

The freedom of family organization from biological or psychological compulsions might still seem an invitation to deny the possibility of family ethics if one were to follow modern anthropology in treating traditional kinship as the model for family relations. Although anthropology pretends to address what is generic to humanity, and by extension, to rational agency, it tends to focus upon traditional societies, ignoring modern life. This peculiar omission of modernity was once justified by the assumption that traditional societies, being primitive or savage, presented original, unobscured human nature. Now the fixation upon premodern communities claims the higher ground of ethical indifference, subscribing to the communitarian dogma that practical norms are cultural givens beyond rational prescription, something ratified by traditional societies' explicit appeal to ancestral ways.

Significantly, in focusing upon traditional societies, anthropology devotes most of its energies to unraveling the complexities of traditional kinship.[30] This reflects how traditional societies lack the separation between household, social and political spheres marking the institutions of freedom arising with modernity, a lack that makes kinship analysis a prerequisite for comprehending each and every traditional practice. Under the traditional scheme, a distinct family ethic becomes unthinkable, for kinship directly functions as an instrument for allotting property, occupations, and authority at all levels of community.[31] Far from being a vice, nepotism figures as a pervasive virtue, for kin solidarity permeates every form of association.[32]

Moreover, since kinship relations in traditional cultures are themselves defined by appeal to natural factors of birth, gender, and age, the anthropological focus upon kinship tacitly universalizes not only the inescapability and primacy of kinship bonds, but the hold of natural determination over community that the lack of demarcated spheres reflects. Only when the hegemony of kinship has proven to be a contingent scourge can the family disengage itself as a discrete institution of freedom and provide the object for a family ethic. The modernity that anthropology spurns presents an empirical testimony to that eventuality.

The Natural and Psychological Prerequisites of the Family

By now it should be evident that the natural and psychological prerequisites of the family are no different than those that apply to any other interaction of freedom. Self-determination requires nothing more than a plurality of rational agents, capable of mutually respecting the exercise of their respective entitled freedoms. Free agents must therefore inhabit a common world physically amenable to their interaction, possess sufficient biological endowments to objectify their wills in recognizable ways, and possess sufficient psychological health to act as a unitary independent individual capable of relating autonomously to others while honoring their rights. How rational agents reproduce, how they are sexually differentiated, and how they must be nurtured are contingent matters obeying no other proviso than that they accommodate the above requirements for engaging in relations of right. As such, the endowments of nature and psyche provide no juridical principles of family ethics, but only enabling conditions of free agency, which, like the orbits of the planets and the bonding properties of water, leave undetermined how to distinguish the just from unjust family arrangements that they equally make possible.

CHAPTER III

Friendship Morals versus
Family Ethics

With family norms no more prescribed by the biology of sexual difference and reproduction than by the psychology of childhood development, the family has the same natural and psychological enabling conditions as any other structure of freedom. Conversely, as current convention increasingly brings home, sexual intimacy, reproduction, and child rearing can occur just as well among informally attached friends as among formally recognized spouses.

This complementary situation brings to the fore the question of how family relations can be differentiated from friendship, since no longer can a distinction be made by appealing to the naturally determined factors of sexual difference, reproduction, and nurturing that tradition relied upon. Given the lingering tendency to identify family relations with the elements honored by tradition, the toleration of premarital sex, unmarried couples, and childbirth out of wedlock fosters the notion that marriage and the other accoutrements of family bonds are redundant formalities, adding nothing of value to what friends enjoy by sharing residences, bodies, and child care. In such an atmosphere it is no wonder that modern law has grown uncertain over whether to extend the same status to friends and their charges as to spouses, parents, and children.[1] Nor should it be any surprise that defenders of gay rights can refrain from militating for same-sex marriage, as if matrimony was an expendable freedom and all that really counted was equal treatment in society and state. Truly, are there any norms that should apply to family members that do not equally apply to friends who engage in those activities traditionally associated with domestic life? Or are marriage and child-parent relations ethically superfluous? And if they are superfluous, does this reinstate property right and the moral standpoint as the only parameters governing conduct, reducing ethical community to a vain chimera?

Adding to the confusion is the peculiar predicament of the treatment of friendship in the history of ethical theory. Whereas modern theorists from Hobbes to Hegel have let friendship virtually disappear as a distinct topic of ethics, the standard bearers of ancient thought, Plato and Aristotle, have tended to elevate friendship above family relations in the order of the good life.

Their privileging of friendship reflects a ranking that results from family practices prevailing throughout much of history up until modern times. Friendship has historically been granted pride of place on two grounds to which the family could little lay claim until recently. On the one hand, friendship has been recognized to be the field for true romance, where personal bonds are those of freely entered love and sexual adventure. On the other hand, friendship has been acknowledged to forge ties of true equality and reciprocity.

By contrast, the family has been assigned a secondary status for just those natural determinations that have marked its traditional organization. On the one hand, the family has figured as a sphere of natural necessity, devoted to procreation and to fulfilling daily recurring subsistence needs. On the other hand, the family has operated as a sphere of naturally determined hierarchy. The relation of spouses has been defined by an unequal gender differentiation, lacking reciprocity, freedom, and equality and thereby lacking true romance and love, as well as true respect and self-respect. The parent-child relation, for its part, involves a natural inequality, readily viewed as a technical management, where, as Kant would put it, right applies to persons treated as things.

Against this historical backdrop, the theoretical privileging of friendship over family has an apt resonance, that easily conceals the contingency of the fit. For just this reason, the classical conception of friendship involves its own deformations, whose exposure paves the way for properly distinguishing friendship and family, as well as for comprehending why modern ethicists have tended to give no special norms to ties among friends.

The Confusion in the Classical Conception of Friendship

Both Plato and Aristotle assign friendship the role of supplying the surrogate ethical community that a naturally defined, hierarchical family cannot provide. Friendship gets characterized as a freely entered unity, whose participants live their lives in common, benefiting from the joint activity in which what each friend receives is the same good that the other obtains, a good that can be had nowhere else but in the fraternity they share.

As Plato indicates in the *Lysis*,[2] friendship can achieve both reciprocity and benefit only by standing in stark contrast to the exchange relations characteristic of the market. In commerce, exchange only proceeds when the parties have different desires and receive different benefits, for otherwise, individuals might as well enjoy the goods they already possess, instead of trading them for something else. Friendship can benefit its participants in reciprocity precisely because they desire the same good and this good cannot be attained in isolation, but only in the joint activity of their fellowship.[3] Plato intimates that the common endeavor uniting benefit and reciprocity lies in the joint search for knowledge of the good, effectively making true friends companions in philosophizing,[4] which raises the specter that success in jointly seeking knowledge will eliminate the rationale for friendship's own preservation. Aristotle escapes this dilemma by identifying friendship's common activity not just in jointly conceiving the good, but in jointly living in accord with virtue,[5] an undertaking that never comes to completion.[6]

Overshadowing these differences is Plato's and Aristotle's agreement that friendship be conceived as an association uniting reciprocity and benefit. When this idea of friendship is thought through, it entails withdrawing its participants from any life in a naturally defined household and ends up obliterating any distinction between friendship and a free family, whose members marry by choice and share an ethical love involving reciprocity, self-determination, and equality. For if friends are literally to live a life in common, they cannot equally dwell within separate private domains, sharing an *oikos* with wife, slaves, and children.[7] Instead, their life in common becomes a life of virtual spouses, provided the natural functions of sexual difference, reproduction, and nurturing of offspring have no constitutive hold on family affairs.

In these respects, Aristotle's description of friendship closely approximates the normative ideal of the family, reconstructed as an ethical association of freedom, whereas his account of the *oikos* straps the household with bonds of natural difference and domination that undermine its ethical community. Aristotle gives expression to these complementary construals by affirming both the identity and difference between family and friendship. On the one hand, friendship and family are alike in that friends have no need of justice,[8] enjoying as they do the same unity of ends that characterize household ties. Accordingly, family relations of parent and child, husband and wife, and between siblings can all be described as examples of friendship.[9] Moreover, whereas deficient forms of friendship based on utility or pleasure have a particular scope and transience making unnecessary a life in common,[10] complete friends are unconditionally good for each other, loving in their counterpart what is best for themselves, and therefore finding living life together most choice worthy.[11] On the other hand, however, the friendship of family members should be set apart from the friendship of companions because of the inequality marking all but one family relation.[12] Paternal friendship is a tyrannical relation, where a father treats children as slaves,[13] whereas the friendship of husband and wife is aristocratic, reflecting a difference in worth that may verge on oligarchy when the difference gets tied to control of wealth.[14] Yet, under tyranny, Aristotle admits, friendship is hardly possible given the absence of anything in common, while under aristocracy, friendship is less feasible than under democracy, where people are equal and have the most in common.[15] Accordingly, the only family relationship that bears resemblance to complete friendship is the community of siblings, for they are equal except with respect to age.[16] Hence fraternity and friendship deserve the link that language has confirmed, but only in recognition of the divide between true friendship and all the other dimensions of traditional family community.

The reason why friendship is given so much more attention in ancient thought lies in this contrast. For complementary reasons, Plato and Aristotle construe the family in ways that deprive it of proper normativity. For Plato, the family is a sphere of nepotism, whose kin partiality stands implacably opposed to the unity of the polis, where the good of the individual must be at one with the good of the community. Hence, the natural functions traditionally rooted in the family must be withdrawn from the particular home and Plato's abolition of any family for the Guardians confirms how the ends of procreation and subsistence can be achieved through other means.[17] For Aristotle, the family is a sphere of natural domination that may be retained as a subordinate equipment for virtue so long as domestic hierarchy frees the head of the household from attending to necessities of subsistence and upbringing, enabling him to participate in the good life of the citizen.[18]

Yet, by presenting friendship as a superior counterpart to family affairs, Plato and Aristotle are equally at a loss to retain any special standing for friends among the institutions of ethical community.

Friendship poses a dilemma for Plato, given his own objections to family parochialism. If friends are partial to one another, but indifferent to the good of strangers, fraternity will collide with concern for the common good and Plato would have to hound friendship out of the polis together with family and poetry. Yet, if friendship can be viewed simply as living together in pursuit of the joint good that its shared life represents, friendship can be redeemed by becoming a universal fellowship, relating all citizens in bonds of fraternity. In that case, however, friendship loses its own specificity, for the virtues of the citizen are now indistinguishable from the virtues of friends.

Aristotle, on the other hand, may maintain the difference between friendship and politics by tolerating the particular scope of fellowship among friends. Yet because he conceives friendship as a form of joint living, where friends take pleasure in each other for freely sharing in activity together and taking pleasure in the same things, Aristotle cannot distinguish between friendship and the form of family he ignores, a free family, whose members choose to become spouses out of love and devote themselves to a life in common embodying reciprocity and equality. Whereas Plato, to be consistent, would have to allow friendship to turn into the universal solidarity of politics, Aristotle ends up reducing friendship to what family affairs would become if freedom and equality replaced natural necessity and gender hierarchy.

Either way, friendship retains no independent worth of its own. Instead, relations between friends that do not substitute for family membership and citizenship become no different in ethical character from relations among strangers.

The Lacuna of Friendship in Modern Ethics

If friendship is to be irreducible to family, social, or political community, it will have to seek its guidelines in property right or morality, the only alternative modes of self-determination. Yet neither property nor moral interaction gives friends any special entitlements or duties to one another.

The norms of property relations and moral accountability pertain no differently to friends than to strangers. Neither property entitlements and contractual obligations nor moral duties are contingent upon shared interests and experiences or mutual affection and attraction. Whether persons are friends, enemies, or indifferent strangers does not affect their property unless they happen to allow such considerations to influence the acts by which they dispose over their holdings. Yet even then, these acts count as dispositions of property irrespective of the interests that accompany them. Respect of ownership in no way obliges individuals to dispose of property in function of friendship or enmity. In morality, interest and welfare do come into play to the extent that moral agents hold each other accountable in respect to the conscientious purpose and intention underlying their actions, incurring praise or blame only for what they do on purpose and only for consequences they intend in light of their own determination of the moral good. In this context of moral accountability, individuals act with interest in the sense of aiming at goals they hope to achieve by fulfilling their purpose, and their welfare consists in achieving their interest. Moral agents respect each others' interest and welfare simply by not allowing their responsibility for their own purposes and intentions to interfere with that of others. This occurs irrespective of the status of other individuals and what feelings they may have for one another. Indeed, as Kant emphasizes, the morality of conduct is most evident when one interacts with those one dislikes.

Accordingly, it can come as no surprise that friendship receives scant attention among utilitarian and liberal theorists, who model normativity on property right and morality, to the neglect of ethical community.

Kant might appear to be the big exception to the rule insofar as he maintains that persons have a duty of friendship.[19] Yet Kant grounds this duty in the adoption of ideal dispositions making prospective friends worthy of happiness, where these dispositions consist in sharing sympathetically in the well-being of one another by joining in exercising a morally good will. This disposition thereby becomes indistinguishable from the general duty of benevolence that Kant mandates for all persons in their relations with strangers and friends alike.[20] Moreover, Kant suggests that this disposition is an unattainable idea because those who strive for friendship can never be sure whether each party acts with equal benevolence and whether benevolence does not conflict with respect.[21] If friends make themselves too familiar, they therefore risk their own dignity. And although friends are morally obliged to point out each other's shortcomings, this may be seen as a lack of respect.[22] The problem of balancing benevolence and respect is irrepressible. Each party, Kant acknowledges, should seek to spare the other of having to provide care, for allowing mutual help to be the end of the relation would undercut respecting one another as autonomous agents. Yet, by refraining from being benevolent to one's friend, one diminishes friendship, whereas by extending aid one diminishes the dignity of the other by putting the recipient under an obligation that is not reciprocated.[23] This outcome leaves friendship as devoid of independent normative stature as before. For, on Kant's account, friendship either becomes indistinguishable from moral conduct in general or remains a problematic ideal.

Friendship deserves no more place of its own in ethics if, like Hegel, one acknowledges property right and morality, without ignoring ethical community. For, granted that property, morality, family, society, and state exhaust the different spheres of right, friendship still engenders no obligations or entitlements specific to itself.

Just as property and moral rights are not conditioned by the friendships of persons and moral subjects, so family relations involve their own entitlements and obligations irrespective of the friendships of their members. Spouses owe each other the same conjugal care and respect whatever other friendships they may have, whereas parents and children retain the same juridical relation whatever their friendships may be. If friendship impinges upon family responsibilities, it thereby wins no juridical place in the home any more than a robber acquires any ownership of what he or she steals.

The freedoms of civil society are equally indifferent to friendship. That commerce involves friends is wholly incidental to its economic character and to individuals' exercise of equal economic opportunity. Similarly, honoring the rights of individuals to equal treatment under the law precludes privileging friends at any stage of the legal process. Amity has no allotted place even in social interest groups, where individuals unite in pursuit of shared ends, for the joint advocacy of such groups is defined by factors specific to civil society (e.g., class interest, consumer rights, environmental concerns, etc.) that are independent of the particular bonds of friendship. By the same token, a public welfare institution cares for the economic well-being of individuals without concern for who their friends may be.

Camaraderie is equally incidental to the political arena. Holding political office is based not on amity, but on election by one's fellow citizens, with strangers playing no different a role than friends. Political activity is partisan on the basis of shared political programs rather than on fellowship. If fraternity is to figure as a virtue of a just republic, it must embody the impersonal concern for upholding the rights of all citizens in a constitutional democracy, with utter indifference to the favoritism friends show one another.

In short, if relations among friends have any normative standing, it will not be in virtue of their amity, but in respect to their rights as owners, moral subjects, family members, social agents, and citizens. Because none of these rights are qualified by the presence, absence, or degree of friendship among the parties involved, friendship warrants no special treatment in the philosophy of right other than as a contrast term from which genuinely distinctive normative relations can be distinguished.

The differentiation of friendship from family ties serves just this purpose of putting into focus what sets household relations apart from informal fellowship.

Family Relations in Contrast to Friendship

Friendship distinguishes itself from family membership at every stage of its development. Individuals become friends as a result of the experience of particular mutual decisions to fraternize, without any single agreement that formally ratifies the friendship for the parties involved or for others. Hence, the beginning of friendship has an informal, indeterminate character that reveals itself only retrospectively.

Once established, friendship unfolds through the pursuit of joint activities, but without entailing a common home in which property gets merged and mutual care becomes a strict responsibility. Friends may hold property in common, but that property will be a particular part of their respective holdings, rather than something inclusive of the private domain of each friend. Similarly, friends do not have any claim upon the present and future earnings of one another nor any claim upon their respective properties apart from particular contractual agreements. Moreover, activity in behalf of a friend is a matter of moral benevolence, rather than a juridical duty. Friends are not obliged to be responsible for nor entitled to participate in raising each other's children. Nor do friends who are children have any claim upon or any obligation to obey each other's parents.

By contrast, the dissolution of friendship might appear to closely parallel the dissolution of family ties. Like marriage, friendship may terminate due to the natural contingency of death or the psychological contingency of a change in feelings of attraction and aversion. Yet the dissolution of friendship does not raise the problem of dividing a common home since friends already retain separate private domains. Similarly, the end of friendship does not pose questions of alimony.[24] Friends do not belong to a substantial unity for whose upkeep they remain responsible. Ex-friends are not responsible for supporting one another or for supporting the children of ex-friends for whom they are not guardians. Moreover, since friendship imposes no juridical duties requiring legal promulgation and enforcement, its dissolution no more involves a publicly recognized formality than does its inauguration. Indeed, whether friendship is recognized by others is a matter of indifference from start to finish. So long as friends do not infringe upon one another's property, moral, family, social, and political rights, their friendship remains a purely private affair, whose integrity includes the prerogative of unilateral termination at any time.[25]

Against these phases of friendship, the outline of family community stands out in sharp relief. Whereas one cannot be placed into a friendship through the acts of others, one commonly[26] first belongs to a family through birth or adoption to individuals who have incurred the publicly recognized obligation of parenthood, an obligation resting not on biological relations of reproduction, but on the acknowledged ethical commitment to raise a child. Alternately, when one does enter a family voluntarily, membership proceeds from a publicly recognized formality, the marriage, with binding consequences for the spouses. Moreover, whereas friendship is entered simply on the basis of mutual willingness, prospective spouses must fulfill formal requirements that today generally involve age, prohibitions of incest and bigamy, and, most questionably, gender.

Once married, spouses distinguish themselves from friends by consolidating their property into a common ownership subservient to the end of maintaining the family well-being, by being obliged to care for the welfare of one another, and, when children are involved, by being obliged to insure their upbringing to autonomous maturity. In fulfilling these duties, spouses are entitled to jointly manage the household property and to take joint responsibility for caring for their children. Whereas friends are never compelled to sustain their relation, the entitlements and obligations of family life are publicly enforced.

Finally, when marriage breaks down, a publicly recognized formality, divorce, is necessary to signal the termination of the juridical relation between spouses. Whereas the breakup of friendship remains a private matter, with no publicly enforced consequences beyond what strangers owe one another, divorce entails distributing family property and future income in function of the entitlements of spouse and children.

Significantly, these differences are not defined by any natural or psychological factors, but only in terms of distinct modes of interaction, involving different rights and duties. For this very reason, the acknowledged discrepancies in friendship and family ties are commonplaces of modern practice, even as the traditional restrictions upon married life and premarital relations go by the wayside. Nonetheless, the familiarity of the divide only delivers an ethical message if it can be supplemented by an authoritative drawing of boundaries, delimiting the structures of freedom. To this end, the abiding differences between friendship and family must be corroborated in the rational reconstruction of the household as an institution of ethical community.

By now, this undertaking has a doubly enhanced plausibility. Natural and psychological factors have proven unable to prevent family relations from being ordered as an association of freedom. On the other hand, the differences between friendship and family suggest that household association cannot be reduced to the moral ties of friends, where commitment remains subjective and fellowship imposes no rights and duties that individuals do not already possess as owners, moral agents, and members of society and state. By contrast, the ways in which domestic ties diverge from friendship from start to finish indicate that individuals acquire new entitlements and obligations by belonging to their families, for whose common welfare they serve as beneficiary and benefactor alike. As the mores of friendship testify, contract institutes nothing but particular disposals of preexisting property entitlements just as moral accountability projects the same perennial norms onto each and every relation. By comparison, family ties engender normative commitments that begin and end with family membership, suggesting the basic logic of ethical community, where agents exercise rights and observe duties reproducing the association within which their self-determining role can alone subsist.

What then are the rights and duties specific to family membership and where should the ethics of family community begin?

CHAPTER IV

Marriage

With What Must Family Ethics Begin?

In order to escape reliance upon unjustified factors, ethics must achieve a theoretical independence analogous to the practical autonomy with which conduct frees itself from arbitrary customs and authorities. To avert succumbing to dogmatic assumptions, ethical theory must refrain from introducing any relations whose normative preconditions and constituents it has not already established. Any appeal to foundations must be avoided, including any surreptitious recourse to accepted beliefs and so-called "moral intuitions." In positive terms, this prohibition amounts to allowing valid conduct to be progressively developed in terms of its own constitution, with the content dictating the order by which it is addressed. Since normativity consists in structures of self-determination, ethical theory must begin with the most elementary structure of freedom presupposed by all others, yet presupposing none itself. If any more complex practice serves as the point of departure, ethics will have taken more basic constituents for granted, compromising the legitimacy of all that follows. Commencing instead with the minimal form of freedom, ethics must then advance to the mode of self-determination that comprises itself out of nothing but a plurality of individuals who already interact in terms of that first form of right. Only then will no unaccounted for material be smuggled in. Each successive sphere of right must meet the same demands of systematic immanence:[1] it must constitute itself entirely out of the resources made available by the modes of freedom already at hand, without merely reiterating the prior relations.

Contrary to foundational argumentation that derives legitimate practices from prior postulates, the initial structure of freedom does not serve as a principle mandating norms that follow upon it. Rather this most elementary form of self-determination figures as a constituent element in the modes of freedom that have their own distinctive rights and duties. Accordingly, each sphere of right retains its self-determined character, instead of becoming a derivative formation owing its design to antecedent factors, whose own givenness is taken for granted. Thereby escaping the flawed architectonic of prior principles and their derivatives, ethics achieves closure when it arrives at an institution of freedom whose own characteristic self-determination unifies all the preceding spheres of right that enter into its own formation. Such a unifying achievement is the work of democratic politics, which upholds all the prepolitical spheres of right in conformity with its own exercise of self-government, doing so for its own sake to the degree that citizens can only engage in political self-determination if they are not oppressed in any other sphere of conduct.[2]

Applied to the family, the demands of systematic immanence entail two complementary strictures. On the one hand, the just family cannot be conceived until after its normative preconditions have been determined. On the other hand, the development of family relations cannot incorporate any terms from other spheres of right that themselves presuppose the household.

The normative preconditions of the family are twofold. Granted that the family can comprise a sphere of freedom sui generis, undetermined by natural or psychological necessity and distinct from the personal morals of friendship, family relations must presuppose the elementary freedom of property relations, where persons reciprocally determine themselves as owners, and the reflected freedom of moral agency, where subjects hold one another accountable for the aspects of their actions prefigured in their conscientious determination of valid purposes and intentions. Although, as we have seen,[3] these two modes of self-determination ultimately require further institutions to overcome violations and incipient conflicts, property and moral rights do not incorporate family, social or political relations as necessary components of their own exercise. They possess their conceptual primacy because no further relations of right can operate without incorporating recognition of the property and moral rights of their participants. Unless individuals are recognized as property owners, that is, as persons, they are tantamount to slaves, subject to the will of another and thereby incapable of enjoying any rights that membership in family, society or state could entail. Similarly, if the moral accountability of individuals is ignored, they can hardly be held responsible for observing the duties or enjoying the entitlements that ethical community involves. For these reasons, which communitarians ignore, ethical community cannot be the exclusive field of normativity in conduct, but must itself presuppose and incorporate the rights of property and morality that function apart from community. Consequently, the family cannot comprise an institution of freedom unless its members enjoy recognition as persons and moral subjects, exclusively owning at least their own bodies and incurring blame only for what they have done on purpose and only for the consequences that they intended with an understanding of what comprise valid purposes and intentions.[4]

Taken strictly, this requirement might seem to exclude any presence of children within the family since individuals remain prisoners of childhood only so long as they are recognized to still be without the complete autonomy that comes with maturity. Lacking autonomy, children might appear equally lacking the status of personhood, rendering them property of their parents, as Roman law maintained. In that case, children would fall beyond the pale of moral responsibility and be subject to whatever discipline parental masters might impose. If, however, children are recognized to be *immature* persons and moral agents, whose immaturity consists precisely in possessing the potential to full autonomy, the exclusive normativity of freedom precludes their treatment as subservient and expendable things. Instead, bringing their potential autonomy to actuality becomes the governing consideration. Then their presence in the family can accord with property and moral rights, just as the presence of children in society and state can accord with civil and political right once childhood gets recognized as a way station to attaining the knowledge and independence needed to exercise one's rights and respect those of others. In that case, children are entitled to be treated with respect for their future autonomy, allowing them to qualify as owners, as beneficiaries of legal protection and social welfare assistance, and as citizens, even if they can only exercise the entailed rights with the aid of recognized trustees. Accordingly, whereas only some members of the family may qualify as fully competent persons and moral subjects, all family members must qualify as at least *potential* persons and moral subjects to enjoy domestic rights.[5]

Conversely, valid family relations cannot be constitutively determined by social and political factors. Although not every social agent or citizen need belong to a family,[6] social and political institutions of freedom still incorporate households within their spheres, such that economic affairs, legality, social welfare administrations, and government all refer to independently given family relations. Moreover, if households are not constituted as associations of self-determination, but allow some adult members to lord unilaterally over others or permit domestic roles to be defined by factors given independently of right, membership in the family will interfere with individuals exercising their social and political freedoms on a par with others. So long, for instance, as family roles are dictated by gender, giving one sex easier access to public spheres, the disadvantaged gender will not be able to participate equally in society and state, despite gender neutral rules of social and political interaction.

On both grounds, family freedom must be conceived prior to and apart from the determination of social and political institutions. Only then will it be possible to conceive coherently how economic relations, legal affairs, public welfare administrations, and political institutions must be structured to uphold the family rights and obligations of individuals while not allowing their family involvements to prejudice their social and political opportunities.

Still, it is one thing to grant that the conception of the family proceeds with individuals who already figure as persons and moral subjects but without any appeal to social or political factors; determining the minimal relation of family freedom is another. With what interaction is family ethics to begin?

Marriage as First Topic of Family Ethics

The obvious starting point is marriage, broadly construed as the interaction whereby individuals become recognized as spouses of one another. Marriage appears to meet the dual requirements of the minimal family relation since 1) marriage occurs between individuals who do not yet stand in any specifically domestic relation to one another, and 2) all further relations among spouses presuppose it, including the relation of parents to their children, even when those parents are separated or divorced. Accordingly, the likely order in determining the structures of family freedom would be 1) marriage, 2) the conduct of married life between spouses, 3) the dissolution of marriage as it exclusively affects spouses, 4) the relation between spouses and their children, and finally 5) the dissolution of marriage as it affects spouses and their children. This path would allow each aspect of family relations to be determined after its preconditions had been established. After all, the conduct of married life among spouses is predicated upon marriage, just as the dissolution of marriage presupposes married life. Moreover, what applies to relations between spouses and children already incorporates the relation between spouses. And if any wider ties were to be introduced within the free family, such as extended households, these would presumably follow upon the former spouse/spouse and spouse/children ties by virtue of incorporating them rather than being part of their determination.

Two other sets of family relations seem, however, to defy integration into this series.[7] On the one hand, individuals with no spouse may have children, whereas, on the other hand, adult relatives may live together forming households without spouses or children.

Unmarried single parents and their children might appear to be just as minimal a family unit as childless spouses, for neither arrangement involves other domestic relations. Nevertheless, unlike marriage, the single parent unit does not function as a constituent precondition of more concrete domestic relations. If, for instance, a single parent marries, the ensuing relations of spouses and children could just as easily arise out of marriage between previously unmarried and/or married spouses who do and/or do not have previous children of their own. Conversely, the rights and duties applying to single parents and their children appear equivalent to those of parents who become single as a result of divorce or death of their spouse. Consequently, single parent households can be treated without detriment in conjunction with the parent/child relation predicated upon marriage.

By contrast, relations between adult relatives[8] involving neither conjugal[9] nor filial ties cannot be similarly incorporated in the ordering proceeding from marriage. Does this signify that an independent parallel development of family ethics applies to households where combinations of siblings, cousins, nephews, nieces, aunts, uncles, or grandparents and grandchildren live together as adults? If the relatives in question do not live as spouses, then in what respect is their juridical relation any different than that between roommates who owe one another respect for their rights as independent property owners, moral agents, bourgeois, and citizens? And if they are otherwise obliged, can this be on any other terms than as veritable spouses, allowing their bond to fit under the heading of conjugal relations and within the ordering of family relations that follows upon marriage? In the absence of any other alternatives, the case of cohabiting relatives leaves the former ordering intact.

Accordingly, family ethics must begin with marriage, that relation whereby individuals who are otherwise juridically determined solely as persons and moral subjects acquire a new conjugal autonomy with rights and duties of its own.

Methodological Quandaries in Conceiving Marriage

In any systematic argument, the starting point of analysis vindicates its own position as a beginning only as a result of the development that follows from it. Although the minimal content of the starting point may already exhibit the exclusion of extraneous, unestablished factors, the ensuing development can alone confirm that the starting point is a beginning from which more follows, what the starting point is a beginning of, and that its role as starting point is nonarbitrary. The development that follows can settle all these matters by exhibiting how every further determination of the emergent subject matter presupposes the point of departure either as a structural constituent or as a term to which reference must be made.

This feature of systematic argument puts the determination of marriage in family ethics in somewhat of a bind. On the one hand, marriage provides a starting point insofar as prospective spouses do not yet stand in any family relations to one another whereas, by way of anticipation, all further household rights and duties are or can be defined by relations predicated upon marriage. On the other hand, marriage contains implicitly the entire scope of household relations. In becoming spouses, individuals knowingly enter a domestic relationship whose prospective character already mandates the terms of its genesis. Consequently, although marriage may conceptually precede the determination of the other dimensions of family ethics, it must reflect in germ the whole panoply of domestic norms. To determine what marriage is, who can qualify as a spouse, which spouses are entitled to marry one another, and how marriage should take place all seems to require an understanding of the valid conjugal life to which marriage provides entry. How can this understanding be at play without family ethics begging the question, presupposing in its first step the very body of knowledge it aims to provide?

A way out of the dilemma lies in distinguishing between the concept of conjugal association minimally ingredient in the process of marrying and the complete determination of valid married life predicated upon marriage. The former concept has a doubly ideal character in that it prefigures what is yet to be realized and it is represented in the understanding of the prospective marriage partners to the degree that normatively valid marriage is a free union entered both by choice and with knowledge of what kind of relationship it will comprise.

To avoid arbitrarily introducing family relations and violating the successive ordering of family, civil society, and state, the minimal concept of conjugal association must involve nothing more than a plurality of individuals recognized as persons (e.g., owners of at least their own bodies) and moral agents, who now determine themselves as members of the most basic ethical community.

That this basic ethical community provides the germ for the determination of family ethics can only be established by following out how the family, reconstituted as an institution of freedom, turns out in all its different dimensions to be the minimal structure of ethical community, presupposed by civil society and state. This retrospective vindication may well satisfy the demands of reflective equilibrium, provided that the family institutions of our day and prevailing ethical "intuitions" happen to conform to the dictates of the philosophy of right. What, however, will give this vindication more than conventional applause is the link it has to the development of the entire system of freedom, starting from the minimal structure of self-determination, property right.

What then is the rudimentary structure of ethical community, as it can be constituted with nothing more than a plurality of persons and moral agents, who as yet participate in no further ethical institutions? To the degree that the family is the basic shape of ethical community, this question converges with that of what is the minimal shape of family association.

The minimal ethical community, simply given without further qualification, comprises a particular group whose members define themselves by autonomously and directly willing the common good of the association as the already embodied structure enabling and obliging them to exercise that volition. The association is *particular* in scope because ethical association can minimally proceed between as few as two individuals and the members *directly* will the good they pursue in common because any indirect willing of it, such as defines the self-seeking interdependence of market relations, involves the added qualification of a mediated connection. Further, because ethical community is a structure of self-determination, the common good its members aim at is not defined apart from the freedom they exercise, as it would be if, following tradition, its roles were derived from natural differences or extraneous cultural antecedents. Rather, the good they will in common consists in the very partnership that they sustain by jointly determining their shared sphere of action.

The role membership involves must accordingly oblige each participant to act in behalf of the common life of their association, where observance of this duty consists in realizing a distinct form of freedom: exercising the right to pursue a common good that other members are equally obliged to promote. Membership must itself consist in having one's welfare be the immediate concern of other member/s, which, given the reciprocity of right, must equally involve treating the welfare of the others as one's own responsibility. If such mutuality is lacking, having one's welfare cared for becomes a privilege of which other family members are deprived and to which they are subordinated. Moreover, the welfare in question must not be a fate imposed upon each member, but something determined by the member's will, as the satisfaction of a freely chosen interest. Otherwise, the association will not be a structure of self-determination, even if all members are treated equally.

One's interest as member must therefore be an interest of a very special kind, an interest that is both shared and inclusive, so that pursuing it automatically promotes all members' aims in common as a work of their coordinate freedom. If the interest were shared but not inclusive, it would merely occasion an ephemeral expedient union of individuals who may as well be strangers, leading otherwise unconnected lives. Accordingly, more is here at stake than a moral interest, for moral agents can never be assured that their personal determinations of good purposes and intentions will count as a unification of welfare and right for their counterparts, whose conscience can always speak with a different voice. Similarly, members cannot interrelate in terms of property entitlements, since these automatically involve respecting distinct private domains, rather than upholding joint interests. To guarantee the fit between welfare and right, that is, between the ends that individuals autonomously pursue and recognition of their legitimacy by others, members of such an association must overcome the divide of their personal property and the disengaged standpoint of conscience. What each autonomously wills must be an end that the other parties should will if they are to perform their role as member, sustaining the union to which they belong. This can be achieved when what members aim at is the flourishing of an inclusive life in common, which encompasses all their private projects and which they share in determining. Under these conditions, members have no interests of their own that are not joined to the interests of their partners, whereas the particular union they reproduce in securing their joint welfare remains a work of their freedom. As a consequence, members are able to exercise a freedom to be had no where else but in such an association: the freedom to codetermine a joint private life, in which one enjoys the right to pursue one's freely chosen interests with the freely given assistance of another insofar as those interests have a shared scope reflecting the same freedom of one's partner.

Taken by itself, this bare notion delineates a basic ethical community particular in scope, with no further terms accounting for how the individuals involved have come to be members of the same union. Because it is particular, the association in question immediately places its members in a dual relation: they are united together as partners in a common, inclusive relationship, and they are equally differentiated from other individuals with whom they are not so united. Since their own status as persons, moral agents, and family members is a matter of right, they stand in relation to others who themselves must qualify as property owners and morally accountable subjects who may or may not belong to their own distinct domestic association.

Since such an association is particular, yet inclusive in scope, it can only be an institution of freedom if its members establish their union autonomously in a manner recognizable by other agents. If any other individuals or institutions were to impose conjugal union upon prospective spouses, the common right and welfare they are obliged to uphold would rest upon an extraneous foundation, rendering their domestic life an homage to a superior power instead of a realization of freedom. Conversely, if conjugal relations are themselves instruments of oppression, bearing the imprint of external or internal privilege, the entry into marriage cannot coherently proceed as an act of self-determination on the part of its participants. Because the mere concept of marriage mandates a path of entry indissolubly linked to what it heralds, the convening of marriage must not be deformed by false preconceptions about domestic life.

To comprehend the normative prescriptions governing the entry into marriage, three key misconceptions must be set aside, misconceptions that have successively dominated the theory and practice of domestic life and still present barriers to conceiving and realizing what marriage should be. These misconceptions consist of predicating marriage upon natural necessities of bisexual reproduction, identifying marriage with a contractual relation, and treating marriage as nothing but a relation of romantic love.[10]

Marriage and Nature

As an immediate ethical association, directly joining individuals into a common private domain, marriage undeniably contains the natural lives of its members with no juridical barrier separating them. Spouses may not be at liberty to rape, assault, and otherwise unilaterally dominate their conjugal partners, but nothing intrudes between them other than their personal volitions. By contrast, because civil society and state relate their participants without eliminating separate personal domains, intimacy is extraneous to social and political freedom. The all-inclusive privacy of marriage, however, places every aspect of welfare and interest at common, albeit codetermined, disposal. This includes the dimensions of sexuality predicated upon bisexual reproduction, provided, of course, that marriage involves rational agents who possess this contingent natural constitution. Since the particular biology of rational agents may vary, allowing for asexual reproduction as well as infertile hybridization, sexual difference and, indeed, sexuality itself need not be present at all. Nevertheless, to the degree that finite rational agents are embodied and marriage involves a joint private domain, conjugal ties automatically entail an intimacy in which individuals are at home in both body and soul.

This does not imply, however, that the natural relations contained within marriage's joint privacy possess any juridically determining role in prescribing either the conduct of married life or the manner by which it is entered. Indeed, if marriage is to be an institution of freedom, natural necessity cannot independently prescribe any norms of conjugal conduct. With respect to the institutions of freedom, all that nature lays hold of are those dimensions of life and recognition that are inescapably naturally determined. These simply comprise the natural conditions of agency in general (e.g., a physical environment allowing for embodied intelligent life) and of the practical interaction of agents (e.g., that agents be close enough spatially and temporally and possess sufficiently similar size, power, metabolic rate, sensory equipment, linguistic apparatus, and so forth to communicate and act with respect to one another's volitions). As such, these natural preconditions apply indifferently to the existence of *all* conventions and thereby leave utterly undetermined what distinguishes good conduct from bad. In particular, they play no constitutive role in determining the distinctive acts of will by which family association operates.

Accordingly, agents who by nature possess the capacity for bisexual reproduction are hardly all obliged to exercise that capacity, either within or without marriage, nor are they obliged to structure their conjugal lives around the requirements of such natural functions. Although the maintenance of family members, as well as of social and political institutions, eventually requires the enlistment of new generations to contribute what can no longer be done by the aged and deceased, this general imperative can conceivably be met without each and every individual engaging in procreation and child rearing, be it within or without wedlock. Moreover, when declining birthrates and/or increasing mortality make it imperative that the private initiative of fertile individuals be supplemented, public incentives can still be employed so as to retain reproductive freedom. Hence, even if reproduction be exclusively centered in the family, fertile rational agents can escape the mandate that their conjugal life should involve procreation.

Were procreation and child rearing a condition for the validity of marriage, the logical consequence would be to follow Bertrand Russell's proviso that no marriage should be binding until pregnancy is achieved,[11] with the addition that marriage should dissolve as a juridical tie as soon as children reach maturity and leave parental care.

While such restrictions would subordinate spouses to an extraneous natural necessity violating domestic freedom, that very freedom requires that spouses be able to exercise the right of codetermining the joint welfare and interest of their conjugal association and to fulfill their corresponding obligations to one another. To do so, however, requires nothing more than the capacities by which an individual functions as a property owner and moral subject. Consequently, individuals need not be of a particular gender, sexual orientation, procreative capacity, or procreative willingness to enter into marriage and enjoy conjugal self-determination. Nor do marital right and duty become annulled when reproductive duties are completed or ignored out of choice or necessity. To enter and sustain conjugal relations, all that are required are the basic qualifications of rational agency: independence of will, sufficient knowledge to exercise that will responsibly, and the capacity to recognize and be recognized by those with whom one will associate.[12] The natural preconditions of these qualifications necessarily enter in as well. Any further natural features do not.

Individuals therefore have the right to marry irrespective of any natural or conventional factors that do not impede their ability to exercise the conjugal entitlements and observe the conjugal responsibilities entailed by domestic unity. Since independent persons and moral subjects already possess that ability, they are all entitled to marry. By contrast, children and the curably insane are deprived of that entitlement until they attain the requisite effective autonomy, whereas those who cannot exercise free agency due to irremediable psychological, mental, and physical impairments are unfit just as much for marriage as for participation in any other sphere of freedom.

Liberating the right to marry from illicit natural restrictions may clarify who can qualify for conjugal relations, but it does not entirely settle the question of which autonomous agents are entitled to marry one another. As incest taboos, among others, suggest, separate considerations may erect juridical barriers between the marriage of certain individuals otherwise entitled to marry any number of other possible candidates. Nevertheless, the same reasons that bar natural factors from prescribing entry into marriage apply to some of the most common objections to marriage between specific rational agents.

First, since imperatives of procreation cannot dictate family ethics, marriage cannot be legitimately prohibited between individuals because they will not produce offspring with one another due to either infertility, choice, and/or the absence of exclusively heterosexual relations. Consequently, prohibitions against marriage between individuals of the same gender or with transsexuals cannot be supported by appeal to the requirements of reproduction.

Similarly, incest taboos applying to marriage cannot be upheld out of concern for the genetic problems of inbreeding. Since spouses are not obliged to reproduce, let alone to restrict themselves to spouses of a different gender, the issue of inbreeding need not even arise between genetically related individuals. By the same token, genetically transmitted disabilities need not bar affected individuals from marriage, be it heterosexual or not. Moreover, in both cases, genetic testing and abortion enable reproduction to proceed without arriving at the feared results. Accordingly, if incest taboos are to restrict who may marry whom, the relevant prohibitions must have other grounds, as indeed they turn out to do.

Marriage versus Contract

If the right of marriage cannot coherently issue from nature, might conjugal freedom instead be a contractual relation, imposing entitlements and duties that first arise through the agreement of the independent persons who would be married, just as in any other contract?

The temptation to appeal to contract in determining marriage has manifold grounds. To begin with, if marriage is not a product of natural necessity, but a work of freedom, and the family is presupposed by society and state, rather than predicated upon social and political relations, contractual agreement seems an appropriate and sufficient vehicle for inaugurating matrimony. Since spouses need have no further status than person and moral subject, and marriage involves a joint private sphere in which property and welfare are consolidated, contract appears to be just the instrument needed to effect the union at stake. Indeed, contract seems indispensable if the autonomy of prospective spouses deserves respect and the liberal route is followed of rooting all obligation in mutual agreement. Then, contract provides not only sufficient, but necessary conditions for establishing marriage as a rightful union. And, as a final confirmation, the rise of modern "love" marriage, where individuals choose one another as spouses without authorization from parents, extended kin, clergy, or any further power, suggests the historical triumph of contract over marriage.

Yet, as tempting as recourse to contract may be, difficulties arise the moment any attempt is made to fit the marriage relationship within the confines of contractual agreement. Even if marriage partners forge their conjugal relation through a mutual agreement, there is something highly incongruent between the reciprocal consent to marry and the exchange of terms in contract. Contract, as a relation of property right, constitutively involves the exchange of factors external to the parties involved. Although these factors can figure as objects of contract because they are recognized to embody the will of their owner, they remain separate from the contracting agents, even if they consist in alienable services. Consequently, parties to contract always remain independent persons, with inalienable ownership of their bodies, just as every contractual agreement always touches only a partial sphere of the private domains of its participants. If any alliances are established through contract, they can concern joint disposal over only a portion of the property, including alienable services, of their owners. In no case can contract touch upon internal, as opposed to external, factors, such as love and sentiment, for the simple reason that all internal matters lack the externality that first enables them to figure as property, embodying the will of a person in something outside the subjectivity of agency.

In addition, the terms of contract are arbitrary, limited only by what the parties are recognized to already own and what they can agree to exchange, provided they do not thereby violate the property rights of others. As long as the contracting parties understand the terms of their agreement, properly represent what is to be exchanged, agree without duress, and respect the rights of other persons,[13] they are at liberty to shape the details of their contract as they please.

Given these inherent features, contract offers at most the kind of caricature of conjugal life to which Kant is led in his *Metaphysics of Morals*.[14] Employing property right to approximate the inclusive union of matrimony, Kant, like Locke before him,[15] construes marriage as a contract wherein spouses trade exclusive use of one another's body, putting at disposal that most intimate of properties. If this contract is taken at face value to give each party the *entire* use of the other's body, then it reverts to an incoherent mutual enslavement, where each marriage partner treats the other as a thing while being used as a thing in turn, as if one could alienate the whole use of one's body and still retain the recognized autonomy to own the use of anything else. If instead, Kant's marriage contract limits itself only to sexual use, leaving each party's body otherwise available for self-selected activity, it becomes a mutual barter prostitution, where spouses interact as separate owners for whom any further union of property, interest, and welfare remains incidental, if not inexplicable. Following Locke,[16] Kant feels compelled to add two crucial features: first, he seeks to sanctify the marriage contract by subordinating the mutual entitlement to one another's body to the end of the procreation of humanity, and secondly, in function of this reproductive imperative, he injects into marriage the mutual support and communion of interests enabling spouses to care for their common offspring. This appeal to the duty of procreation as the ultimate basis for family unity, is, however, extraneous to the freedom of contract and therefore reflects a substantive aim whose role in marriage requires a different justification. For this reason, Kant tellingly admits that individuals do not become spouses proper until the marriage contract has been followed by sexual intercourse directed at procreation.[17]

Moreover, the injected communion of interests remains not merely extrinsic, but antithetical to contract, which presupposes the separate status of contracting parties, who persist as independent owners before and after each and every contractual relation. Even if individuals were to merge all their available property through contract, the resulting joint venture could still not achieve the inclusive unity of matrimony. Individuals can never contract away the entirety of the use of their body, since doing so would relinquish the basis for any recognized independent conduct. Nor, by the same token, can they contract to be perpetually responsible for the welfare of another, whose interests are joined to one's own. To achieve such a merger would once more require eliminating the distinction of independent persons on which contract is predicated. Accordingly, contract is incapable of establishing the community of interest of matrimony, which enables spouses to have equal claim upon one another's care and earnings at least as long as marriage endures.

A similar incongruence underlies the long-standing recognition that the marriage "contract" involves restrictions upon the freedom of the parties that conflicts with the autonomy of property right, as well as liberal contract doctrine.[18] Whereas contractual freedom leaves the terms of agreement open so long as person and property are not violated, the terms of marriage involve prohibitions limiting both the choice of marriage partners and the conduct of conjugal life by standards completely extraneous to the respect of personhood. On the one hand, individuals who otherwise are entitled to contract with one another are barred from marriage by, for example, incest taboos applying to consenting adults, prohibitions of polygamy, and restrictions to heterosexual unions. On the other hand, individuals who otherwise are entitled to enter contracts under terms of their choosing find themselves only able to marry in accord with fixed strictures of marital rights and duties that are reflected, among other things, in recognized grounds for marriage annulment and divorce.[19] Although the content of these restrictions has varied historically and is certainly subject to dispute, a common recognition persists that the marriage agreement involves compulsory principles that are not subject to contractual revision, rendering marriage what some have called a "preformed status contract."[20] The prevailing refusal of courts to allow wives to contract away rights to support and to enforce contracts between husband and wife reflects this anomaly of a marriage contract whose terms are beyond determination by the parties to the agreement.[21]

Given the acknowledged fixity of the terms of marriage, it is not surprising that the marriage agreement commonly lacks the full disclosure of terms that is required to be made to all parties of binding contracts. Although Okin sees this reflecting how marriage has been the paradigmatic contract between unequals,[22] the absence of comparable disclosure more essentially reflects how the terms of marriage are determined apart from the particular volitions of contracting parties. Since the terms of marriage are independently available, they need not be articulated in conjunction with the particular agreement in order to be known to the prospective spouses.

Furthermore, the relation between the entering into contract and the performance of its terms is significantly different from that between the marriage agreement and the assumption of matrimonial roles. Whereas, as Hegel points out,[23] the performance of a contract can occur well after the reaching of agreement, the act of marriage immediately ushers in the practice of matrimony, with all its attendant rights and obligations. The key to this discrepancy lies in how the marriage agreement gives its newlyweds a qualitatively novel status, in distinction from contract, which simply enacts a particular property arrangement between persons who already are immersed in property relations. In effect, individuals have already left behind the external relation of unattached persons the moment they publicly agree to become conjugal partners, which is why Derrida, commenting on Hegel's treatment of marriage, can suggest in his cryptic way that individuals never become married, but always are already married when giving notice to the community of the unity into which they have coalesced.[24]

By way of anticipation, it bears noting that a similar disanalogy applies between the termination of contract and divorce. On the one hand, whereas validly entered contracts cannot be unilaterally annulled unless specific terms of contract so provide, the rise of no-fault, unilateral divorce challenges such contractual procedures. On the other hand, measures that counteract the ease of divorce on demand (by requiring spouses to undergo waiting periods and public scrutiny before obtaining divorce) are just as incompatible with the right of contract as the handling of postdivorce property divisions and support in accord with fixed, independently stipulated family rights and obligations.

These anomalies are all symptomatic of how marriage is not a property relation, but a form of ethical community. Although legitimate marriage may proceed from a freely entered agreement, the nature of matrimony precludes that the agreement fit the form of contract. That freely entered agreements could be anything but contractual may be a mystery to liberalism, given its denial of ethical community. But to paraphrase Bradley, if marriage is still to be described as a contract, it must at least be acknowledged to be a contract to end all contract.[25] Unlike contract, which always leaves its parties in the position of separate property owners, ready for further contractual engagements, the very terms of marriage render the marriage agreement the last act of will that its parties can make as separated, independent persons until their marriage is no more.[26] By establishing a conjugal unity, the parties to the marriage agreement will to be manifestations of a common domestic will,[27] relinquishing their external relations to one another as independent persons, mediated by separate alienable property, without which they cannot contract with one another.[28] Persons can only stand in a contractual relation by means of external alienable factors in which their wills are recognized to be discretely embodied. By contrast, the marriage agreement unites the private domains of its participants, such that nothing in the joint property and welfare of the established family can count as external to any of its members. Marriage thus joins spouses in an immediate unity to the degree that they unite into a common household without any third intervening factor providing the basis of their relationship. For this reason, as Derrida emphasizes in his commentary on Hegel's theory of marriage, there is no marriage *contract,* properly speaking; the free inclination of individuals to become spouses excludes contractual agreement precisely because it does not forge an association mediated by external factors, as abstract juridical bonds of contract constitutively do.[29] Although, as Hegel points out, freely entered marriage does involve the arbitrary, personal choice of with whom one marries, this is not an agreement over a particular external factor. Matrimony instead concerns the entirety of the juridical personalities of its participants, whose decision to conjoin their property and welfare into a unitary domestic domain, relinquishing their separate private spheres, is precisely what removes the conditions for contract to define the relation between spouses.[30]

Nonetheless, the immediacy of the union does not cancel the plural, intersubjective character of matrimony. To the degree that marriage confers upon spouses distinctively conjugal *rights* with respect to one another, they retain separate individual agencies as marriage partners, with specific entitled prerogatives. These rights, however, do not consist in the independent license to dispose of property of one's own, of which freedom of contract is an extension.

If matrimonial right has any specificity, it resides in the entitlement to comanage family property and welfare, sharing the right to be cared for by one's spouse while being obliged to provide equivalent care in return.

The independent ownerships underlying contract only touch upon matrimony from without: beforehand, with prenuptial agreements excluding particular property from the family sphere; during marriage, when spouses represent the joint personhood of the family in property relations with outsiders; and afterwards, when marriage breaks down and ex-spouses face one another as separated private individuals.

At most, the increasing frequency of prenuptial agreements, especially among remarrying divorcees with children, suggests that spouses can retain contractual relations with one another, but not that marriage is itself a contract. Prenuptial agreements are entirely incidental to marriage, whose joint private domain can perfectly well include all property that spouses owned before matrimony. This does not signify that spouses relinquish self-ownership, becoming virtual slaves of love. To the degree that spouses unite into a common domestic association in which each of their wills retains an equal and equally essential realization, the norms of matrimony proscribe any unilateral submission of the body of one to the will of the other. Each spouse retains ownership of the one property that is inalienable in principle: a person's own body. This cannot be forfeited, since doing so reduces an individual to a rightless factor, incapable of participating in conjugal or any other form of right. Accordingly, although matrimony does not relate spouses as separate owners of *alienable* property, it neither relates them as objects of property nor removes their standing as persons and moral subjects. Their personhood has instead been enlarged to include the common property of a joint household, just as their moral interest and welfare has expanded to include the mutual care and support enabling family members to determine as their interest a common good already embodied in the household to which they belong. For this reason, spouses can commit malicious and nonmalicious wrongs against one another that do violence to person and property, even if matrimony establishes a joint private sphere. There is a crime of marital rape, not to mention other forms of marital abuse. Since all such violations involve individuals whose marital status makes each responsible for honoring the rights of their spouse, any violation of one's rights by the other comprises a violation of matrimonial duty as well. Conversely, whenever spouses ignore their matrimonial duty to respect the shared interest and welfare of their counterparts, they strike at an autonomy that incorporates the agency of owner and moral subject.[31]

If these implications underscore how marriage need not involve prenuptial restrictions upon matrimonial ownership, they equally reflect how unless prospective spouses consolidate some of their property and become individually responsible for each other's welfare, they will not have advanced from being independent owners and moral subjects to attain the additional status of members of a domestic ethical community.

Indeed, whether marriage overrides all prenuptial agreements limiting the extent of joint ownership remains a controversial question. To decide the issue requires determining the valid conduct of married life, as well as the proper treatment of divorce and the due ramifications of the death of spouses. Whatever the verdict of these investigations, prenuptial agreements can hardly turn marriage itself into a contractual relation. At most, prenuptial agreements pose the issue of whether matrimony has any legitimate place for spouses' retaining antecedent contractual agreements with one another.

Liberal feminists are thus employing the wrong standards when they appeal to norms of contract to uphold the rights of spouses against the oppressions of gendered household, social, and political institutions.[32] What lies at stake is not the freedom of contract, but the ethical freedom of marriage.

Marriage and Love

With neither natural difference nor contract capable of defining the distinctive unity of matrimony, love readily appears to be the missing factor providing marriage its essential character. Given the normativity of freedom and the incommensurability of marriage and contract, the replacement of parental arrangement by "love" marriage seems to signal the reconstruction of conjugal life upon the foundation of romance.

Certainly, of all ethical relations, matrimony is most amenable to love. Social and political community can operate with no more than interdependent interests and shared programs for governing. Whether individuals be strangers, friends, or lovers is a matter of indifference for their membership in society and state. Marriage, however, forges an intimacy in which mediating rationales for unity fall by the wayside. Within the coalesced privacy of matrimony, spouses join immediately together in their unique individuality, which is the only proper object of love, whose own immediacy of feeling is receptive to the individual rather than to universals or particular types. Consequently, a "love" for humanity in general is more a duty of benevolence than anything commensurate with romantic passion. By the same token, one does not love another because of embodied qualities, as if any other exemplar would do. No recipe for Mr. or Ms. Right can conjure romantic feelings by itself. Although certain features of an individual may more attract a lover, which qualities elicit romantic passion is a purely subjective matter opaque to any rational prescription.[33] Conversely, because love does not derive from particular qualities, it can remain attached to a person whose characteristics change. Love is therefore historical, depending not upon abstract features, but on an encounter with an actual individual. It follows, as Nozick duly reasons, that love is no more transferable to persons with similar qualities than it is subject to redistribution when the loved one benefits from "unearned" natural endowments that play a role in attracting romantic passion.[34] In sum, individuals love one another in their given totality without any mediating grounds providing sufficient explanation for the "mystery" of amorous attraction. As Kierkegaard observes, the less "why," the more love.[35]

Yet, if love appears to have a place in matrimony sharply contrasting to love's wholly incidental role in social and political community, can marriage retain any distinction from the informal romances in which individuals live as lovers, but not as spouses? If marriage is defined by love and informal romance is a permissible exercise of interpersonal freedom, how can matrimony possesses any normative character beyond the moral ties of friendship? And in an age where freedom is increasingly accorded legitimacy, with widening toleration of unmarried couples,[36] how can marriage appear as anything but a completely redundant relic, adding nothing to romance but inconvenient entry and exit formalities?

Maintaining a distinction between marriage and romance, of course, need not exclude love from matrimony; it only requires that the essence of marriage not reside in that factor. Or, to put matters conversely, upholding a meaningful divide between freely entered "love" marriage and informal cohabitation demands that matrimony add something normatively salient that romance lacks. Marriage must somehow transfigure love and infuse it with an ethical dimension otherwise wanting.

How marriage is irreducible to love can be gleaned from the

oft observed limitations of romance, with which modern thinkers have so frequently sought to redeem matrimony from the caprice of passion. Romantic love rests on what is accidental: a passion for the individual that, being immediate, is therefore groundless and inherently ephemeral. In distinction from lust, romantic love does not depend simply on physical attraction, nor is it contingent upon beauty. Although no merely natural necessity dictates when and where or for whom love strikes, romance does not issue from a decision, be it unilateral or bilateral.[37] It retains a receptive, contingent basis that escapes reduction to a determination of will. Lovers may proclaim the lasting, unselfish character of their relation, but romantic passion provides no such guarantees. Although lovers may profess enduring devotion to one another, that devotion remains contingent upon the personal feeling of each party, which may evaporate at any moment. Thus, as Kierkegaard observes, romantic love becomes prey to ridicule and irony for building a union that claims unqualified eternity for itself upon a purely subjective, temporal, and conditional foundation.[38] If romance tries to escape such anomaly by reducing itself to a purely casual affair, whose transience is openly acknowledged and even relished, the bond of love becomes even more contingent upon arbitrary desires and interests, further reducing the meaning of romance while rendering inexplicable why a marriage based on such love should involve more than a fleeting affair.

From the point of view of romance, any attempt to give love a "true eternity"[39] through a determination of will binding spouses to a lifelong commitment only violates the liberty of personal passion. For if marriage has nothing to offer beyond romantic love, matrimony becomes a prison the moment either spouse has lost that special feeling.

Romance and matrimony could appear to become happy bedfellows in a "conditional marriage,"[40] which individuals enter with the understanding that they will cohabit so long as it pleases them, but separate with no strings attached whenever a happier option comes along. Although conditional marriage thereby minimizes trust and weakens the resolve of spouses to uphold their union,[41] these liabilities need not disturb individuals for whom ethical community has little attraction. Reduced to a minimal conjugal commitment, marriage can serve their needs of "personal growth and self-fulfillment," providing a "lifestyle enclave" in which individuals exchange feelings and pleasures,[42] indulging their psychological gratifications with an ease approaching freewheeling romance.[43] The very success of this solution, however, calls into question the reality of marriage to the degree that under such conditions matrimony appears indistinguishable from informal cohabitation.

Conditional marriage seems to approximate contemporary matrimonial arrangements where no-fault divorce on demand prevails.[44] Moreover, such arrangements are equally amenable to the middle course of the marriage of convenience,[45] where prudential calculation of personal costs and benefits provides a utilitarian measure for individuals to become and remain married, just as lovers, friends, or strangers might calculate when and whether to live together. Such marriages nonetheless remain genuinely distinct from informal unions so long as spouses still enjoy juridical rights and duties that cohabiting lovers do not. Lovers may well find their own freedom affirmed only in being drawn to one another,[46] and this romantic union may lead lovers to care for one another and share property in ways completely paralleling matrimony. Modern states have increasingly recognized such behavior as grounds for extending the rights and duties of spouses to informal unions, transforming them into the equivalent of respected common law marriages.[47] By itself, however, lovers' concern and sharing remains purely contingent upon personal feeling, whose own durability is itself accidental. Marriage, on the other hand, upholds the rights and duties of spouses even when their passion has lapsed. Only the recognized decision to divorce brings these entitlements and corresponding obligations to some end.

Such differences reflect how the marriage bond involves acts of will going beyond the limits of romantic passion. These limits revolve around the receptive, inward and subjective character of the feeling of love from which romance proceeds. To the degree that feeling is receptive rather than self-determined, it lacks the dimension of responsibility without which duty can hardly apply. Further, insofar as feeling is internal and not directly embodied in ways that automatically affect the agency of others, it cannot be subject to external regulation.[48] Consequently, if one's ardor for another cools, no obligations are violated if one limits oneself to treating one's former love with the same respect that one is morally bound to show to any other person.[49] When love is over, the affair is simply finished.[50] By contrast, insofar as matrimonial rights and obligations pertain to conduct impinging upon individuals who belong to the same domestic community, marriage is susceptible to external mandate and regulation, upholding a very sharp divide between the treatment of spouses and nonspouses. Although romantic love may enter into matrimony, the recurring traces of a distinction between spouse and lover testify to a field of irreducible marital right involving an exercise of freedom above and beyond what animates informal affairs.

What is the affirmative character of this added element that allows marriage to transfigure the romance it may contain and contribute an autonomy somehow lacking in the liberty of the affair? Given the exclusion of natural determination from right, what freedom marriage adds must be entirely independent of procreation and child rearing, even if these biologically conditioned functions can enter into family relations as a further field for domestic right. Hence, the question that needs answering is what further entitled autonomy does marriage confer upon individuals simply in virtue of becoming spouses?

This autonomy conceivably has two dimensions: a negative side, involving liberation from a confinement that marriage might remove, as well as a positive counterpart consisting in the new exercise of freedom that matrimony provides.

Negatively speaking, the unmarried may well fall into the double bondage to which they are condemned by Judge William, the voice of Part II of Kierkegaard's *Either / Or*. First, because single persons owe no one an accounting for their private behavior, they are slaves to their own whims in their personal life even while they conform to public norms of social and political rectitude.[51] Second, lacking the obligation to be strictly open with any one else,[52] unmarried individuals are strangers in the world, liable to become enslaved to those on whom their solitary domestic upkeep depends (housekeepers, etc.).[53] These shortcomings might appear to be abetted by friendship and romance, wherein singles share in an intimacy that tempers their solitude, self-indulgence, and dependence upon strangers. Yet to the degree that these informal intimacies lack any objective, juridically binding commitments, the liberation they provide remains hostage to the very subjective caprice and atomism they are to counter.

Accordingly, marriage can be said to contribute a positive freedom in which the immediacy of romantic love becomes mediated by an objective bond,[54] formally recognized by spouses and outsiders alike to empower spouses with juridical entitlements that are not simply expressions of the passions of individuals. The *recognized* prerogative to codetermine a joint domesticity is a right that unmarried lovers never attain without making the transition to conjugal partners, be it through formal marriage or public recognition as a "common law" couple. Partners in romance each may feel sufficiently enamored to share everything, but the shared feeling to do so is something different from enjoying the objectively acknowledged entitlement to comanage a consolidated private sphere in which the merging of the right and welfare of each party is obligatory. For this reason, what distinguishes marriage from romance is not preserving love in time, supplementing first love with mundane faithfulness, as Judge William maintains in *Either/Or*.[55] Cohabiting lovers can inject their romance with such an inner history without assuming the mutual rights that individuals first acquire as spouses. This irreducible empowerment, embedded in the elementary ethical community of marriage, is the key element that gives marriage a rationale in consonance with, rather than in opposition to, freedom.

The romantic argument against marriage ignores this salient point, as well as the place for romance both within and as prelude to marriage. Domestic rights are not inherently inhospitable to the continuance of romantic love between spouses. Although romantic love may itself be a stranger to family duty,[56] marital obligations need not stifle romance so long as romantic love ties spouses to one another, rather than to anyone else. When the resolve to marry supervenes upon falling in love, it does introduce an element of reflection on whether love should be mediated by conjugal right. Nevertheless, such reflection does not automatically sound the death knell for the immediacy of romance, whose amorous feeling can just as well persist.[57] The transition from informal cohabitation to marriage thus need not involve any restriction upon the liberty of the heart, although many a case may exhibit the contrary.

Indeed, to be consistent, individuals can hardly assume the roles of autonomous spouses unless they choose one another with the same independent resolve with which romantic lovers act upon their passion. Even if marriage involves more than romance and need not be animated by an abiding romantic love,[58] the transformation of matrimony into an institution of right, demarcated from society and state, readily fosters the notion that marriage should issue from romantic love, rather than from external mandates, such as parental arrangement.[59] For when the separation of kinship from economic and political affairs has been achieved, with nepotism prohibited, hereditary rank abolished, inheritance restricted, and social inequality reduced so that family ties no longer decide economic opportunity,[60] marriage loses its former economic and political significance, enabling personal attraction, manifest in romantic love, to be matrimony's central facilitator.[61] Nevertheless, as much as romantic love may then be an amenable springboard for freely entering marriage, the abiding difference between cohabiting as lovers and living as spouses indicates that the decision to marry cannot simply be a consequence of romance.[62] Whether mutual feelings of romantic love should even be a prerequisite for becoming free spouses can only be decided by delineating the boundaries of this irreducible ethical resolve by which individuals step beyond the frontiers of nature, contract, and romance.

The Eligibility to Marry

To the degree that marriage establishes an ethical community among spouses, where individuals acquire domestic rights and duties predicated upon membership in their new family association, the act of marrying must have an objectively certified form enabling others to recognize newlyweds as spouses. If such recognition is wanting, individuals' resolve to marry will remain a shared subjective wish, lacking the objectivity required to confer upon individuals the respected freedoms to which spouses are entitled. This objectivity has two complementary sides: first, that the act of marriage take a certifiable form that is universally acknowledged, and second, that the particular individuals' new status as spouses become a public matter at least capable of being an object to the awareness of all rational agents who are obliged to honor the conjugal rights and duties that individuals acquire upon marriage.

Although what arrangements marriage must employ to win this dual recognition involves purely positive details, resting on convention rather than on reason, the formal convocation of marriage and the preliminaries that may precede it are conditioned by the rational strictures that mandate who is eligible to marry whom. Because these strictures delineate the limits of the right to marry, they must be specified before the marriage process can itself be fully prescribed.

As an ethical association, marriage presupposes that its participants be persons and moral agents, who accordingly possess the recognized rational agency to exercise their rights as property owners and moral subjects and to respect the corresponding rights of others. Since the family does not incorporate social or political relations, spouses need have no other standing than that of persons and morally accountable agents in order to enter into marriage and exercise domestic freedoms. In other words, as long as individuals possess the basic rational agency of an autonomous

adult, making them capable of personhood and moral responsibility, they qualify for marriage, irrespective of any other factors,
such as race, ethnicity, nationality, religious faith, occupation,
wealth, or mental and physical differences, that do not hobble their
ability to exercise property and moral rights. Age requirements
for marriage thus legitimately enter in as an index of physical,
psychological, and intellectual independence, provided nothing
better is available to furnish a universally applicable standard for
the maturity that autonomy presumes. Since, however, individuals of the same age may have greatly disparate physical, psychological, and intellectual capabilities, age requirements need to be
supplemented by further standards that specify what minimal
physical and mental condition individuals must enjoy to be able to
recognize the rights of others and to exercise their own. So long as
these elementary preconditions of rational agency are met, individuals qualify as prospective spouses.

In line with these considerations, the right to marry has been
progressively widened by modern developments of the last two centuries relaxing requirements of parental and family consent[63] as
well as lifting bans against marriage of paupers, interracial and
interdenominational couples, and victims of disease (such as epi-
lepsy, tuberculosis, alcoholism, and venereal sickness) and of alleged genetic disabilities (which do not preclude the capabilities
allowing individuals to function as persons and moral subjects).[64]
Nonetheless, additional restrictions still come into play when it
comes to authorizing who may marry whom. These abiding restrictions generally consist in the prohibitions of same sex marriage,
incest, and polygamy, with the last carrying with it the interdiction
of bigamy. Given the exclusive legitimacy of self-determination, the
validity of any such restraints must be measured according to
whether they comprise conditions for the realization of freedom
within or without the family or represent forms of oppression usurp-
ing conjugal rights.

Same Sex Marriage

Because family right, like all other right, consists in enacted structures of self-determination rather than in derivatives of nature,
objections to same sex marriage that appeal to what is putatively
"natural" or what is imperative for bisexual reproduction have no
independent validity. Even if heterosexual mating were not just
the predominant but the sole form of sex among bisexually repro-

ducing creatures in nature, the tag of "unnatural behavior" would still be devoid of normative significance. Who agents should marry depends on how conjugal life can comprise an institution of freedom, something that requires more than patterns of behavior issuing from natural dispositions. All that nature can dictate to ethics is conformity with the natural conditions of free agency, conditions that cannot fail to be already met in the very existence of responsible individuals, whatever be their gender or sexual orientation.

Further, since bisexual reproduction need neither occur only among spouses nor be a feature of every marriage, heterosexual marriage need no more be a prerequisite for the reproduction of the species than the fertility of each and every spouse. Consequently, objections against sexual activity among individuals of the same gender without or within marriage cannot be rationally sustained by citing its nonreproductive or otherwise allegedly "unnatural" character. Not only do such grounds apply equally to much heterosexual behavior, but they are extraneous to the properly normative consideration of whether sexual activity between individuals of the same gender is a violation of the rights of the participants or of anyone else. So long as the sexual activity involves freely consenting adults, does not violate the privacy of others, observes due care for the health and safety of the participants and any other potentially affected individuals, and does not violate the trust of spouses or other lovers, it is hard to see how such behavior violates rights in any sphere any more than would heterosexual behavior that meets the same standards.

In order to sustain a prohibition of sex between consenting adults of the same gender, such sex would have to subvert their autonomy, either through undermining the preconditions of freedom or by violating the rights of one another. Yet since the physical and psychological differentiation of heterosexual and homosexual/lesbian sex leaves completely undetermined what ethical qualities (respect, loyalty, tenderness, caring, etc.) may accompany its respective lovemaking, any inherent ethical "depravity" is groundless. Moreover, since sex with any gender can be performed safely or unsafely, the mere orientation of sexual activity has no connection to the health that rational agents need as a precondition for self-determination.

What determines the legitimacy of sexual activity is not what genders are involved, but whether sex is consensual and kept within limits of time and care not impeding individuals' exercise of their domestic rights and duties or of their entitled freedoms and corresponding obligations as owners, moral subjects, social agents, and citizens. The freedom to codetermine the joint private domain of domestic property and welfare is simply indifferent to the sexual orientation of those involved. Indeed, although the coalesced privacy of marriage is the most apt institutional setting for sexual intimacy, the fulfillment of conjugal right and duty need not involve any specific carnal activity, be it due to physical and psychological limitations, spatially and/or temporally divergent occupational and political commitments, or mere lack of interest.[65]

Accordingly, any proscription of marriage based upon the sexual identity of the prospective spouses is not only devoid of legitimacy, but a violation of the right to marry. This applies as much to the prevalent prohibition of same sex marriage as to any restrictions specially placed upon the marriage options of hermaphrodites or transsexuals, such as the bans in England and France against transsexuals marrying individuals of the same former sex.[66] Whether the sex of an individual be defined by external anatomical difference, chromosomal composition, or psychological sense of gender, the right to marry individuals of the same, opposite, or intermediate sexuality remains an unimpeached entitlement essential to upholding the family as an institution of freedom. To the degree that basic family rights should never be trampled upon with impunity and that no further rights are thereby jeopardized, the entitlement to marry irrespective of gender deserves constitutional protection.

Incest and Marriage

In contrast to prohibitions of same sex marriage, incest taboos appear to be an irremovable bedrock of family and social life. The virtually universal ban of incest in some form or other seems to reflect an unconditionally valid core. In respect to the normativity of freedom and the due differentiation of discrete spheres of right, incest prohibitions seem to garner legitimacy from two widely held views of modern anthropology and psychology. First, by guaranteeing that individuals marry outside their household, establishing the plurality of interacting families between which distinct social and political arenas can emerge, incest taboos seem to be the indispensable prerequisite for the disengagement of kinship ties from society and politics.[67] Second, from the point of view of psychoanalytic theory, incest taboos plays a key role in the development of an autonomous personality.[68]

The first view, that the incest taboo is a precondition for overcoming tribalism and liberating social and political arenas from kinship, only holds, however, if marriage among kin is overwhelmingly followed and individuals interact socially and politically solely along lines of kinship. In the absence of incest taboos, however, individuals could still choose to marry beyond bloodlines, just as they could choose, no matter whom they married, to work, trade, and politic with people outside their clan.[69]

Similarly, the role of incest taboos in early childhood development does not directly carry over to marriage prohibitions. On the one hand, age requirements for marriage combined with general prohibitions of child molestation and statutory rape could independently proscribe the sexual experiences that psychoanalytic theory fears. On the other hand, because marriage between consanguine adults involves individuals who have already reached independent maturity, their cohabitation would no longer involve the psychological endangerment to autonomous self-development that incest in childhood presents.[70]

Moreover, even if incest taboos are preconditions of autonomous personality and of a free society and state, the boundaries of incest prohibitions and their application to family right remain far from self-evident.

To begin with, incest taboos, which restrict mating, are not strictly identical with marriage prohibitions keyed to kinship or "affinity" relations.[71] Since marriage need not involve sexual relations between spouses, individuals can conceivably marry those with whom sex would be incestuous without necessarily physically committing incest.

More to the point, the acknowledged limits of incest have so varied historically that the legitimating grounds for prohibiting marriage between kin are clouded in controversy. Whereas Egyptian pharaohs and Inca kings were required to marry their own sisters, at the other extreme the Catholic Church banned marriage within the third degree of relationship (e.g., between second cousins) between 1550 and 1917.[72] Any founding of incest taboos on allegedly universal feelings of repugnance not only illicitly subordinates right to feeling, but ignores historical diversity.[73] However incest boundaries be drawn, during most history and prehistory, life in isolated communities has left people sharing a multiple consanguinity, well reflected by how in rural England the pool of potential spouses was generally confined to a radius of five miles, the distance a person could walk to and from on a day off from work.[74] Given that the mere mathematics of the pyramid of human ancestry guarantees that no spouses can be more than fiftieth cousins, the prevalence of geographical limits to available marriage partners makes it plausible, as one expert maintains, that four-fifths of marriages have been with second cousins.[75]

If such facts suggest that incest prohibitions cannot pretend to exclude all kinship from marriage partners, the violation at issue in one principal focus of incest taboos requires no reference to family roles. Sexual relations between adult and minor family members, be they married or not, comprise violence to the person of the minor for the very reasons that sex between an adult and a minor should be considered a punishable felony of statutory rape. Even if the minor has consented, the minor still lacks the recognized mature independence to make sex with an adult count as a mutually chosen act. Consequently, sex between parents, grandparents, or any other adult relatives and their minor kin is already prohibited by due provisions penalizing statutory rape and molestation of minors. For this reason, France has deleted the felony of incest in favor of punishing any adults who abuse their position to engage in sex with minors.[76] Similarly, owing to the age requirement that duly permits only mature, autonomous individuals to marry, no separate prohibition of marriage between adult and minor kin of any degree of consanguinity would be needed, even if marriage does not automatically entail subsequent sexual relations.

The only factor that would warrant added attention is the violation of custodial duty perpetrated by adult family members who abuse their minor relatives. This violation of a distinctly domestic duty, however, does not concern marriage eligibility of custodians and their minor charges, which age requirements would already preclude.

If general prohibitions of sex and marriage between adults and minors thus remove the need for any separate incest taboos covering adult and minor relatives, the same cannot be said for cases where kin marry one another after reaching maturity. In these circumstances, which can involve both grandparents and grandchildren, parents and children, uncles or aunts and their nieces or nephews, cousins, siblings, or steprelatives of each and every gender and sexual orientation, additional proscriptions require some further rationale.

Historically, modern legal systems have tended to narrow incest prohibitions to marriage between parents or grandparents and their descendants and between siblings, whether full or half-blooded.[77] Germany makes no other unconditional exclusions, permitting marriage between parents and adopted children. By contrast, in England, the United States, and France, marriage is banned between adoptive parents and their children. France permits marriage between adoptive siblings, as well as between aunt and nephews or uncles and nieces, whereas England and the United States prohibit marriages between aunts/uncles and nephews/nieces, unless, in the American case, aboriginal cultures are involved. In addition, England bans marriage between stepparents and stepchildren when they have earlier lived together as parent and child, whereas France prohibits marriage between brother- and sister-in-law unless the marriage making them in-laws has already been broken by divorce.[78]

To determine which, if any, of these prevailing incest restrictions have ethical legitimacy, the tribunal of right is once more the sole authority. Neither secular nor religious tradition can provide unqualified guidance, since no convention nor any allegedly divine commandment can claim authority if it diverges from what can independently be determined to be just. Moreover, since none of the proscribed matches involve minors, they cannot be banned by directly relying upon age requirements for marriage or the prohibitions against statutory rape and child molestation.

A familiar alternative involves basing the forbiddance of incestuous marriage upon the dangers of inbreeding. Although this move appeals to the natural process of genetics, it need not be at odds with the exclusive normativity of freedom. Since rational agency has biological preconditions, genetic dangers fall within the scope of right, whose conscious upholding of the prerequisites of persons and their entitled freedoms supervenes upon any evolutionary dynamic wherein natural selection favors the survival of genetically diverse species.[79] If marriage was automatically tied to procreation, mating between individuals of a certain consanguine relation had a reasonable likelihood of producing offspring with an impaired rational agency, *and* genetic screening of fetuses and abortion was unavailable, there could be genetic grounds for limiting marriage options accordingly. As long as inbreeding were not the exclusive marriage option, particular instances would not by themselves comprise much of an evolutionary threat to the survival of the species, but they still could handicap the exercise of freedom of any immediate offspring who suffer disabling congenital defects. Under such conditions, the dangers of inbreeding would not justify extending incest prohibitions to individuals lacking consanguine ties, such as adoptive children and their parents or grandparents, stepparents and their stepchildren, and certain half-siblings. Analogously, given that the gender and sexual orientation of individuals should not restrict those they are eligible to marry, a genetically supported incest taboo would not prohibit same-sex marriages among family members, be they with one's siblings, parents, grandparents, or other relatives. If these options are to be banned, some other rationale would have to be found. This, however, does not preclude a genetic basis for forbidding incestuous marriage between close heterosexual blood relatives of the opposite sex.

What does subvert reliance upon the dangers of inbreeding even here is the illegitimacy of tying marriage to procreation. Because matrimony can have normative validity as an ethical association even if spouses do not procreate, the genetic argument cannot justify absolute prohibitions of marriage between individuals whose inbreeding would pose biological dangers sufficient to undermine their offspring's rational agency, let alone the survival prospects of their species of rational agents.[80] This holds true even if prospective marriage partners have no access to birth control, genetic screening and abortion. If they were informed of the genetic dangers, they would share responsibility for any resultant impairments to the autonomy of whatever offspring they produced. They could even be held responsible for reckless conduct if they produced offspring, who, against all odds, suffered no genetic damage, provided one can be held liable for negligence even when no harm results.[81] Nevertheless, since the mere forging of a marital union does not entail offspring, even when the spouses want children or when birth control and abortion is lacking, risks of inbreeding cannot justify narrowing the marriage options of individuals. Of course, when birth control, genetic screening, and abortion are available, marriage can easily escape the dangers of genetic disabilities. Consequently, right is duly served by the policy followed by every nation today of permitting marriage between unrelated individuals who suffer from inheritable disease or disabilities.[82]

The failure of the genetic argument, of course, does not rule out alternate grounds for supporting incest taboos in marriage eligibility. In fact, the pitfalls of the appeal to the dangers of inbreeding leave room for wider incest restrictions than genetic risk would entail. This is apparent when one examines the consideration that gives the most coherent underpinning to the scope of contemporary incest prohibitions: that marriage eligibility should be shaped so as to diminish the risk of sexual abuse of minors by their elders in the family and of the accompanying betrayal of parental and conjugal duties. The age and competence requirements for marriage may already ensure that only autonomous, that is, adult rational agents, are eligible to marry. Nevertheless, if marriage is permitted between individuals who antecedently interacted as child and grownup in the same family, a situation arises encouraging adult family members to develop sexual and/or romantic liaisons with minor kin under the veil of household privacy. The danger of such abuse of minors within the family and of its attendant damage to family ties will accordingly be diminished by proscribing marriage between any individuals who previously interacted within the family as child and adult.

This proscription would apply most directly to parents and their offspring and to adoptive parents and their children, including stepparents and stepchildren who acquire their relation of "affinity" (a nonconsanguine family connection) before both have reached maturity. The prohibition would apply more indirectly between individuals and their grandparents, be they consanguine, adoptive, or stepgrandparents, as well as their aunts and uncles and any other relatives whose family position enabled them to interact with the former while the former were still children. The least direct application would be to relatives of the same generation, such as siblings, be they consanguine, adopted, or stepsiblings, and cousins. Prohibiting marriage between siblings or cousins would only ward against adult abuse of children in the family if an age difference exists sufficient to put minor siblings and cousins in jeopardy of abuse by their adult counterparts. Given, however, that age requirements of maturity would eventually place all siblings and cousins, with the exception of simultaneously born twins and cousins, in the situation where one is a minor while the other is an adult, it would be reasonable to extend the prohibition of marriage to them, provided their family relations place them within the same private domain. Although siblings who live together would fit this proviso, cousins would not unless the family were an extended one, in which aunts and/or uncles maintain a joint household, or a polygamous home in which the very distinction between cousin and sibling tends to disappear. Whether either extended or polygamous families have legitimacy remains to be examined. If they do not, then incest restrictions on marriage eligibility would directly apply only between children and their parents and between siblings. Grandparents and aunts and uncles would be ineligible marriage partners only to the degree that they intruded into the home during childhood. Individuals, by contrast, who become stepgrandparents after their stepgrandchildren reach maturity, would not be ineligible marriage candidates. The strict banning of marriage with grandparents, but not with aunts or uncles, followed today in France and Germany,[83] is compatible with these grounds so long as aunts and uncles have a significantly lesser place in the family than grandparents. If extended families turn out to be antithetical to family freedom, any differences in the presence of grandparents and aunts and uncles within the home would be a matter of convention, rather than a dictate of right. The corresponding incest extensions would therefore be contingent upon empirical observation of whatever pattern happens to prevail.

The restricting of marriage eligibility to discourage the abuse of minors by other adult family members and consequent disruptions of marital life fits the parallel development of an increasing prevalence of nuclear families and a progressive reduction of marriage prohibitions between family members related by "affinity."[84] For as joint, extended family arrangements become supplanted by households consisting only of spouses and their children, subsequent marriage with other relatives poses a diminishing threat to childhood and family unity. The same rationale serves to undergird how prohibitions of marriage between half-siblings have been weakened in face of accelerating divorce rates that have made it increasingly common for half-siblings to grow up in separate homes.[85]

By contrast, as Glendon observes, the "family discord theory" does not provide a rationale for why some American states ban marriages between persons related by adoption, while permitting stepparents and stepchildren to marry.[86] An approach consistent with that rationale would require prohibiting marriage equally between adoptive and stepparents and stepchildren, not to mention between both types of siblings, insofar as each group shares the same household intimacy. On the other hand, dispensations from such restrictions would seem appropriate for individuals who have not lived in the same home, nor interacted in terms of their nominal family ties.

Needless to say, any such prohibitions are not predicated simply upon the preferences of the family members involved or on any unhappiness that results. If that were so, incest taboos could be cast aside whenever, for example, one spouse accepted the other's premarital or marital designs upon their child or other family members were successfully left in the dark about the whole affair.[87] What properly lies at issue instead is crafting marriage eligibility regulations that do not compromise the rights of children and the obligations of parent and spouse.

Further limitations upon marriage eligibility are not necessary to uphold domestic right or other entitled freedoms. No one's property, moral, household, social, or political rights are jeopardized by marriage between consenting adults who have not grown up in the same family but are relatives either by blood or affinity. Accordingly, the only incest marriage prohibitions that would be warranted are those that do discourage abuse of children and the related betrayal of custodial responsibility and marital trust.[88] To dismiss these restrictions would require demonstrating that general prohibitions against child abuse and statutory rape already provide sufficient deterrent to adult family members to prevent family rights' being compromised by a possibility of future marriage. In the absence of such a demonstration,[89] the limitations on marriage eligibility of parents, and siblings who have shared homes is not an imposition on marital freedom, but rather an element in the realization of the domestic rights of spouses, parents and children.

Monogamy, Polygamy, and Bigamy

Questions of gender, sexual orientation, and incest all bear upon marriage eligibility irrespective of whether individuals are to be permitted to marry one or more than one spouse. Consequently, they can be considered prior to and apart from the issue of whether marriage should be restricted to monogamy. Yet once gender, sexual orientation and degree of family relation have had their role in marriage eligibility determined, the debate over the exclusivity of monogamy takes on a character quite different from the traditional terms in which it has been addressed.

Ordinarily, arguments in behalf of the exclusive legitimacy of monogamy have focused upon the prevailing historical forms of polygyny and the much rarer instances of polyandry, rather than on the bare concept of polygamy (understood as marriage between more than two spouses, irrespective of their gender and sexual orientation). Given the approximate parity between populations of men and women, polygyny and polyandry can only be exceptions, unless they figure side by side in the same community.[90] This conjunction has not occurred due to the very two contingent factors on which the exceptional character of polygamous marriage has historically rested: the dominance of one gender in most spheres of life and a sharp differentiation in social and political position[91] among the members of the dominant gender. On this basis, polygyny has taken shape as a marriage form for men of wealth and rank who lord over their wives, choosing unilaterally when to take new spouses, how to divide their attention among their harem, how to raise and educate their children, and how to manage the household property. With male privilege channeling inheritance through fatherhood, the women of the harem are, for their part, to be sexually monogamous.[92] In the rare incidence of matriarchal society, polyandry exists in a parallel form, with the woman enjoying a privileged position with respect to her many husbands. Under either condition, monogamy exists side by side with polygamy, reflecting the predominant position of one gender as well as pervasive inequality outside the household. Monogamy thus hardly exists as a model of freedom and equality, either while polygamy persists or after civil society and democracy have undercut the traditional privilege on which polygamy rested without entirely suppressing residual gender inequalities.[93]

Despite these common shortcomings, arguments limiting marriage to two spouses have generally contrasted monogamy as a model of domestic reciprocity and freedom to the nonreciprocity and despotism of historical polygamy.[94] Such arguments are to be credited for appealing to freedom as the deciding factor and for rejecting the historical forms of polygamy due to the oppression they display by permitting one spouse of one gender to wield unmatched power over a plurality of spouses of a different gender. Given, however, that monogamy can, and often has, incorporated an analogous lording of one gender over another, the question must be addressed of whether monogamy has any privileged connection to marital freedom.

In this respect, it will not suffice to argue, following Engels, that sexual love is by nature exclusive, that marital freedom depends on marriage being based on nothing but sexual love, and that such marriage must therefore be monogamous.[95] The natural exclusivity of sexual love is far from evident, simply given the diverse complexities of polygamy, adultery, and nonmarital romance. Yet even if sexual love were exclusive and marrying on its basis reflected liberation from external obstacles to the free choice of marriage partners, more than two individuals could still freely decide to form a joint household. Just as two prospective spouses can agree to marry even if their "true passion" lies elsewhere, unrequited or not, so individuals can freely resolve to forge a polygamous family without sexual love being the deciding factor. In each case, all that is necessary is that the parties to matrimony personally share the ethical commitment to take on the domestic rights and duties that define their roles as spouses.

To play that role of belonging to a joint private sphere whose right and welfare is codetermined, individuals must enjoy completely equivalent entitlements and obligations regarding entry into marriage, the subsequent management of family property and earnings, the provision of care for one another, and the upbringing of any children for which they are joint guardians. A monogamous marriage can readily meet these requirements so long as spouses act with reciprocity and mutual respect for one another's equal share in codetermining the household.

By contrast, the nonbinary character of a polygamous family makes the achievement of reciprocity and codetermination a more complicated affair. Kant and Hegel have argued that a reciprocal joining of right and welfare is unattainable in polygamy since the spouse who marries a plurality of individuals of the opposite sex enjoys the entire sexual attention and care of his or her counterparts while dividing his or her favors among them.[96] If such an imbalance were inherent in polygamy and touched upon the essential rights and obligations of matrimony, polygamy could not satisfy the requirements of marital right. The argument offered by Kant and Hegel, however, presupposes features that may accurately reflect the historical practice of polygamy, but hardly constitute irremovable aspects of marriages with more than two spouses.

First, because Kant and Hegel both illicitly limit marriage to a heterosexual union, they assume that spouses are heterosexual and that they divide into a plurality of individuals of the same gender wedded to someone of the opposite sex. If, however, this limitation is eliminated, the possibility exists of polygamous marriages involving individuals, be they bisexual, asexual, or all of the same sex, who divide their affection and care so that all spouses have the same relation to their counterparts. No spouses would then be surrendering their entire person to another who offers only a portion in return. Each would have an equal claim upon one another, albeit a divided one.

Further, even if sexual and/or romantic involvement were not equally distributed among every spouse, this need not pose a juridical problem to the degree that one can retain one's ethical rights and duties as spouse independently of romance and sex. Although in any marriage, whether monogamous or polygamous, a lack or imbalance in affection and sex can express a breakdown in the shared intimacy of matrimony, this need not be the case if the spouses remain committed to treating one another's right and welfare as a common concern. The latter may not be easy, and the difficulty may be particularly acute when polygamy involves heterosexual individuals of different genders in different numbers. Yet just as the waning of romance and sexual activity or even adultery need not automatically entail a divorce agreement eliminating

marital rights and duties, so an imbalanced sexual life among polygamous spouses need not impel some or all to break their household apart.[97]

What rather is essential to marital freedom is the ability of
each spouse to have an equal say in the running of the household,
including not only the use of property and earnings and how children will be raised, but also the decision of who may be admitted
into the family as an additional spouse. Whether in a monogamous
or polygamous arrangement, marital right requires that family
roles not be mandated by gender or sexual orientation. Further,
since any new spouse becomes a member of a joint private domain
in which no one deserves a privileged role, marriage decisions cannot legitimately be unilaterally undertaken. If one spouse wishes
to marry anew, he or she must obtain the agreement of all the
other spouses, as well as the consent of the prospective newlywed
to join in marriage with all of them. Analogously, respect for the
marital right of each spouse would mandate that any divorce and
its accompanying property and child custody settlements should
proceed between the separating individual and *all* other spouses,
with the latter jointly deciding their side of the outcome.

In all these dimensions of domestic life, polygamy must reform its historical embodiments to embody reciprocity and codetermination. Yet even in doing so, polygamy retains a division between
the inclusive unity of the family in which each spouse's right and
welfare has been subsumed and the partial attention that each
spouse gives to and receives from every other.

Hegel maintains that any such division contradicts the reciprocal relinquishing of personality into the joint, undivided domestic unity distinguishing marriage from other ethical associations.[98]
Although he directs this objection against the traditional polygamous arrangement where a husband lets his desire dictate which
wife to receive, Hegel's point can be generalized as the claim that
polygamy of any form connects one spouse with another through a
particular appetite, transforming marital love from an ethical right
and duty into a matter of personal preference.

Such an argument fails in two respects. First, even if polygamous spouses are obliged to divide their love and care, while each
giving up their entire privacy, the common good of the family resides precisely in this divided interaction in whose pursuit household right and welfare is maintained. By being all for one and one
for all, polygamous spouses do not undercut the unity of the household any more than the addition of children into the family under-

mines the undivided conjugal relation of monogamous spouses. So long as each family member remains equally responsible for caring for the others, sharing property and income, and comanaging an inclusive common household, the presence of more than two spouses does not itself erect distinct private domains undercutting domestic unity and trust. Fulfilling household obligations to all one's spouses and children may entail psychological challenges more imposing than those of monogamy, but the historical practice of polygamy already suggests that more than two spouses can live in common without necessitating psychological harm for themselves or their children.[99]

Accordingly, polygamy can conceivably be reconstructed in accord with marital right. Overcoming the hierarchy and lack of reciprocity condemning polygamy's traditional embodiments, a legitimate incarnation would join spouses of any gender and sexual orientation in a marital union involving the same rights and duties of household codetermination that apply to a monogamy liberated from the heterosexual male privilege imposing a gendered hierarchy upon family life. Whether this involves insurmountable challenges of consensus and coordination can be concretely assessed only in the course of determining the norms of marital conduct, of child rearing by parents,[100] and of the dissolution of marriage by divorce and death.[101]

In the interim, it remains evident that bigamy would still count as a violation of domestic right. Even with the legitimation of a reformed polygamy, a spouse committing bigamy would violate the conjugal rights of both the party to the bigamous union and the spouse or spouses of the preexisting marriage. On the one hand, the perpetrator of bigamy would be forming a new domestic union, establishing a separate sphere of privacy at odds with the preexisting marital commitment to merge one's entire right and welfare with that of one's spouse or spouses. On the other hand, the bigamist would be doing this without obtaining the consent of any of the other spouses either to consolidate into a single family or to divorce so as to properly resolve the conflicting domestic responsibilities. Unlike a polygamist who enjoys the same marital rights and responsibilities as all of his or her spouses, the bigamist would be creating parallel households, dividing his or her domestic life in a way automatically incommensurate with the reciprocity marital freedom requires. The objections raised by Kant and Hegel against polygamy would now ring true, indicting bigamy as a malicious violation of domestic right. Consisting in marriage by a married individual that neither consolidates all spouses into a single family, nor does so with the consent of his or her other spouses, bigamy would remain a domestic crime, warranting punishment as well as possible compensation.

Marital Right and the Extended Family

The abiding wrong of bigamy and the potential right of polygamy have important implications for the legitimacy of extended families, where a plurality of married individuals, traditionally involving siblings and their spouses and parents, live together in a common home, sharing property and income. Needless to say, if this arrangement follows the traditional pattern where elders control the management of the household, lording over children who have become married adults, the extended family deprives the latter of their domestic autonomy, subjecting them to a tutelage fit only for minors. Similarly, if the extended family follows the tradition of limiting itself to heterosexual couples who are related by some specific blood line, it shackles itself to natural determinations that should not limit the shape of family life. A problem still remains if the privilege of elders is removed and each household unit (of spouses and their immediate children) is granted an equal say in family affairs, as well as if joint families are not limited by blood relation and sexual orientation. The question then arises how the extended household can count as a juridical family while each married unit remains a discrete entity, whose spouses retain rights and duties to one another that are different from those they have in relation to the other family members. If such distinctions remain, the relations between married units cannot exhibit the inclusive reciprocity of a joint right and welfare that distinguishes domestic association from friendship and other social partnerships. If, conversely, the difference between family units is eliminated, the extended family becomes indistinguishable from a polygamous household, where every spouse is as much the partner of every other as every parent is the guardian of every child.

Consequently, even when the extended family has cast off the traditional ties that conflict with marital freedom, household right does not attain any new reach. Whether monogamous or polygamous, domestic ethical community genuinely consists solely of the relations of spouses and of parents and children. Further groupings by family name and blood relation have no ethical standing and impose no rights or duties of their own.[102]

Preliminary Formalities to Marriage

Freed from traditional fetters, marriage might appear to be bound by no preliminary formalities once individuals decide to take their matrimonial vows. Prior approval by family elders or religious authorities might be sought for purely personal reasons, but the right to marry can no longer be contingent upon such externalities. Nevertheless, because domestic right has implications for how and with whom individuals may marry, certain formalities are necessary to insure that the entitlements and correlative obligations of prospective spouses are duly honored, in conformity with the domestic and nondomestic rights of others. Insofar as domestic right imposes eligibility requirements upon marriage in function of the autonomy of spouses, marriage must not be concluded until the parties have been certified to be mature rational agents who, irrespective of gender, sexual orientation, race, ethnicity, nationality, or religion, 1) satisfy the minimal incest prohibitions mandated by family freedom, 2) understand the basic rights and duties of spouses, 3) independently resolve to marry, and 4) are not committing bigamy. This certification, comprising the marriage license or its equivalent, must be made public since the domestic rights and duties conferred upon individuals by marriage require recognition by others.

Obtaining certification on these issues is contingent upon whether and how the relevant information is made available for public scrutiny. The time and effort required to guarantee marriage eligibility will accordingly vary. Where public registration of births, deaths, marriages, divorces, and other relevant personal data lags, there may be need for a public notice of intent to marry, followed by a waiting period during which objections to eligibility can be aired and investigated. Where detailed public records are available, but enforcement cannot be taken for granted, marriage may proceed after a rapid check of the relevant information. And where not only the needed facts can be examined, but violators can be readily apprehended, public notification and waiting periods can be dispensed with in favor of merely accepting at face value information entered in filing for a marriage license.[103]

Given the intimacy of marriage and the dangers of venereal disease, it is not surprising that many nations require medical examinations before granting marriage licenses. Generally, the results only serve to inform individuals of their respective medical conditions, rather than barring them from marriage. This purely informative role is in accord with right, first, because individuals should be informed of any infirmities that threaten the health of their prospective spouse and secondly, because any further restrictions would infringe upon the freedom to marry in ways that do not contribute to the realization of self-determination. Prohibiting marriage between individuals with sexually transmitted disease would commit the same injustice as banning marriage between individuals known to carry inheritable disorders. Each prohibition would ignore how affected individuals could fulfill their matrimonial rights and obligations without undermining the health either of one another or of offspring.

Granted the purely informative role of preliminary medical testing, the question arises concerning to whom results should be divulged. In some countries, such as France,[104] only the person examined is informed. This respects the privacy of the individual involved, especially when releasing the results to the prospective spouse may lead to cancellation of marriage plans and public ostracism. Yet should one be left in the dark regarding central health concerns of the individual with whose private domain one is to be joined, especially when ignorance may leave one's immediate survival at the mercy of one's spouse's candor? If medical exam results are disclosed merely to prospective spouses, the due privacy of both parties can be maintained without undermining either one's survival. Moreover, if one or more spouses allow disclosures to become public, any resulting injustices can be warded off by strictly enforced anti-discrimination policies.

These provisos are variously fulfilled in current marriage policy. For example, in England, marriage certificates are only issued after a twenty-one-day waiting period following a public notice of intent, whereas in France, medical certificates as well as divorce papers and death certificates of prior spouses must be filed, and public notice must be given at least ten days in advance of marriage.[105] The opposite extreme is followed in the United States, where in many states intended marriages need not be publicized, premarital medical exams are not required, marriage license applications are simply filed and accepted without any waiting period or investigation, and so-called common law marriage is recognized with no preliminary formalities at all.[106] Combined with freedom to change one's name at will and strict obstacles to obtaining privately information about the civil status of others, such lax U.S. practices place marriage as well as family support obligations at risk.[107]

Formal Versus Informal Marriage

The imperatives of domestic right that call for premarital procedures provide grounds for not automatically recognizing informal cohabitation as "common law marriage." If informal cohabitants are simply granted marital status without further ado, they risk having domestic obligations imposed upon them, without having satisfied the provisos that allow marriage to be in conformity with right. Some preliminary formalities must intervene to certify that informal cohabitants are freely deciding to become spouses with the corresponding rights and duties, have met the necessary eligibility requirements, and obtain public recognition for their union.

Obtaining such public recognition underlies the need for formalities for the solemnization of marriage that at least in part permit others to know the marital status of the newlyweds. Without some public certification that marriage has been duly concluded, the domestic rights of spouses lack objectivity, putting in jeopardy any marital claims they may have with respect to one another. The very fact of their marriage would rest upon subjective assurances, whose authority could always be questioned, either by others or by one or more of the spouses. Any children would have their right to parental care and support equally jeopardized, at least insofar as custodial obligations rest upon marital status.

Because right resides in the foundation-free, self-grounding normativity of self-determination, certification of marriage, like that of any ethical relationship, is a purely secular affair, whose principles are completely independent of religious dogma. Consequently, the solemnization of marriage must ultimately rest upon some civil formality, even if spouses choose to have a nuptial ceremony that has religious trappings. Moreover, given the imperatives of enforcing domestic obligations during and after marriage, the civil practice by which marriage obtains public recognition should be accompanied by some sort of registration that makes publicly certifiable the marital status conferred upon the newlyweds.

These provisos can be fulfilled either by making a civil ceremony compulsory for valid marriage (the rigorously secular path followed in France and Germany) or by permitting both civil and religious marriage ceremonies (the pluralistic approach of Great Britain and the United States),[108] provided the ceremonies are accompanied by a civil registration guaranteeing recognition by all individuals regardless of religious affiliation. By contrast, if only religious marriage ceremonies are recognized, the right to marry is compromised for interfaith or irreligious couples, who face the Hobson's choice of forsaking marriage or sacrificing their freedom of belief by converting to a religious faith they do not share.

The Grounds of Choice in Marriage

As long as individuals meet the eligibility requirements, preliminary formalities, and nuptial procedures for marriage, they have complete latitude in choosing a prospective spouse who agrees to marry them.[109] In conformity with this freedom to marry, individuals are at liberty to allow nothing but mutual inclination to be the deciding ground for their choice. This mutual inclination may or may not be informed by romantic love, erotic attraction, or other factors, including living standards or parental approval. Such grounds only begin to undermine the autonomy of marriage when they intrude due to compulsion. Even if parental approval is no longer required it can intrude upon the freedom to marry when, for example, individuals are economically dependent upon parents and parents use this dependence to compel marriage decisions to their liking.[110] Similarly, if individuals are unable to support themselves, economic necessity can obstruct certain marriage possibilities that individuals would otherwise freely pursue.[111] In this respect, domestic right cannot be upheld unless civil society and the state secure the equal social and political opportunity of all.

Marriage and Family Name

Historically speaking, marriage and naming have been intertwined, reflecting the contingent circumstances that individuals possess family names, that kinship relations intrude upon wealth and power, and that gendered traditions have compelled one spouse or other to take on the family name of their marriage partner. Once marriage is reconstructed as an institution of freedom compatible with social and political self-determination, traditional appellations become at best relics of oppressive institutions, relics rendered innocuous only through the repudiation of the practices they reflect. With civil society and democratic self-government depriving kinship of any social or political privilege, and with the disengaged family freeing itself of domination by the wider blood ties of clan, family name loses its role as a conduit for rank, wealth, and authority. Further, with marriage becoming a relation of free and equal spouses, whose gender, sexual orientation, and descent have no bearing upon their domestic rights and duties, there is no longer any domestic basis for one spouse having the privilege of making his or her family name that of all spouses and children of the new household.

The need for public recognition of domestic status may make marriage registration imperative, but this need not entail that spouses publicly identify their conjugal relation by taking any common name or by adopting visible signs of matrimony such as marriage rings or other forms of dress. So long as means are available to certify who is married to whom, spouses are at liberty to name themselves as they will.[112] Convenience may be served by adopting family names, in addition to some other unique identifier (such as a social security or national identity number). Moreover, expedience may warrant following traditional practice in restricting family name to that of one spouse,[113] but any such device can have no bearing upon domestic rights. Naming must remain a pure formality, devoid of any ethical significance, if marital freedom is to be upheld.

CHAPTER V

The Conduct of
Married Life

Once marriage is determined in concept or reality, family right confronts the ethical topic presupposing no other domestic relation and thereby immediately facing newlyweds themselves: the conduct of married life. The moment individuals become spouses, they acquire a new set of uniquely domestic rights and duties, prescribing the conjugal conduct that commands normativity by building a mode of self-determination sui generis.

These matrimonial entitlements and obligations do not yet involve the specific rights of parents and children, which need not apply to spouses as such. The ethic of parent-child relations is properly treated after the married conduct of spouses both because child rearing is an option, rather than a duty of matrimony, and because child rearing by single parents introduces no special ethical relationships that are not already contained in the parenting of spouses.

The mode of ethical freedom that spouses exercise by themselves is defined by the twofold relation in which marriage immediately sets its newlyweds. On the one hand, spouses stand internally related in function of the common private domain into which they have joined together. On the other hand, because conjugal association is a particular ethical union, spouses stand externally related to other individuals, who may be married or single. In this connection, spouses no longer face outsiders simply as property

owners and moral agents, but as members of a family, whose particular joint right must be upheld in all external transactions. By
the same token, those outsiders who are married figure as representatives of a family of their own, whose shared well-being should
be equally respected in any dealings with other spouses or single
individuals.

The historical privileging of one gender over another and the
proscription of same sex marriage have led to unequal distributions of the internal and external roles of spouses, with wives restricted to domestic affairs and husbands appropriating the representation of the household to other individuals, families, society, and the state. Once marriage is liberated from gender and
heterosexual privilege, however, the internal and external roles of
conjugal life become matters for every spouse, conferring the same
rights and responsibilities on each one.[1]

Although these internal and external roles are concurrent functions of matrimony to which spouses are equally entitled, their
conception has a specific order. Insofar as marriage unites the property and welfare of spouses, internal conjugal relations center upon
the conduct of spouses regarding the common household property
and their common welfare. Since the external relations of spouses
involve representing the joint matrimonial property and welfare,
the external role of spouses must be conceived in function of their
internal role, even if both roles are coeval dimensions of married
life. Consequently, the ethics of married life begins with the relations of spouses to one another.

The Internal Relation of Spouses

Because the free family incorporates neither social nor political relations, but presupposes personhood and moral accountability, the conduct of spouses within the household revolves around the community
of ownership and interest forged by domestic association. Property
provides one element integrated into conjugal community insofar
as spouses must already qualify as persons. Interests take their
place alongside property insofar as spouses must equally be morally accountable subjects, whose autonomously chosen ends comprise a rightful welfare to the degree that they cohere with the
personhood and analogously self-selected aims of others. The interest consisting in achieving such ends can figure as a factor of
conjugal self-determination because it constitutes the attainment
not of externally given goals, but of aims already defined by the

autonomous selection of purpose and intention by moral subjectivity. Within the consolidated association of marriage this interest and the property that underlies it take on a new cast. Their domestic transformation involves no introduction of any socially or politically derived modifications. Although spouses are equally entitled to exercise social and political rights, conjugal right and duty have their own character given independently of any reference to society or state.

The family unites right and welfare to the degree that spouses are entitled to codetermine the control of domestic property in conjunction with treating the achievement of each other's ends as a common concern. Consequently, property right is doubly transformed within marriage: not only are the acquisition, use, and disposal of household property joint rights and responsibilities, but that codetermination of property is subject to the proviso that it should serve the welfare of both spouses.[2] In order for conjugal life to remain a structure of freedom, the welfare in question must be determined in respect to the autonomy of the spouses involved. In this regard, physical and psychological needs can comprise an *element* of their welfare insofar as the exercise of freedom has physical and psychological preconditions. Beyond these prerequisites, however, the content of domestic welfare must be determined by the wills of spouses, so that the further ends in whose satisfaction such welfare consists are self-selected. What makes these self-selected ends not just moral, but domestically ethical in character is that they must promote the joint private existence that spouses have undertaken. Needless to say, not all self-selected ends meet this proviso. What distinguishes marital welfare from any atomistically determined satisfaction of interest is that the self-selected interests of spouses must be in harmony with those of their counterparts in order to enjoy conjugal validity. In pursuing one's legitimate interest as a spouse, one is no longer just caring for oneself, but equally for the other, just as the legitimate welfare of one's spouse promotes life together.[3] This formal requirement provides a framework for determining what marital conduct spouses can engage in without violating their conjugal duties. Due to the reciprocity of marital right, whereby what one spouse is entitled to do is mediated by the opportunity of the other, upholding conjugal welfare will not involve conforming to a set of ends dictated apart from what spouses agree upon as modalities of marital life.

Since property entitlements are the most basic rights, the internal conduct of spouses is first defined by the entitlements and obligations pertaining to joint marital property.

Marital Property Relations

Marital property relations are usually considered within the concrete empirical framework where families are observed existing within societies and states and where their property is found qualified by economic and political relations such as earnings, social welfare benefits, taxation, and statutory regulation. Since, however, society and state contain families, whereas household relations are defined independently of these further spheres, marital property must first be considered in its own right, without reference to the complications that supervene once the relation of family to society and state is addressed. Any other route would take for granted institutions whose own determination presupposes property relations, morality, and the family.

Consequently, at this stage in the development of family ethics, marital property must be considered solely in terms of how its acquisition, use, and transfer should be shaped so as to conform to conjugal right and duty. Although these basic aspects of ownership become incorporated in the economic and political relations in which spouses get enmeshed, the basic norms of marital property are first to be determined in abstraction from these developments.

As we have seen, property relations undergo two basic modifications in conjugal association: 1) ownership becomes joint, and 2) marital property becomes subordinated to the common welfare of the spouses.[4] These transformations entail, on the one hand, that spouses are equally entitled to determine what property will be acquired, how it will be used, and how it may be relinquished or transferred to others, and, on the other hand, that joint decisions regarding marital property should promote satisfaction of the aims that spouses have agreed upon without duress and misunderstanding and without subverting their autonomy as family members.

Meeting these demands requires uprooting traditional arrangements that place control of domestic property predominantly in the hands of one spouse (most commonly, given the predominance of patrilineal households, the husband), while protecting the inheritance of the other spouse from mismanagement by the titular head of the household and keeping title to it in the bloodline from which it comes.[5] Joint ownership is compromised whenever one spouse acts as juridical head of the household or when kinship relations beyond the nuclear family[6] restrict spouses' ability to control domestic property. Both arrangements usurp the right to codetermine marital ownership, which is undermined even if spouses themselves acquiesce to oppressive traditions. Just as political self-determination requires institutions of self-government and not just acceptance of one's rulers, so marital freedom involves more than simply consenting to any household regime. As a mode of ethical freedom, marital self-determination can only occur within a domestic order whose constitutive roles are structures of right.

Framing a marital property regime compatible with conjugal freedom has largely informed the more recent[7] attempts of modern legal systems to specify the rights and duties of domestic ownership. Three basic alternatives appear possible:[8] the property of spouses can be thoroughly united under an all inclusive joint ownership, with or without a mix of separate and joint management; spouses can retain separate ownership and management of all their assets and income; or finally, spouses can order their property in intermediate arrangements, where some property is separately managed and/or owned and other property is jointly held. Modern legal systems have tried all these options under the guise of regimes of community property (where ownership is jointly held), separation of assets (where spouses separately administer and own all property that they individually contribute), and community of gains and deferred community (where spouses independently manage the assets they bring into the marriage, but share either all income or all property when the marriage ends). In grappling with the demands of conjugal solidarity, equality, and independence, these domestic property regimes cast in relief the dilemmas that household ownership must resolve to accord with right.

The community property system might appear to provide the simplest and most adequate fulfillment of conjugal right. To the degree that community property makes joint ownership the rule, it would seem to realize the freedom of spouses to codetermine household affairs with little compromise. In practice, however, community property has had a more complicated implementation, reflecting not only a recalcitrant tradition, but difficulties endemic to marital ownership.

As originally instituted by Napoleon in the French Civil Code of 1804, the community property system gave a decidedly limited realization to the joint character of marital ownership. Although wives were allotted a half-share of jointly held domestic property, conjugal ownership was compromised by two independent restrictions: first, immovable property (real estate) owned separately at marriage or acquired after marriage by gift or inheritance was excluded from the joint community property, together with moveable properties either gifted under the condition of separate ownership or retaining special personal significance; secondly, the husband still enjoyed privileged authority to manage marital property.[9] This retention of control by the husband clearly stands at odds with the freedom and equality of marital right. Similarly, the exclusions from joint ownership of "real" property acquired separately before marriage and of gifts and inheritance received after marriage reflect a residual clan domination over conjugal life, whereby the imperative of maintaining the property of a bloodline subverts the right of spouses to preside jointly over their common private domain.

The restrictions on real and movable property, can, of course, be detached from the imperatives of oppressive ancestral traditions. As George Wright points out,[10] the separate ownership of postmarital gifts could also operate independently of clan property interests, as when a friend might give someone property not to be shared with the latter's spouse. Although Wright wonders what would be wrong with such a possibility, the independent ownership it entails would establish an enclave of separate interests and inequality limiting and potentially undermining the remaining unity of property and welfare that gives conjugal right its distinctive character.

These problems might be thought to be secondary in view of how restrictions on communal property can be seen to follow the same justification commonly made for prenuptial agreements limiting joint marital property: that such exclusions are necessary to protect the welfare of spouses and their dependents in face of the possibility of divorce. From a systematic point of view, such concerns presuppose that divorce is legitimate and that divorce settlements take a form that can compromise the right and welfare of spouses and children, a result that may equally depend upon how public welfare benefits are administered. Moreover, it is debatable whether prenuptial agreements fairly serve these aims when the spouse with greater personal resources will be in a stronger bargaining position to set the terms of those agreements.[11] It would be premature to address these issues at this juncture since divorce, economic inequality, and the public administration of welfare presuppose marriage and the conduct of conjugal life and must therefore still await their own rigorous accounts.

Nevertheless, a further issue does apply to these same exclusions that falls within the confines of marital conduct and provides an important rationale for the other two forms of marital property regimes. Namely, a strictly followed community property regime would require all spouses to participate together in every property transaction. Such a requirement not only seems all too cumbersome for managing family property within or without the home, but imposes drastic limits on personal initiative that are only ameliorated if one assumes a preestablished harmony between spouses on each and every acquisition, use, and disposal of household property. Not surprisingly, early efforts to free household property from male domination did not involve the institution of a pure community property regime, where, in effect, the husband can veto every initiative of his wife. Instead, the new reforms entitled wives to pursue an occupation of their own without the consent of their husbands[12] and simultaneously "democratized" the patrician techniques to preserve family wealth, giving wives control over their own earnings and any separately gifted or willed assets.[13]

These concerns for practicality and autonomy provide strong rationales to temper the community property regime. The abiding question, however, is how far can domestic property be separately managed without disrupting the unity of conjugal life? Do the marital right and duty to codetermine household property and care for one another's welfare translate into the entitlement to control independently one's own acquisitions (including earning activities, income, and bequests)? And if so, how should this independence be constrained, if at all?

An intermediate solution is provided by the community of acquests system, operative in France, where community property is retained, but circumscribed first by excluding all inheritance and all property acquired separately before marriage, and secondly by entitling spouses to manage their earnings independently until these have been converted into other holdings, as well as to engage alone in professionally related property dealings. In addition, each spouse is authorized to manage the community property through independent actions so long as transactions do not involve factors crucial to domestic welfare, such as family homes, furnishings, and business.[14] A pure community property regime would leave no scope for liability for damages for mismanagement of marital property,[15] since damages would have to be drawn from the same joint property into which they are reimbursed.[16] Under the community of acquests system, however, the allowance of separately controlled incomes, inheritance, and prenuptial properties makes it possible for spouses to be held liable for damages to one another for mismanaging community property.[17] At the same time, the power to dispose freely of personal earnings gives spouses the sort of latitude exhibited in a 1984 French case in which a husband was found entitled to channel substantial portions of his earnings to his mistress so long as he still adequately supported his wife and child.[18]

The above-described community acquests system clearly attempts to balance the fulfillment of shared marital obligations with the granting of independent discretion in property dealings, avoiding the difficulties of a joint micromanagement of all transactions and providing a measure of independence to each spouse. The requirement that properties essential to marital welfare be strictly comanaged prevents latitude in personal property dealings from completely undermining the enduring common ownership on which the mutual care of spouses depends. Meanwhile, the freedom to control personal inheritance and gifts, prenuptial possessions, and earnings secures a degree of independence from domination by the other spouse. Yet the possibility of glaring disparities in what possessions each spouse controls equally threatens the freedom of the less endowed, for whom marital support and care may not eliminate a fundamental inequality facilitating domination at home by the more propertied person, especially when the breakdown of marriage threatens to leave spouses in very different conditions.

This threat is partially reduced by the system of deferred community followed in Sweden and other Scandinavian countries. As in the community of acquests regime, spouses in the system of deferred community separately control all property they independently acquire for the duration of the marriage. Once, however, the marriage ceases, these acquired assets are divided equally just as would occur if a community property regime had been in effect.[19] Deferred community thereby ensures that the end of marriage does not privilege the spouse with greater property, unless, of course, the earning potential of one spouse still outstrips the other. At the same time, deferred community allows for convenient and independent management of the household property that each spouse has personally provided.

The community of gains regime, instituted in Germany by the 1957 Equality Law, presents a middle course between the deferred community and the community of acquests systems by permitting spouses to manage separately all assets they bring into the marriage, while excluding gifts, inheritance, and premarital holdings from the equal division of marital property that follows the demise of the marriage.[20]

In each of these three departures from community property, the allowance of separate control need not undermine the joint welfare of spouses provided properties deemed essential to that welfare (commonly identified as conjugal residences, furnishings, and personal effects) are not subject to unilateral disposal. Further, the divided management of personally acquired property will conform to marital duty provided it fulfills the demands of care that spouses owe one another.

This proviso applies to every regime of marital property since the form of marital ownership does not itself guarantee how the welfare of spouses will be mutually served. Differences in personality may, for example, enable one spouse to use the veneer of consensus to dominate another. The latitude for independent property management provided by deferred community and community of acquests or gains systems can then provide a protective buffer to the weaker spouse, unless the disparities in the separately managed properties give one spouse decisive advantages. Thus, although community ownership formally fits the marital principles of codetermination and equal sharing, separate control of certain conjugal properties may promote the equality of spouses, especially when the vestiges of gendered traditions still linger.

The separation of assets regime, followed in the United Kingdom and the United States, exhibits this connection between independent control and marital equality in its most extreme form. Here spouses each enjoy the same control over their assets and earnings as single individuals.[21] Although this gives wives, for instance, a control equal to that of their husbands, it raises two questions: First, does separation of assets disadvantage one spouse when his or her earnings and holdings are markedly less than that of the other spouse? Secondly, does this complete division render spouses indistinguishable from cohabiting lovers?

One factor that seems to mitigate each of these concerns is the countervailing tendency of spouses to acquire and use property jointly, without registering the particular contributions they each may have made.[22] Thus, even though under separation of assets spouses enter marriage with divided holdings to which they add divided earnings, a parallel accumulation of joint property establishes itself, potentially diminishing the significance of differences in personal assets and distinguishing spouses from romantic roommates. Indeed, the prevalence of joint savings accounts and joint real estate tenancies with right of survivorship resembles a voluntary community property arrangement for particular assets.[23]

A second mollifying factor is the commonplace addition of guarantees that nonowning spouses retain "a right of occupation" in the marital home, protecting them from eviction by the owner spouse or by purchasers or mortgagees.[24] A similar role is played by restrictions on spouses' contractual freedom to ensure support of their children.[25] On both grounds, separation of assets does not prevent spouses from remaining joined together in ways distinguishing them from informal couples.

Such qualifications are not, however, necessary ingredients in the separation of assets system. If they are not added, marriage does seem to lose all trace of the joint ownership without which the conjugal merging of right and welfare becomes an empty fiction. Yet, even if the above modifications do become mandatory features of a revised version, the separation of assets system, like deferred community, community of acquests, and community of gain regimes, still allows the household to become an arena in which the relative disadvantage of the spouse with less income and assets retains its force, especially when one spouse is occupied as a "homemaker" with no income at all.[26] Although the developments of a full-fledged civil society have tended to increase the importance of public and job-related benefits (such as family assistance, social security, and public health care) relative to traditional forms of property,[27] this has not blunted the risks of the various departures from community property. Instead, the enhanced significance of a spouse's earning power and benefits makes separate control of such resources all the more dangerous for the spouse who has less of each. Only if disparities in property, earning power, and benefits have no differential bearings upon the domestic welfare of each spouse can limitations on community property be benign variations on family right. This will depend upon the interaction of civil society and the family, a topic that can be systematically addressed only after the family and the various civil institutions have been determined in themselves.[28]

If conjugal right stands in jeopardy from marital property regimes embracing different degrees of separate control and ownership of assets, can a community property system be practical and amenable to the domestic autonomy of spouses?

To begin with, joint marital ownership is hardly incompatible with spouses separately deciding how to acquire, use, and transfer particular properties. Spouses, for example, may retain equal title to earnings, purchases, and exchanges and yet individually make the requisite decisions as trustees of the common household capital. As long as joint ownership is maintained and decisions do not undermine marital welfare, spouses are entitled to use their discretion in administering property. Community property would thus not deprive spouses of the right to decide upon an employment without the consent of their mates so long as their occupation does not imperil the assets or mutual care upon which family welfare depends. Nor would community property prevent one spouse from separately deciding how to manage property (including labor power) in his or her occupation. Once again, so long as such latitude does not undercut marital welfare, it accords with conjugal duty. Moreover, because whatever property gains accrue through such discretion are jointly owned, the independence of spouses does not threaten their equality, as it can under separate assets regimes. Differences in earning power now become absorbed within the unity of community property, which wards against any of these disparities translating themselves into domestic privilege. Accordingly, community property need have no practical disadvantages in comparison to rival domestic property regimes.

Similar considerations apply to consolidating personal inheritance, gifts, and sentimental items under community property. Such consolidation promotes domestic equality and unity in accord with marital right so long as it does not violate duties to spouses and children of former marriages (duties that remain to be determined), nor subjects spouses to having their private effects unilaterally disposed of by their mates, nor subjects spouses to exploitation by predatory individuals who marry only to reap the benefits of divorce settlements. Each of these potential abuses can be countered by measures that may modify the latitude of community property, but need not transform it into a different regime. The right of ex-spouses and their children to support can be retained as a claim upon the *jointly* owned property of spouses. Private effects, as well as essential household assets such as residences and business, can be protected from unilateral disposal. And divorce settlement regulations can ward against predatory divorces.[29]

As for insulating marriage from domination by the more forceful spouse, community property can guarantee every spouse the autonomy of having equal control of household assets without being subject to the disadvantage brought by unequal ownerships in separate assets regimes. This benefit will be particularly important for homemakers, who will retain an equal say over *all* family income and wealth, a say that can be freed from domination by such measures as mandatory deposits of assets and income in joint accounts from which each spouse can freely draw,[30] albeit within the limits imposed upon all domestic property relations by the imperatives of marital welfare. Such measures will facilitate every spouse's having an equal say in such key marital decisions as place of residence or the initiation of expensive education and career training, decisions that cannot be unilaterally taken to the degree that they essentially affect the opportunities of all family members.

The above considerations underscore how the alternative marital property regimes not only have no advantages over community property, but suffer from distinct liabilities that community property wards against. As a consequence, marital right is best served by consolidating the property of spouses under a community regime sufficiently flexible to combine domestic equality, autonomy, and the unity of conjugal welfare.

Moreover, since none of the above considerations hinge upon the number of spouses, they apply equally to monogamous as well as to polygamous marriages, provided that each has overcome traditional oppression that privileges spouses of one gender, crowning them as heads of households lording over their mates. Further, since domestic property issues pertain to spouses irrespective of sexual preference, the consequences of the different marital property regimes are the same whatever be the sexual orientation of spouses, provided genders are treated equally.[31]

As noted, to avoid circularity, the valid marital property regime must first be conceived in abstraction from divorce and the domestic rights and duties that persist between ex-spouses and their children. Nonetheless, these factors will certainly have an impact upon how household property should be managed. For this reason, the initial specification of marital property applies directly only to spouses who do not have dependents from previous marriages and for whom the possibility of divorce does not yet affect their own domestic affairs. After divorce has been addressed, marital property will have to be further determined, taking into account how responsibilities arising out of marriage breakdowns modify spouses' control over family assets.

The Scope of Mutual Care and Welfare in Marital Conduct

The ownership and management of property forms an important, but limited side of internal marriage relations. Equally significant are those dimensions of marital conduct where spouses exercise and fulfill their domestic right and duty by doing more than acquiring, using, and transferring property. This part of marital conduct bears upon all activities between spouses that fall within the scope of their consolidated domestic welfare. Because marriage merges the private domains of spouses into a joint haven, every matter falling within that sphere, from household chores to sex, love, and companionship becomes a potential vessel of marital obligation. To determine those elements which spouses have a duty to perform and a right to claim can only be decided by viewing them through the lens of the ethical freedom of marriage.

Like all forms of freedom, marital self-determination has biological and psychological prerequisites. Consequently, if spouses are obliged to uphold one another's domestic freedom, they are responsible for ensuring the physical and mental health of their marital partners. When spouses are personally unable to provide sufficient care in these respects, they are obliged to obtain feasibly available assistance to enable their partner/s to retain these basic conditions for self-determination. Although a developed civil society will publicly guarantee its members provision of health care, food, and shelter, as well as the further resources needed for equal economic opportunity,[32] marriage remains a first bulwark of care by making the welfare of each spouse a personal responsibility of the other/s, which public concern may supplement, but not preempt.

These responsibilities for upholding the preconditions of domestic freedom pertain solely to the levels of physical and psychological well-being that individuals must enjoy simply to possess and exercise their rational agency. They do not address the further physical and psychological satisfactions that contribute to a happy marriage and the personal happiness that it fosters. Rational agency does not require any particular level of such happiness, which is why mere differences in personal contentment have no bearing on one's entitlements and obligations. Ensuring one's spouse romance, tenderness, sexual fulfillment, personal encouragement, and loyalty only becomes a matter of marital right and duty when it can be tied to the content of domestic welfare, a content that is not a *precondition* of marital conduct, but rather the substance and aim of conjugal activity.

If the content of domestic welfare were fixed independently of the mutual determination of spouses, marriage would be transformed from an institution of freedom into an embodiment of externally imposed virtues, whose vulnerability to the dilemmas of foundational justification would undermine the normativity of matrimony. To escape this difficulty, domestic welfare must be conceived strictly in terms of marital self-determination, whereby what makes a course of conduct domestically legitimate is its conformity with achievement of spouses' mutually concordant interests. What these interests are is a matter for the spouses themselves to determine.[33] Nonetheless, what is not left to their discretion is the abiding requirement that their chosen interests not undermine either their other rights or their roles as free and equal domestic partners.

Taken together, these parameters allow for a certain range of possibilities challenging many of the traditional, as well as not so traditional canons of marital virtue.

To begin with, sustaining romantic love can hardly be an *unconditioned* imperative of marital conduct. Although the liberation of marriage from external proscription and social and political significance may have left the resolve to marry free to follow the lead of romance, neither the presence nor the preservation of romantic love can be an object of marital right and duty. Because romantic love is tied to the receptivity of feeling and possesses an inward character unsusceptible of external enforcement, spouses cannot be held responsible for being or remaining in love with one another, either by the inner tribunal of conscience or by the outer authority of ethical community. Moreover, since the presence of romantic love leaves open exactly how spouses treat one another, romantic attractions can hardly be constitutive of the activities building an ethical association.[34] Romance only bears upon the entering into and preservation of marriage *if* both spouses agree on treating romantic love as an essential element in their matrimony. In that case, the demise of their romantic feelings can spell for them the destruction of the common welfare that their marriage is meant to sustain. It remains to be seen whether this recognition alone is sufficient ground for dissolving their marriage. In any event, since romantic love has no necessary connection to conduct, spouses are at liberty to make romance a subordinate and potentially expendable element of their domestic welfare, just as the care they owe one another remains unimpeached and untouched by the coming and going of romantic ardor.

A similar indeterminacy surrounds the role of sexuality in marriage. As we have seen, the freedom of marriage from natural determination liberates spouses from any duty to procreate with one another. Further, since sexual activity can be engaged in within or without marriage and with or without any ethically relevant interchange between the participants, sex can hardly be an obligation for spouses. Whatever be the sexual preferences of spouses, marriage does not itself dictate that they should engage in sexual activity either of any particular type or with any particular duration and frequency. If they are jointly interested in a particular sex life that does not endanger their health or otherwise jeopardize their exercise of right, engaging in such sex accords with their domestic welfare just as would a life of abstinence to which they were agreeable. The presence or absence of sex affects marital welfare only if sexual activity is imposed upon an unwilling spouse or if a spouse is deprived of desired sexual activity. Unilaterally imposed sex comprises an assault on the person of the unwilling spouse and therefore clearly comprises a criminal violation of marital right. By contrast, when one spouse refuses to engage in the safe, nondemeaning sexual activity that another spouse desires, domestic welfare is jeopardized *only if* the spouses consider this to be an essential breach of marital harmony, rather than an incidental disagreement. If the sexually unfulfilled spouse treats this conflict as an irreconcilable difference, that attitude may be sufficient to fracture marital unity provided it spills over into a general breakdown of mutual care. Nevertheless, this possibility hardly makes having sexual relations a general marital duty. If this is not a shared concern, spouses can fully care for their joint welfare without having sex.

This is part of why marital duty is not automatically violated by spouses living apart on a limited or even a permanent basis. Provided spouses have agreed to dwell in different locations but still to share property and to promote a joint welfare, the absence of direct physical contact need not interfere with their fulfillment of marital obligations.[35] The same could be said of individuals who are physically unable to have sexual relations or any other physical contact beyond the sensory impressions of linguistic interaction. Provided their communications enable them to make decisions concerning property and care, they remain capable of exercising marital freedom and obeying marital duty, even if they have no romantic love to disclose. By contrast, if one spouse unilaterally deserts another to lead a separate life, the marital duties to care mutually for and to share property with one's spouse/s are violated.

Given the codetermined character of marital welfare, the right to have one's spouse care for one does not automatically translate into a particular apportionment of household chores. Although neither gender differences nor any other given factor can independently determine how spouses should distribute their activity between domestic and external affairs, a purely equal division only serves the right of spouses if they have agreed upon no other arrangement. In that case, there is prima facie ground to expect equal participation in all spheres of marital life, since otherwise, some spouses will be unfairly burdened while others take advantage of privileged opportunities within and without the home. Because, however, the shared interest of spouses may reflect an agreement to distribute unequally household functions temporarily or for the duration of marriage, spouses can legitimately resolve to concentrate on different areas of domestic life, without relinquishing their obligation to support one another and their right to codetermine their life together.

Such agreement is, however, compromised whenever it is directly coerced or indirectly elicited by discriminatory practices within and without the home that encourage one spouse to bear the burden of household chores. The latter depends largely upon whether civil society illicitly tolerates labor markets that discriminate by gender or sexual preference, by, for example, barring genders and sexual orientations from certain occupations, setting different wages for comparable work, or penalizing the career advancement of parents who take off from work to give birth and care for children.[36] Under such conditions, household prosperity will be promoted by relegating the discriminated spouse to household chores and favoring the career of the advantaged partner. Hence, even if spouses then follow the "rational" course of agreeing to unequal sharing of domestic duties, their acquiescence is tainted by unfair compulsion.

A related problem arises if unequal divisions of housework occur in an environment in which marriage separation and divorce settlements leave homemakers disproportionately disadvantaged with respect to both ensuing child care responsibilities and social and political opportunities. Under such all too familiar circumstances of our gendered societies,[37] any significantly unequal apportionment of household responsibilities must be suspect, both for its unfair consequences after marriage breakdown and for the asymmetrical compulsions it introduces within marriage by making one spouse more dependent upon its preservation.[38]

If, however, the principles of right are upheld, purging gender discrimination from other institutional spheres and regulating the withdrawal from marriage to prevent lopsided disadvantage, mutually chosen unequal divisions of housework need not introduce illicit hierarchies within marriage, let alone ones that will then infect and distort all those other arenas.[39]

External Marital Rights and Duties

Since how spouses should act to one another provides the basis for what they are entitled and obliged to do in respect to others as representatives of their family, the determination of the valid marital property regime and of the proper boundaries of marital care and welfare already sets guidelines that govern these external relations.

The norms of conjugal community property, as adjusted to allow for practicality and legitimate independence, already entail that spouses can separately acquire, use, and transfer household property in relation with others, provided three requirements are satisfied: first, spouses must not thereby fail to care for the welfare of their marriage partners; second, they must not unilaterally dispose of essential household property, such as domiciles, furnishings, and personal effects; and thirdly, they must place all gains within the community property, abstraction here being made from responsibilities to dependents from prior marriages. So long as these imperatives are fulfilled, spouses are at liberty to engage in external property transactions of their choice, including engaging in independent occupations and business investments, as well as making loans and gifts. In exercising this discretion, the unity of community property leaves spouses jointly liable to creditors [40] and tax authorities[41] for any of their separate transactions.[42] The joint ownership of assets and income also entitles individuals whose spouses have been injured or killed by third parties to sue them for damages.[43]

Less evident is whether the limited independence of conjugal community property entitles spouses who are victims of adultery to sue third parties for disrupting their marriage, or conversely, entitles spouses to channel income or other wealth to extramarital lovers. Although a tort of adultery has been rejected in the United States because it can be a vehicle of spite and blackmail,[44] the more fundamental question is whether extramarital affairs violate conjugal right[45] even when the perpetrator continues to share property with and care for the cuckolded spouse. If adultery is not an unconditional marital wrong, it can be disqualified as a tort without appeal to threats of blackmail.

Although the presence or absence of romantic feeling and sex between spouses has no necessary connection to marital right and duty, love and/or sex with outsiders seems less immune to dictate by family ethics. Even if spouses have resigned themselves to observing their marital obligations without sharing in romantic love or an active sex life, extramarital affairs would appear to challenge the conjugal fusion of right and welfare whether or not the affairs involve love without sex or sex without romance. How can spouses fulfill the marital imperatives of treating each other's welfare as their own if they give their heart elsewhere and/or engage in physical relations of the most intimate sort with someone else? Continuing to share property and to care for one's spouse in other respects would be little solace if extramarital relations signify a rupture in the exclusive unity of conjugal association. Two somewhat overlapping questions here apply: first, is extramarital involvement automatically a violation of conjugal right, and secondly, does it do fatal damage to marriage?

Significantly, neither of these questions reduces the issue of adultery to a moral problem, to be decided in terms of the accountability that applies to individuals simply as moral agents, rather than as members of marital community. Much of the contemporary debate concerning adultery has, true to its liberal parameters, ignored the specificity of domestic *ethical* right and duty and instead judged infidelity by moral standards of honesty and benevolence.[46] The ensuing moral casuistry then typically debates whether adultery must always involve deception, and if so whether the deception is active or passive, and whether sexual intimacy should be associated with love and intimacy, and if so, whether exclusivity and possessiveness should be upheld.[47] Since neither honesty nor love and intimacy nor a general commitment to sustain a romantic relation are constitutive, let alone exclusively constitutive of marriage, but may pertain just as well to friendship, adultery, as something applying only to matrimony, must be considered in respect to the conjugal rights and duties of spouses.

Historically, the treatment of adultery has reflected the restriction of marriage to heterosexual couples, the unbroken tie between procreation and sexual intercourse, and patrilineal concerns for securing inheritance to the "proper" bloodline, concerns magnified by the traditional ties between kinship and economic and political power. Under these conditions, a wife's adultery could figure as a far more invidious crime than a husband's, since what is put at risk is not merely the personal relation of spouses, but a patrilineal succession on which social and political alliances are based.[48] Once, however, the family is duly disengaged from society and state and marriage becomes reconstituted as a freely entered association of equal partners, for whom sexual relations need not be connected to procreation nor to any particular genders or sexual orientations, any wrong ascribed to adultery must be shown to reside in a violation of the rights of spouses.[49]

This could appear to have a double edge, since, from the modern standpoint, the attainment of the right to marry freely enables marriage to be based increasingly upon mutual romantic attraction. Although this perspective affords sympathy to the extramarital romances of individuals imprisoned in traditional externally arranged marriages, it equally heightens the significance of fidelity for spouses who have had the liberty of "love" marriages.[50] Does this mean that fidelity is a duty of conjugal right, subject to external enforcement, or do spouses have the right to decide for themselves whether infidelity counts as a breach of marital obligation? And if any latitude is permitted, does marriage then become a nonbinding commitment, where spouses replace the unrealistic illusions of romantic love with a sober technique of arriving at some shared agreement on how much adultery their relationship can bear?[51]

The answer is simple if an extramarital relation involves one spouse's unilaterally letting lovers use household property or unilaterally channeling income and property out of the joint ownership of marriage. In such cases, the responsible spouse has ignored the conjugal property right of his or her partner/s and committed a malicious wrong for which both compensation and punishment are warranted. Similarly, if the person having an affair thereby neglects duties of care to his or her spouse/s, an obvious violation of conjugal right has occurred, calling again for compensation for any damages incurred as well as punishment for maliciously transgressing that right. Yet what of the less obvious case where property is not involved and duties of care are otherwise fulfilled? Because marital welfare has normative validity insofar as it is freely determined by the spouses involved, what decides the issue is whether extramarital affairs oppose the interests that spouses have chosen to pursue together. Given the exclusive and all-inclusive private unity of marriage, adultery would ordinarily threaten marital welfare by initiating personal relations that signify to both spouses a lapse in commitment to one's domestic obligations. Whereas other personal ties of friendship and kinship need not pose any challenge to conjugal solidarity, extramarital romance and/or sexual relations are commonly recognized to be incompatible with the exclusivity of conjugal trust and care. Whether, however, they *must* be so recognized, is another matter. Sexuality and personal intimacy are hardly inseparable companions. If sex can be performed in a perfunctory, purely sensual way, with no impact upon the participants' ethical commitments to others, it is far from clear that extramarital sex *must* undermine marriage. By the same token, romantic involvement, with or without sex, does not itself introduce any new rights and duties between lovers, nor otherwise automatically compete with spouses' fulfilling their marital obligations to one another. Conceivably, spouses could expressly agree to forge a shared domesticity in which some (or even any) extramarital affairs are tolerated. And even in cases where spouses define their domestic welfare as something incompatible with any form of "open" marriage, they could subsequently agree to regard breaches of marital fidelity as forgivable transgressions, leaving their marriage in place.[52] Consequently, adultery infringes upon conjugal right only in those cases where spouses have chosen to tie their domestic welfare to certain standards of fidelity. Since neither sexual preference nor the number of spouses figure in the above considerations, they apply irrespective of sexual orientation and of whether a marriage is monogamous or polygamous.

The Violation and Enforcement of Marital Right

The correlative rights and duties that inform conduct between spouses are just as subject to violation as those that apply to property owners and moral subjects. For although spouses are able to exercise their domestic freedom only within the framework of marriage, they still retain a choosing will that can always transgress marital obligation. Since individuals can choose to violate any right in good faith, inadvertently, negligently, or with express disregard for the entitlements of others, the different duties of marital conduct can be violated in each of these ways.[53]

Accordingly, the norms of joint ownership underlying the community property of spouses can be violated nonmaliciously or maliciously, just like the norms that govern the property of single persons.

Nonmalicious violations of conjugal property rights can occur in two basic ways. On the one hand, spouses can always disagree over what comprises the boundaries of legitimate use and disposal of joint property, leading to conflicts in which each side wills in accord with what it takes to be the valid matrimonial rights of others. Arguments over how community property and income are to be employed can always lead to such situations, where each spouse claims in good faith to uphold marital right against the nonmalicious usurpations of others. If no agreement is reached, the clash of right persists. On the other hand, spouses can inadvertently use and dispose of property in ways that undermine the welfare of their marriage partners or inadvertently keep gains and other possessions outside joint ownership.

Malicious violations of marital property right can also occur in two ways, exhibiting the dual forms of crime generic to wrong:

spouses can very knowingly usurp the joint ownership rights of their counterparts, doing so either openly, as a brazen crime, or covertly, as an act of fraud hiding behind an apparent respect for marital right. Similarly, spouses can intentionally pursue property transactions that conflict with care for their marriage partner. In addition, spouses can violate each other's marital right with negligence, creating situations that unreasonably endanger their property and welfare.[54]

In the case of nonmalicious violations of marital property rights, the perpetrator is liable for damages to remedy the loss and injury to the victim. This liability is only enforceable to the degree that the perpetrator has some separate resources, since, otherwise, whatever would be taken from the perpetrator would already belong to the victim.

By contrast, in the case of malicious violations of marital property right, the perpetrator is both liable for damages and subject to punishment. Although provision of damages may remedy the particular wrong incurred by the victim, only punishment strikes at the general wrong, which consists in willing against marital right, whose nullity must be upheld.

The difficulty of righting these wrongs with the resources provided by marital relations themselves is analogous to the problem facing owners when confronting violations of their property rights. Just as property relations assign no single person or group of persons privileged authority to identify nonmalicious or malicious wrongs, assess damages, determine punishment, and ensure that victims and perpetrators receive their due, so marriage provides no third party entitled to adjudicate marital wrongs and enforce resulting judgments. Unless conflicting spouses agree to settle nonmalicious disputes among themselves, they are left in a deadlock that no outside single or married persons can legitimately settle. Similarly, marriage gives victims of marital crime no other option than to judge and punish the perpetrator, risking not only resistance or flight, but also the possibility that their response will be judged a new marital crime of its own. Without the intervention of further entitled institutions lying beyond the spheres of property, moral accountability, and the family, any spouses' attempts to right marital wrong remain liable to being personal acts of revenge of dubious effect and legitimacy.

This outcome equally applies to violations of marital rights to care. These violations can also occur with or without malice and accordingly call for damages and/or punishment. Once more, nonmalicious disputes among spouses over whether they are observing their duties to promote their common welfare (including doing a fair share of household chores) cannot be authoritatively settled unless the spouses come to an agreement among themselves. Similarly, the institution of marriage provides victims of malicious violations of matrimonial care with no authoritative power from which a recognized adjudication and enforcement can be secured. Again, the righting of marital wrong must rely upon an institutional intervention from outside the sphere of domestic association, an intervention whose character can be determined only when the relation of family to civil society and state is at issue.

CHAPTER VI

The Ethics of Parenting

Child rearing, parenting, and relations between spouses are hardly coterminous interactions. Children may be brought up entirely outside of families by alternate public arrangements just as parent-child relations may involve single custodians or informal couples without mixing parenting and marriage. Parenting may therefore be a component of family ethics whether or not the family has any privileged role to play in upbringing, just as parenting may entail norms common to single custodians and spouses, as well as principles specifically addressing how raising children bears upon relations between spouses. Before parenting can figure within family ethics, however, the permissibility, if not exclusivity, of child rearing within the household must be secured.

Although the family can exist as a community of spouses without incorporating parent-child relations, upbringing presents an inescapable ethical challenge. Child rearing by no means resides in the contingent peculiarities of human neotony, by which humans stand distinguished from other creatures by the extended helplessness and dependency of homo sapiens offspring. Even if newborn humans were able to meet their own natural needs quickly enough to forego the assistance of adults, they would still require the psychological formation and education that rational agents of any biological constitution need in order to comprehend, internalize, and participate in the forms of conduct by which individuals exercise their various rights and duties. Since rational agents are unconditionally entitled to take part in each of the different spheres of right, provision must be made to equip them with the prerequisites for this opportunity.[1] And since these prerequisites involve at the very least whatever assistance is required to ensure the physical, psychological, and educational competence needed to act autonomously, the raising of rational agents to such capability must be furnished.[2] In order for this imperative to be achieved within the domestic framework of parent-child relations, several famous objections to child rearing in the household must be overcome.

Objections to Child Rearing in the Family

The legitimacy of raising children in the family has been repeatedly challenged on two related grounds. On the one hand, child rearing in the home has been condemned as a subverter of social and political justice. On the other hand, upbringing by parents has been repudiated as a source of psychological malformation, depriving children of the autonomous personality that they should possess on leaving the home.

The social and political objection can be formulated as part of a wholesale repudiation of domestic association, rejecting the family as a cauldron of partiality that is irreconcilable with the common good to which politics should be directed. Plato gives a classic statement of this view in suggesting that at least the rulers of the community should be collectively raised in complete ignorance of their biological parents and siblings to preclude the formation of any nepotism that would hinder citizens from viewing the good of the state as their own. In here assuming that public institutions cannot be safeguarded from nepotism as long as public officials belong to families, Plato presumes a radical incompatibility between private and public ends that exhibits the same externality of universal and particular embodied in the separate reality of the intelligible world of forms. Just as it is questionable whether universals can have their constitutive generality without being inherently related to a plurality of individuated particulars, so it is questionable whether a common good can be realized without a plurality of agents individuating their own conduct in pursuit of particular ends distinct from those of politics.[3] Moreover, in separating the good from the particular ends of individuals, Plato succumbs to the basic pitfall of conceiving the good as something given to reason, independently of willing. Not only does this render problematic the realization of the good, but it makes the good figure as a prior foundation, whose own justification becomes unattainable in the absence of any higher standard to certify the exclusive legitimacy of its privileged content.

Once self-determination is recognized to be the one form of conduct that escapes grounding in any independent foundation, the family wins back normativity provided it is structured as an institution of freedom that can be integrated within a system of right realizing the totality of self-determination. To demonstrate this achievement, it is necessary not only to conceive the structures of family right, but to see how the institutions of social and political freedom presuppose household freedom as an enabling condition for their own forms of autonomy and incorporate families in conformity with social and political right. Applied to the particular domestic issue of child rearing in the family, this strategy of legitimation requires showing, first, how parent-child relations can be reconstructed in function of domestic self-determination, and secondly, how these relations can be made compatible with the rights of individuals in civil society and the state. The former demonstration falls within the conception of family freedom, whereas the latter can only be subsequently established in conceiving the family in relation to civil society and the state.

Fulfilling these demands will meet the more limited objection to child rearing in the family made by such liberal theorists as Rawls and Fishkin. They bewail an allegedly intractable opposition between equal civil opportunity and the divergences in upbringing that families unavoidably introduce, yet they refrain from calling for the abolition of the family or the imposition of collective child rearing, even though they, like all other liberal theorists, have no coherent argument for why there should be families.[4] Their restraint is prudent, for the liberal misgivings can be set aside as long as child rearing can occur as an extension of domestic freedom while families and civil society can be so integrated as to prevent household and social rights from compromising one another.

A different response is required to meet the challenge of psychological objections to child rearing in the home. These objections need not appeal to standards of psychological health extraneous to the normativity of freedom so long as what is questioned is the ability of parents to assist the child to develop a personality capable of exercising rational autonomy. Then, the legitimacy of domestic upbringing will properly hinge upon whether parent-child relations impinge upon the child's attainment of the psychological conditions for free agency.

Various alternative critiques seem possible within these confines. Margaret Mead, for example, suggests that upbringing should be handled by trained professionals, instead of allowing parent amateurs to play with the psychological growth of children.[5] Yet is upbringing a technical enterprise, calling for special expertise, or rather, is child rearing an ethical obligation, demanding nothing but rational agency and the will to uphold domestic right? Parents may be obliged to seek professional help when specialized technical problems arise, such as concern physical and psychological health, but is child rearing reducible to such efforts, where form is imposed upon matter and technician and patient have no constitutive personal, let alone, ethical relationship?

Elsewhere, Mead supplants her advocacy of substituting professional upbringing for family child rearing with a call for freeing childhood from the particular domestic context of the modern nuclear family. This contemporary household structure is alleged to cripple the young psychologically by privileging monogamy and exclusive fidelity, fostering the jealousies of the Oedipus and Electra complexes of which Samoan childhood is blissfully ignorant.[6] In a similar vein, Ruth Benedict rejects child rearing within the nuclear family for isolating children from adult realms of sex and work, turning childhood into a period of play, rigid sexual taboos, and servility to adults from which any transition to mature independence is a distressing, ill-prepared departure.[7] Poster extends these criticisms into an encomium for Kibbutz collective child rearing, claiming that raising children in common dormitories provides a needed escape from the intense, exclusive emotional identification with parents entailed by a nuclear family separated from society. Facilitating childhood identification with a far wider range of adults, collective upbringing allegedly allows parents to share love and affection with their children without encroaching upon their psychological independence by monopolizing the role of authority figure.[8]

Significantly, precisely this separation of love and authority is bewailed by Lasch in his objections to the deformations of modern child rearing. He claims that the vision of collective kibbutz child rearing is actually a dystopic extension of much more far-reaching developments wherein civil society has increasingly appropriated functions of child rearing (through, for example, public day care, schooling, and social work interventions), socializing upbringing so that authority is divorced from parental love, eliminating the emotive dimension that enables children to internalize social norms. Only within the intense emotional cauldron of the nuclear family, so starkly described by Freud, are love and discipline united sufficiently to permit children to overcome their fear and aversion to authority and to gain an autonomy that coheres with socialization.[9] Hence, not only is child rearing permissible within a nuclear family, but child rearing should occur nowhere else, since otherwise, the psychological preconditions for ethical conduct are endangered.

Jeffrey Blustein makes a parallel argument to legitimate the family by claiming that the psychological health needed for moral autonomy depends upon the intimate caring relationship that only upbringing by parents can provide.[10] Early childhood experiences of parental love are alleged to be necessary for individuals to sense their own worth as *unique* individuals, which supposedly enables them to have the capacity to love others, a capacity not only enhancing life, but, if we are to follow Rawls's moral psychology, enabling a sense of justice to evolve out of close personal relations.[11]

All of these arguments and counter arguments are both highly speculative and highly suspect. On either side of the divide rigid assumptions are made about how parents will act toward children within nuclear families, how parental conduct will affect the psychological development of children, and how this development will impact upon children's ability to take their place as autonomous adults, competent to enjoy their different rights and observe their correlative duties. On all these counts, doubts can be raised concerning the description of alleged behavior and the necessity of its effects. Even if autonomous maturity rested upon childhood experiences of a discipline united with emotional attachment, nothing guarantees that nuclear families will reliably provide that tonic, nor that upbringing outside the home will fail to provide its own supply.[12] Moreover, short of generating psychoses that disrupt personal identity and self-control, alleged differences between childhood in kibbutz dormitories, nuclear families, or Polynesian clans hardly entail that any one form will bar the way to mature rational agency.[13]

So long as the family can be a setting in which children are brought up to autonomy, child rearing in the home has legitimacy and comprises a field for parent-child ethics. To disallow this possibility requires demonstrating that domestic relations automatically prevent children from gaining the prerequisites for playing their entitled roles as property owners, moral agents, family members, and, by way of anticipation, participants in civil society and citizens. On the other hand, even if one were to acknowledge either that family upbringing must or may be supplemented by public child rearing or that collective upbringing better serves social and political justice, the relation between public custodian and child would still entail ethical principles fully in harmony with what applies to parents and children. In either setting, the ethical task of child rearing remains the same: namely, having adults serve as guardians who ensure that their charges receive the biological, psychological, and educational prerequisites for attaining a functional mature rational agency. Although other adults may play a contributing role to the upbringing of a child, be it as intermittent caretakers, teachers, doctors, etc., the parental role commands primary, if not exclusive responsibility, for the raising of that minor individual.[14] That the norms applying to public custodians can be met by parents, be they single or spouses, should suggest that upbringing in the home is legitimate, provided family freedom can be prevented from disrupting the freedoms of society and state. Conversely, that public custodians can satisfy the same imperatives should suggest that domestic child rearing need not have exclusive legitimacy. Accordingly it makes sense to proceed to develop the ethic of parent-child relations, recognizing that it contains a core applying to single parents, informal lovers, spouses, and public custodians alike, while acknowledging that the final legitimation of domestic child rearing hinges upon how relations between the family and civil society and the state can be resolved.

Historical Presuppositions of Ethical Parenting

Although parents may be single, informally attached, or married, they can only engage in child rearing in conformity with right if historical conditions have insulated their parental vocation from all the extraneous restraints that tradition imposes.

On the one hand, family relations must have been liberated from the clan domination of the extended household and from all remnants of hereditary rank and of the mixing of kinship with social and political position. Otherwise, parents are not independently responsible for their children's upbringing, nor is that upbringing free of subservience to concerns unrelated to the attainment of autonomy on the part of the child. On the other hand, the family and civil society must have demarcated themselves from one another and from the state. This dual disengagement enables parents to raise children autonomously, free of undue meddling by other kin, social groups, or rulers. It equally safeguards childhood from all forms of social and political bondage by transforming economic and political association into arenas of self-determination open to all mature, independent free agents, but closed to children. As is evident, these complementary historical prerequisites are part of the same development in which the overcoming of traditional institutions has its positive outcome in the rise of the institutions of freedom.

Accordingly, only with civil society and self-government extricating social and political relations from kinship does domesticity arise as an independent domain in which children can become a part of the life of their parents and parents can become independently responsible for their upbringing. By contrast, in medieval Europe, male children of all estates left home once they reached the age of seven: those of the poor to work, those of the rising bourgeoisie to begin apprenticing under an artisan, those of the nobility to serve as pages at court. Not until schooling became a common secular right for all children and labor became a free undertaking of autonomous members of society, for which children therefore could not qualify, did children of both genders finally spend enough time at home for parents generally to experience their childhood and figure as the authority chiefly in charge of their upbringing.[15]

Such historical preconditions make possible independent child rearing not only by heterosexual spouses and of their progeny, but by spouses, informal cohabitants, and single individuals of any gender and sexual preference, with the children for whom they care being just as well unrelated as related. In each of these cases, the residual existence of institutions lacking the demarcations of domestic, social, and political communities of freedom would pose obstacles to a parenting independently devoted to raising children to autonomy.

The residues of such obstructions to right are encountered when the relation of parent and child is limited to progeny or restricted by any other factor, such as gender, sexual orientation, race, ethnicity, or religion, that has no necessary bearing upon the capability of individuals to fulfill their parental duties.

The Qualifications for Parenting

Since child rearing owes its normative validity to its reconstitution as a relation of freedom, the biological relation of procreator and offspring does not independently confer exclusive or permanent parental rights and responsibilities. To the degree that individuals have produced offspring intentionally, through negligence, or despite reasonable birth control precautions, they are initially responsible for the care of their young, granted that custody of their offspring has not been antecedently assigned to others.[16] This is simply because these individuals have, through actions for which they are accountable,[17] brought into existence a potential rational agent who needs in the first instance their care in order to reach that potentiality, which is an end in itself. The parental relation thus does not issue from the biological relation to offspring, the helplessness of the newborn, and the proximity of at least the biological mother; as Blustein points out, custodial responsibility follows only if child rearing is so arranged that no one but the biological parents are expected to be primary caretakers for their offspring.[18] Then, responsibility for producing a child translates into responsibility for its care. It is thus not surprising that under modern conditions of nuclear households, the decision to reproduce is typically associated with the ethical resolve to become parents responsible for the child's upbringing.[19]

Although liberal thinkers, starting with Hobbes, have rightly recognized that "parental dominion" cannot rest on the mere natural facts of birth, they betray once more the incompatibility of social contract arguments and domestic association when they attempt to root the right and duty of parents in some replica of consensual agreement. Since neither newborn infants nor adopted children can qualify as competent parties to contract, the absence of an explicit agreement preceding child rearing can hardly be remedied by appeal to any tacit agreement as a basis of parental right. Hobbes's answer is to claim that the dependence of the child on parental care is analogous to the submission of individuals to any power that preserves their lives in return: just as the conquered become subjects to their conqueror, so the helpless infant becomes subservient to its child care provider.[20] Yet if children lack autonomy, their position under parental control does not reflect any act of will on their part any more than the assumption of parental responsibility can be predicated upon any agreement between parent and child. Parents who have voluntarily produced offspring are *immediately* ethically responsible for their upbringing because, in the absence of any intervening arrangement, they have brought into being a potential participant in the institutions of freedom, whom they can respect as such only by providing the care necessary to secure the realization of that potential.[21] If they were to evade their parental obligations by appeal to any prudential consideration, they would be treating freedom as an expendable factor, instead of as the locus of normativity.

The only way parental obligation could be circumvented in accord with right would be if child rearing somehow jeopardized the autonomy of parents, not in the sense of impinging upon their contingent desires, but in the sense of undermining their capacity to exercise their respective rights and duties as person, moral subject, family member, and ultimately, civilian and citizen. That such a predicament could even arise would largely depend upon whether the family and the other institutions of freedom had been duly integrated so as to prevent their different rights from conflicting with one another, as well as upon whether emergency conditions had disrupted such arrangements.

Different consequences follow if an individual contributes to reproduction unwillingly. This can occur due to coercion, as in cases of rape, or due to deceit, as in unauthorized inseminations of donated sperm. Reproduction also fails to possess the full-fledged voluntary character necessary for imputing responsibility when the parties either lack the mental capabilities to comprehend their deed or lack the emotive capacities to act independently. Such deficits may result from permanent disabilities or simply be due to immaturity. In all of these cases, the unwilling individual's biological connection to resulting offspring does not entail any parental rights or obligations, unless the ensuing delivery of the child depends upon a competent decision by that person. If anyone is personally obliged to care for the resulting child, it should be the agent who has compelled someone else, either by force or deception, to participate in reproduction. If, on the other hand, none of the participants are competent to take responsibility for their offspring, child care should be provided from some other source.[22]

Where reproduction involves responsibility, the right to continue as a parent persists only until or unless other individuals have obtained the recognized right and duty to take over guardianship. Given the basic imperative of child rearing, this transfer of custody should occur whenever the biological procreators fail to provide the necessary care. This can be due to the biological parents not qualifying as independent rational agents because they are themselves still children or because they lack certain physical, mental, or psychological capabilities. Alternately, the failure can result from the death or incapacitation of otherwise competent parents, or be due to an ethical lapse, where mature and capable biological parents abuse or simply abandon their children. And finally, the failure can derive from destitution brought on by market forces or by war and political upheavals that public institutions are unable or unwilling to remedy.

On the other hand, biological parents can decide to transfer custody of their children to other agreeable parties. Such transfer will accord with parental duty provided it serves the interest of the children by ensuring adoption by more or equally capable guardians. Since any transfer of child custody involves a relinquishment and an assumption of domestic rights and duties, it must take a form that is duly recognized by others.

These options indicate how an ethical parenting all too often cannot but call upon guardians who are not biologically related to their children. Since these guardians qualify as parents in virtue of an ethical commitment to rear their charges in accord with their right to be raised to independent autonomy, the limits of who can be a parent must be drawn in respect to the capabilities for fulfilling that commitment.

The task at hand is governed by the telos of the attainment of the capability to exercise one's rights and duties as property owner, moral agent, spouse and parent, and ultimately member of civil society and self-governing citizen. Since engagement in the institutions of freedom has physical, psychological, and cultural prerequisites, a prospective parent must be competent on three fronts. To begin with, a parent must be able to care for the physical well-being and growth of children, providing food, clothing, shelter, health care, as well as physical culture. Second, a prospective parent must be capable of tending to the psychological prerequisites of autonomy, furnishing adequate emotional care and support, as well as basic cognitive and linguistic skills. Finally, a prospective parent must be competent to provide the cultural upbringing enabling the child to comprehend the functioning of the different institutions of right, to recognize the rights and duties of others, and to make other agents cognizant of his or her own autonomous actions. The latter formation requires the imparting of appropriate communication skills, as well as the general knowledge and cognitive facility to comprehend the significance of conduct and participate without disadvantage in the different spheres of right. It also entails an emotive dimension, where feeling and disposition are cultivated to facilitate the conformity of the desires of the child with ethical conduct.[23] To the degree that civil society and the state have responsibilities of their own to ensure that individuals receive the training and formation specifically required to allow them to take advantage of their social and political opportunities, which involve respecting the correlative rights of others, a prospective parent must at least pose no obstacle to the participation of a child in any such public education. Consequently, to qualify as a parent, individuals must be mature rational agents capable not only of independent action, but of providing either directly or indirectly the physical nurture, psychological support, and cultural formation that the young need to make the transition to a minimally competent participant in the institutions of freedom.

Ensuring that an individual so qualifies as a parent cannot be left to private discretion without inviting all the difficulties that afflict any personal initiative to uphold right. Strangers and intimates alike may disagree about the qualifications of a prospective parent and any judgment they reach will have a questionable enforcement if left merely to private hands. Once more, public authority must resolve the issue, guided by appropriate legalization of family right. Although current practice tends to limit public scrutiny of parental qualifications to prospective adopters, the need is just as pressing with the natural parents of children.[24] Although requiring a license for parenting, as Blustein suggests,[25] is one method for publicly certifying parental qualifications, the likelihood of reproduction by unlicensed parents makes this an unwieldy option. A more effective measure would involve making training in parenting a requirement of mandatory public education and attempting to ensure that all able individuals complete that schooling with success. On that basis, generally individuals who qualify for marriage would equally qualify as parents, eliminating the need for the separate licensing of childless marriage and parental marriage that Blustein proposes.[26]

No factor indifferent to these requirements should disqualify individuals from either retaining rights and responsibilities as parents of their offspring or from adopting unrelated children. Accordingly, gender, sexual preference, race, ethnicity, or nationality cannot legitimately prevent otherwise qualified individuals from assuming the role of parent. Indeed, given that nonhuman finite rational agents could conceivably evolve on earth or elsewhere in the universe, parenting can no more legitimately be limited to a common species being than marriage can be restricted to individuals of the same race.

By the same token, marital status does not of itself prejudice the right of an individual to be the recognized parent of offspring or unrelated children, or conversely, prejudice the right of children to support from their guardian.[27] A child's custodial entitlements are just as unimpeached by birth in or out of wedlock as a guardian's parental obligations are unaffected by being single, informally cohabiting, or married.

An individual who is raising children alone may face practical difficulties in organizing round the clock care for children that could be avoided if other adults were there to share parenting responsibilities; yet no such difficulties are insurmountable if third party care is available. Otherwise, being single does not deprive one of any of the capacities needed to fulfill the imperatives of child rearing. The parental qualification of a single person might be challenged by those who argue that a key element in proper personal development is the childhood experience of witnessing an enduring love relation between adults, such as married parents ideally provide, an experience that allegedly enables children to recognize the value of enduring intimacy and to acquire the capacity to enter into such relations.[28] If one accepted this argument, the permissibility of child rearing by divorcees or widowed parents could be questioned, just as could parenting by any spouses whose marriage failed to live up to the ideal. Alternately, long-standing cohabitant lovers could conceivably provide an equivalent experience for children. In any case, the underlying argument makes psychological assumptions of a very speculative character, while assuming that children have no exposure to love relations or marriage beyond their immediate custodians. It is far from clear whether any particular relation of married parents will necessarily produce certain attitudes in their children, nor that acquiring any such attitudes has any necessary relation to exercising one's autonomy as property owner, moral agent, spouse and parent, civilian or citizen. Unhappily married parents who remain together for the sake of their children may very well be deluding themselves.

On analogous grounds, whether cohabiting adults are married or unmarried does not itself preclude their having parental responsibilities for children living with them. Blustein, for one, argues against child rearing by unmarried parents by claiming that married parents will give better child care because they perform their parental duties with greater happiness, concentration, and integration with their love for one another.[29] Yet, just as spouses may be emotionally alienated, fragmented, and unsatisfactory parents, so unmarried parents may just as well tend to their children with more joy, dedication, and shared intimacy than their married counterparts. Such indeterminacy cannot be excluded for the simple reason that none of the vaunted qualifying features for parenting are unique to what distinguishes the juridical relation of spouses from the informal bonds of cohabitants. Indeed, as the example of divorced parents indicates, albeit by way of anticipation, individuals can be the recognized parents of the same children without being ethically committed to one another as spouses.

This separability of family roles allows for various parental arrangements. Adults who are neither married, divorced, nor cohabiting can conceivably fulfill the obligations and enjoy the rights of parents of the same children through the same varieties of custody arrangements that prevail among divorced parents. Alternately, cohabiting but unmarried adults can be the parents of children with whom they share full or partial custody, since once again nothing in their own relation necessarily interferes with their capacity to fulfill their parental duties. Similarly, informal cohabitants can have different custodial relations to children living both with and without them. For example, individuals may retain exclusive custody of a child, while their roommate has neither any parental right nor any parental duty to care for that child. Alternately, informal cohabitants may each have children of their own living together without sharing any parental commitments. In each case, the mere fact that individuals share a domicile does not constitute the ethical domestic entitlements and obligations of either conjugal or parental relations. Although informal cohabitants are ethically responsible for any offspring they voluntarily produce, granted that parental care has not already been preassigned by private agreement or public mandate, they remain at liberty to transfer custodial obligations *provided* the welfare of their children is not thereby compromised.[30]

Matters are more complicated when spouses are custodians of children who are not their joint offspring and/or other individuals retain some parental duties. Conjugal and parental relations may be separable, but the generality and extent of this separability have to be more precisely determined. Given that divorce may result in custodial arrangements placing children either temporarily or continually in the home of one parent while the other remains responsible for support, the question arises whether stepparents can acquire any parental rights and duties regarding the upbringing of their stepchildren. If they can adopt their stepchildren, does this automatically sever the parental right and responsibility of noncustodial parents? Or in cases of rotating joint custody, do stepparents and divorced parents all have equal parental status?

Alternately, can spouses observe the equal sharing and reciprocity of marriage without having the same parental relation to children that live with them? Although being spouses may not automatically impose parental duties upon both for nonresident children of one, can one spouse fail to be the juridical parent of a stepchild who lives with them both? Alternately, can one spouse fail to assume parental responsibility for a child that another spouse has born either previously to their marriage or produced with the former but contrary to the former's will? And in the case of polygamous marriages, are all spouses equal parents of any children who are brought up within the household? The answers to these questions hinge upon how conjugal relations in general and divorce in particular affect parental rights and duties. Accordingly, a full settlement of the issue must await the treatment of these topics.

In the meantime, marital status can still count as a factor *not* affecting parental qualifications, except perhaps in the above situations, which await sorting out. By contrast, other conventional factors such as religious practices, profane behavior, imprisonment, or occupation can legitimately disqualify an otherwise competent individual from playing the role of parent if they conflict with fulfilling the duties of child rearing. If the public welfare institutions of civil society succeed in eliminating social disadvantage and make parenting an economically viable option for all, there need be no occasion for the right of children to a proper upbringing to be compromised by the poverty of parents. Given that such success is an imperative of social justice (which is established in the systematic conception of civil society), allowing economic inequality to undermine equal parental opportunity would not be a legitimate ground for disqualifying individuals as parents.

Whether individuals who must forfeit parental rights due to temporary difficulty have any guarantee to reassume custody when this difficulty is overcome depends not upon their sentiments or other distress, but rather upon the abiding governing consideration for the ethic of child rearing: the imperative to raise children to autonomy. If this task is best achieved by returning custody to a formerly parentally incapacitated person, then reassumption of custody is warranted. Since upbringing depends upon the psychological condition of the child, the respective sentiments of the child for the former and present custodians are significant, if not decisive, factors for determining future custody.

Needless to say, the range of personal situations that may prevent an individual from fulfilling custodial duties heavily depends upon encompassing social and political conditions. By themselves, property relations, moral conduct, and domestic association are hardly sufficient to shield individuals from such problems as crime, poverty, civil unrest, and war that can disrupt parental care. How civil society and the state are obliged to meet these difficulties and secure the social and political conditions for upholding family welfare lies within the consideration of the relation of the family to these two subsequent spheres of right.

Modes of Assuming Parental Duty

Parental duty can be taken on in two ways: by voluntarily engaging in sexual reproduction leading to the birth of a child, for whom no alternate custodial arrangements are mandated, or by making the ethical commitment to adopt a child. Either way, the assumption of parenthood must take a form recognizable to others, since what lies at issue is a relation of right and duty to which all other agents owe acknowledgment.

Since voluntary reproduction gives individuals immediate parental responsibility for their progeny, the relation of voluntary parent and offspring must be made public as soon as possible following birth so that one can know who has the right and duty to rear the newborn child. It makes no difference whether a child is born in or out of wedlock. In both cases, those responsible for its birth have equivalent parental obligations and equivalent grounds for making known their custodial duties. Since an ethical responsibility is at issue, establishing a mere biological connection is not enough to impose parental duties. The voluntary nature of an individual's role in procreation must also be certified. Once such certification has been made, the individual must equally be certified to be competent to fulfill the duties of parenting. Whatever form of scrutiny that certification involves, if the individual satisfies its standard, that individual is entitled and obliged to provide for the upbringing of the child. If that individual ignores or otherwise fails to meet this responsibility, he or she is liable for the compensation and punishment that await any malicious violation of right, be it perpetrated with negligence, fraudulent deceit, or open crime. Since parental responsibility here applies independently of marital status, unwed parents are just as liable as spouses for any of these consequences of broken custodial obligations.

So long as voluntary biological parents fulfill their custodial duties, no other party is entitled to intrude unilaterally and either share or usurp parental responsibilities. Such intervention would violate the right of parents to bring up children to autonomy, a right that conforms to the normativity of self-determination by sanctioning parental independence so long as it fulfills the requirements of enabling the child to become an independent participant in the institutions of freedom. Accordingly, if one of the biological parents of a child ceases to play the role of guardian because of death, disease, injury, imprisonment, or malicious abuse of parental responsibility, no other competent adult can step in to supplement that deficit without the consent of the other remaining parent, so long as the latter is able to bring the child up alone. Since single adults can qualify as parents, family right entails that single adults should be enabled to fulfill their parental obligations, an imperative whose realization calls for specific social regulations that fall within the relation between family and civil society.

In cases where a plurality of parents is responsible for the same children, the failure of some of them to fulfill their parental obligations will call for different responses depending upon the nature of the breakdown in child care. When one parent nonmaliciously violates custodial norms, either accidentally, out of ignorance, or due to psychological or physical infirmity, provision should be made for whatever assistance, counseling, or treatment will enable that parent to resume proper parental supervision. The child, of course, will need the remaining parent or parents to step in to overcome the deficit in care, either through their own direct efforts or by obtaining additional help from other parties. When the nonmalicious violation of parental duty involves damage to property related to upbringing and the offender does not share all income and possessions with the other custodial parent/s, compensation is mandated. In cases where the transgression of parental duty is malicious, the malefactor further faces punishment. In addition to punitive fines (that do not take away from domestic resources for child care) and detention, this can require both forfeiting custodial rights and vacating the home in which children are raised, leaving the remaining parent/s in exclusive control of upbringing.

On the other hand, when children have been removed from the care of all their biological parents, be it owing to disability, death, or abuse, their right to be brought up to autonomy calls for the provision of some type of guardian who can fulfill the imperatives of child rearing. Insofar as married as well as unwed individuals can legitimately qualify as competent parents, those eligible individuals who choose to take on the ethical responsibility of child care have a right to apply to adopt children who stand in need of parenting. Only factors that interfere with the ability to fulfill the imperatives of child rearing can legitimately disqualify an individual from adoption. Accordingly, matters such as race, ethnicity, religion,[31] gender, sexual preference, and marital status cannot bar otherwise qualified individuals from becoming the recognized guardians of children to whom they have no biological connection.[32]

The resources of property relations, moral accountability, and domestic association provide only private means of selection between aspiring parents. On this basis, the recognized authority is absent that would give any objective standing to decisions that select some and exclude other would-be parents from adopting children. Neighbors, kin, and other personally connected individuals might all take an initiative in arranging for new placements of children who need a new home. Yet, any decision they take could always be disputed by others who question their standards, their judgment of prospective parents, and their privileged role in deciding the fate of the children involved. Of course, authority is equally lacking in any private initiative to brand parents as unfit guardians and to place their children up for adoption by others. Even when parents decide to give their own child up for adoption, they hardly have license to choose whatever guardians they please, let alone to lord over any selection process. In any case, the plurality of family members and single individuals may fail to provide any willing and eligible individuals to adopt children in need.

In all these respects, upholding the rights of children and parents alike depends upon a public intervention that civil society is obliged to provide in its efforts to realize the rights of persons and family members in conformity with social justice. The very limits of parent-child relations make evident that instances will perennially arise in which the upbringing of children will require public efforts. To prevent child rearing from being a privilege of the socially advantaged, public intervention will be required to furnish supplementary aid to qualified prospective and current parents who lack the means to provide for children.[33] And even if equal opportunity to parenthood is publicly guaranteed, cases of misfortune and maltreatment will still arise requiring public agency to aid children in need of new custodians by not only certifying the eligibility of adopting parents, but providing care where no private placements are available. Although public measures could conceivably take the form of unilateral assignments of children to individuals, this would unfairly place a burden upon those selected. A more just solution would involve public incentives encouraging more individuals to adopt as well as public facilities for collectively raising children who lack adequate home care. Needless to say, mandatory public education in parenting as well as general certification of the parental competency of biological parents would do their share to increase the pool of competent candidates for parenting by adoption.

However adoption occurs, it must have a public, recognizable form allowing third parties to certify who is responsible for the care of the children involved. Without that acknowledged visibility, the rights of adopted children and adopting parents risk dissolving into a welter of uncertainty, where every competing claim is no more than a subjective assurance.

Once adoption takes place in a publicly recognized manner, the biological parents cease to have any domestic rights or obligations to their offspring. Since the need to establish parental authority in a public manner already calls for the public registration of births, with certification of the *responsible* biological parents,[34] adopted children have the opportunity to discover of whom they are offspring. Although that discovery establishes no juridical rights, it has ethical significance for the adoptive parents when it provides access to medical information relevant to the care of the child.[35]

The Parent-Child Relation

The ethics of the parent-child relation are the same whether child rearing is occasioned by consanguinity or adoption, children are born in or out of wedlock, or custodians are single or plural. In every case, the respective rights and duties of parent and child are predicated upon the abiding imperative of upbringing: that the child be given the care needed to achieve independent autonomy as a property owner, moral agent, family member, and ultimately, civilian[36] and citizen. This care involves not only ensuring the physical and emotional health and development of children, but providing them with knowledge of their rights and the ability to exercise them, which, given the connection of right and duty, entails imparting children with a knowledge and respect for the corresponding rights of others.[37]

Unlike other structures of right, the parent-child relation rests upon a constitutive asymmetry. Whereas the parent qualifies as a person who should actually exercise the rights of every sphere of self-determination,[38] the child is subject to parental care to the degree that childhood comprises a period of maturation during which an individual is still developing the capabilities for participating in the institutions of freedom. Since children are only potentially autonomous, the relation of right and duty is different for them. Although the respective rights and duties of parent and child both follow from the imperative of raising children to autonomy, parents do not share authority with their children in determining how child rearing is to proceed, nor can a child be held accountable in the way in which parents should be. Consequently, the authority of parents or any other custodians over children does follow from a child's right to self-determination, contrary to the denial of liberal theorists, such as Blustein, who identify self-determination with liberty.[39] Of course, if freedom meant simply doing as one pleases, parental authority would restrict a child's autonomy. Since, however, self-determination involves the exercise of rights, where choice must be made to fit the practices of recognition specific to each of the different spheres of right, the parental authority that provides children with the means and tutelage to acquire the knowledge and disposition to respect the rights of others and exercise one's own entitlements is completely at one with respecting the child's right to self-determination.

It is important to note that providing children with the capability to exercise their rights is not equivalent to furnishing them with what John Rawls characterizes as primary goods, namely those factors necessary for realizing any ends one might choose as part of a coherent plan of life.[40] Because rights have a specific content, the prerequisites for their exercise involve something more determinate than the preconditions for liberty,[41] which have often been illicitly enlarged by presupposing certain given institutions not necessarily mandated by rational self-interest.

The same concrete character of rights precludes the strictures on upbringing that Rousseau mandates in *Émile*.[42] Although Rousseau develops his educational doctrine in function of a commitment to autonomy, because he construes freedom as the natural capacity of liberty, he regards social relations as restrictions upon rather than realizations of autonomy. He therefore dictates that children be raised in isolation from society, shielded from acquiring the artificial needs for commodities as well as from obtaining the training necessary for participating in the interdependent activities of the market. To the degree that self-determination consists in relations of right including property relations, family association, economic freedom, and political participation, the autonomy of children would be retarded if parenting did not break the cocoon of Rousseau's stoic autarchy and progressively introduce children to the practices of these different spheres of freedom, in each of which a relation to other is ingredient in the agent's own self-determination.

Broadly speaking, parents have the right to oversee the up-bringing of their children, provided they thereby furnish the child with all the physical, psychological, and cultural care necessary to reach autonomous maturity. When parents violate their obliga-tions, they are liable for compensation to their children or their children's trustees for injury and damages, as well as subject to punishment for intentionally or negligently transgressing the norms of child rearing.[43] Children, on the other hand, generally have no right to disobey parents so long as the latter act in accord with the imperatives of child rearing. When, however, children are disobedient, they are neither liable for compensation for any resulting damages or injuries, nor are they subject to punishment in any strict sense of the term. Because children are not recog-nized as full-fledged independent rational agents, any property assigned to them must take the form of a trust or custodial endow-ment controlled by an adult.[44] If children destroy property or injure persons, liability rests with their guardians, who are responsible for their behavior. When damage and/or injury is suffered by par-ents themselves, the question of compensation is therefore moot unless civil welfare institutions have provided a safety net of so-cial insurance. Analogously, since children are subject to parental tutelage only insofar as their independent responsibility remains qualified, when children are maliciously disobedient, any ensuing discipline counts more as training than as retribution.[45] Accord-ingly, what determines which discipline is appropriate is its con-tribution to the physical, psychological, and cultural/ethical matu-ration of the child,[46] a contribution consisting both in restraining the given desires of the child and bringing them to conform to the imperatives of right, which define willing in accord with reason,[47] remaining within the bounds of one's own entitlements and thereby respecting the equal rights of others. Indeed, only in the case of children can "punishment" so serve the aim of ethical formation without disrespecting the autonomy of the recipient. In every other case, where the perpetrator is recognized to be a fully responsible adult, punishment must be restricted to retribution, since any at-tempt to "rehabilitate" would be tantamount to treating the per-petrator as not fully responsible for the crime, and therefore not fit to be tried or punished.[48]

An analogous asymmetry holds with respect to property and welfare. Whereas spouses unite into a common private domain in which property and welfare are fully merged, parent and child cannot achieve reciprocity on either score. Because children are potential, but not fully actual persons, they cannot be held responsible for caring for a parent or for siblings. Although parents may demand of children that they contribute to household chores, such service is warranted not by any domestic obligations of mutual care but rather by the imperatives of training the child to become a responsible individual, capable of respecting the rights of others, including caring for future spouses and children.[49] By the same token, children are not co-owners of the family capital, but rather beneficiaries of the judicious employment by parents of that portion of income and property that needs to be used to underwrite upbringing. Because children do not qualify as independent persons, they have no right to participate in controlling household wealth. Whereas, when marriages break up, spouses are entitled to share what had been their community property, when children reach maturity and leave the care of parents, they have no automatic right to any of the family property. Moreover, when parents (be they married or unmarried) separate, children have no claim upon the divided property of either, independently of what must be drawn upon to shoulder the costs of upbringing.

Although parents may put part of their holdings in a trust for their children, this is not required by the demands of child rearing. Since such trusts hold property for transfer to children upon maturity, they play no role in meeting child care expenses. Because children receive the benefits of trusts only upon becoming adults, what they receive is no longer part of custodial support, but rather an optional gift of parental beneficence that should not conflict with the obligations of spouses to one another or with the requirements of equal social and political opportunity.

The asymmetry of parent-child relations has posed a quandary for many thinkers past and present. Given that children are subject to parental authority in virtue of not yet being independent rational agents, they might appear to inhabit a middle ground in which, as Kant awkwardly puts it, they count as persons who are to be treated as things.[50] Since children lack a fully developed will and thereby cannot competently exercise the rights and duties of property ownership, moral accountability, or family association, they would seem to lack ownership of their own body. This circumstance might appear to render children "things" susceptible of appropriation by parents, who would then fit the ancient Roman scheme where children are the property of their guardians, who may accordingly do whatever they choose to their immature human chattel. Yet just as slavery is distinguished from the domestication of animals by the implicit recognition that slaves are intelligent creatures rather than "things," so child rearing rests on the acknowledgment that children are potential persons, who will eventually attain the status of those who bring them up.[51] Hence, although children may not yet have self-ownership in the strict sense of being recognized to have made their body the embodiment of their free will as a person, their existence as potential persons leaves their body susceptible of appropriation by only one will, the will they will themselves develop as the outcome of proper child rearing. Consequently, children never figure merely as things, nor as persons who are treated as things. From the outset, the treatment of children is governed by a recognition of developing autonomy that sets definite limits upon how parents and every other individual may interact with them.

An entirely different problem arises when children lack the capability to become rational agents. In that case, they stand in need of a care that is not limited to childhood.[52] The custodial issues that then arise are no longer problems specific to parent-child relations. Instead, what lies at stake is how individuals should be treated who have irremediable disabilities that prevent them from ever exercising the rights or observing the duties that give conduct its legitimacy. Because such disabilities can occur with greater or lesser intensity, making a clear cut divide between competent and incompetent individuals poses problems of judgment that have no easy solution.

A similar problem of differentiation applies to the very boundary between childhood and maturity that circumscribes parent-child relations. Although childhood may be characterized as the period in which an individual is developing into an independent person, determining exactly when that process has been traversed is far from straightforward. The speed of maturation may vary not only from individual to individual exposed to the same general course of upbringing, but from one path of upbringing to another. Since the departure from childhood entails the assumption of new rights and duties and a transformation of relations between erstwhile parent and child, it must have an objectively certified form. An age limit may provide a convenient instrument, readily certifiable and easily applicable. Yet given the variation in rates of maturation, some objective test might seem to be a more accurate barometer. Both alternatives must grapple with the difficulty of drawing a line between childhood and entry into the adult world.

The increasing development of rational capabilities during childhood presents an obvious challenge to the maintenance of parental authority and child obedience. Although parents remain obliged to provide for the physical, psychological, and cultural needs of their children, the very success of child rearing progressively elicits a growing independence whose very cultivation requires a drawing back of parental intrusion. This process brings into relief the general problem of defining the limits of parental prescription and the correlative right of children to exercise any discretion of their own. Do parents have authority to control their children's personal appearance and dress, to police their choice of reading, music, television, film, and other cultural exposures, to restrict their friendships, dating, and sexual activity, and to have access to all their children's personal communications and medical records? Is there any sphere of privacy from which a child can legitimately exclude parental supervision?

No matter how far a child has advanced toward maturity, as long as childhood persists, the governing imperative of parenting remains the same: the parent is entitled to supervise the child as much as necessary to promote the development of a competent independence. Parents do not have the right to interfere with children's attaining a basic education or taking advantage of whatever other formation society and state provide to assure the young their due social and political futures. By contrast, a parent can legitimately forbid any activity as well as any range of discretion that interferes with valid upbringing. If, however, a child's course of behavior does not conflict with the tasks of maturation, a parent would be wrong to restrict it. Indeed, such overreaching prohibition would not simply be chastised as an arbitrary encroachment. Because the legitimate challenge of upbringing is to enable a child to become a rational agent capable of exercising the rights and duties of the different spheres of freedom, adequate parenting must make a point of encouraging a child's personal initiative in the various areas of life.[53] Since the permissibility of a particular behavior depends upon the particular maturity and character of the child, as well as circumstances that affect the significance and consequences of the behavior, the philosophical conception of family ethics can only prescribe the general principles within which parental discretion must operate.

The Resolution of Parental Conflict and Abuse

Yet, given the resources of domestic association, who is to determine authoritatively when a parent is either too lax or too strict in curbing child behavior? This problem has two dimensions: one concerning how wed or unwed parents of the same child should resolve disputes over upbringing and another concerning how third parties should intervene to curtail parental abuse.

The moment children are raised by more than one guardian, whether the custodians be unwed or monogamously or polygamously married, the possibility is always present that disputes will break out between parents over how to raise their children. Each party to such disagreements must judge what shortcomings plague their counterparts' parenting and what should be done to remedy the problem. Yet, child-parent relations give no parent special privilege to decide either what the facts are, what is wrong with certain parental conduct, and what measures should be taken. Unless the parents come to an agreement on their own, they have no way of independently escaping an impasse. If one parent attempts to curtail the actions of another, the former is liable to be accused of violating the parental rights of the latter.

Hobbes attempts to circumvent this dilemma by arguing that since no subject can obey two conflicting masters, parental authority, like sovereignty, cannot be divided. Accordingly, one parent must reign supreme, as master guardian. Yet how is one parent to be anointed in this privileged role, when each is otherwise an equal person? In the absence of further institutions capable of imposing a selection, Hobbes allows for two alternatives, familiar enough for social contract thinking, but equally inadequate to determine domestic association: either the parents contract with one another to assign dominion over the child or the mother retains authority in virtue of first having the power of life or death over the infant, who is therefore allegedly obliged to obey her, with the qualification that dominion passes to whoever may replace the mother as provider of nourishment and care.[54]

Hobbes's appeal to contract as a vehicle of deciding parental dominion assumes that parental authority already possesses the external character of an object of property that would allow it to be assigned by a contractual agreement. If that were the case, individuals would be at liberty to relinquish their parental obligations at will and to transfer them to anyone they choose in exchange for any factor that is agreeable.[55] What prevents domestic rights and duties from being assignable by contract is the same feature that precludes social and political entitlements and obligations from being contracted away: they all are elements of ethical community, where right and duty derive not from personal choice but from antecedent membership in a standing association. Here right and duty do not pertain to something external to the agent, for what provides the content of right in ethical community are ends that cannot be dissociated from the roles by which domestic, social, and political associations reproduce themselves. Although the parent-child relation may issue from either voluntary procreation or adoption, once established, parenthood rests upon the specific domestic unity of parent and child, whose character is no longer a matter of choice.

Of course, when Hobbes roots parental authority in a contract between parents, he must assume that the contracting parties already dispose of what is to be apportioned. The only resource he has to offer on this score is his alternative explanation of parental dominion, whereby the mother or her replacement rules over the child by preserving its life. Even if preservation of life were the only reason for an individual to become subject to another, this rationale would neither apply to children, who lack the competency of will to impose duties upon themselves through calculations of self-interest, nor resolve the problem of disputes among parents. First of all, wherever parents cooperate in providing for the needs of their child, obedience would be owed to both. Second, if only one parent initially cares for their child, this fact retains authority only so long as no other spouse (or informal cohabitant) ever contributes to custodial care. In effect, Hobbes's solution eliminates the problem by eliminating the plurality of parents. This even extends to future generations, since, as Hobbes doggedly reasons, if one parent has dominion over a child, that parent equally retains authority over the children of that child and over their children's offspring.[56] What results is a sanctification of an extended family, where the sovereign elder is the one and only parental authority to whom all contemporaneous generations remain subject children. If Hobbes had been even more ruthlessly consistent, he would have had to acknowledge that parental authority stands at odds with civil liberty and political association, robbing its perennial children of any independence, including the opportunity to enter any covenants.

Locke, by contrast, maintains that parental authority equally falls to each parent, insofar as they both concurrently cause the generation of children.[57] If Locke took this as a literal example of his labor theory of property, he would have to conclude that children are mere property of their parents, granting parents a license conflicting with the bounds of child rearing. Instead, Locke describes children as the workmanship of God, to whom parents are accountable for their own existence, which is equally the product of divine labor. What puts all parents under the obligation to nourish and educate their progeny is therefore a divine trust to care for offspring until they reach the age of reason when they can comprehend the law of nature and its imperatives of liberty, as well as its civil counterpart.[58] Needless to say, applying a labor theory of property to a monotheistic creative divinity makes little sense, given how right of any sort requires a plurality of wills, a plurality lacking when, besides the Almighty, the only other agents are God's *own* creatures. Yet even if parental authority could somehow issue from the divine, the inherent limits of that authority remain. Although Locke may assure us that God has endowed parents with feelings of tenderness and concern to temper their power over children, and that delinquent parents forfeit that power to foster guardians,[59] the possibility of unresolvable disputes can no more be dismissed than can the prospect of intractable civil conflict where factions questioning the rectitude of civil government have no recourse but to revolt.

Because parental authority rests upon neither any tacit agreement with children, nor any contract amongst care givers,[60] conflicts among parents over upbringing represent one more instance in which family relations stand in need of further institutions to uphold domestic right. By themselves, families provide no third party with authority to settle disputes among parents. Unless parents can agree among themselves upon how to treat their children, their dispute remains an open breach, potentially obstructing their fulfillment of parental duty. Not only are their children left in a quandary over whom to obey, but other individuals are left in confusion over what decisions have been authorized concerning child rearing arrangements involving outside parties. Of course, even when parents settle their dispute, this hardly guarantees that they conform to the imperatives of child rearing. Yet, once more, family relations are incapable of providing any resource for authoritatively certifying whether parental solidarity serves the rights of a child or for protecting children from abusive parents. The ethic of parenting may provide unambiguous standards for child care: namely, that parents provide children with the physical, psychological, and cultural nurturing enabling them to become autonomous individuals. When it comes, however, to applying these standards to particular cases, domestic association has no resources for authoritatively identifying when standards are violated and for authoritatively determining and imposing the requisite compensations and punishments.

Although the dangers of spousal abuse are equally deadly, parental mistreatment of children has the additional evil of being inflicted in private upon individuals who lack the independence to break through the veil of domestic seclusion and make known their oppression. In such cases, good Samaritan duties to intervene have all the more urgency;[61] yet without authoritative civil institutions at hand to judge violations, apprehend and punish malefactors, and protect and compensate victims, private initiatives remain subjective solutions to subjective accusations. How civil institutions should monitor parental conduct and enforce child rights is a topic for the relation between the family and civil society.

Parent-Child Relations after Maturity

The very success of child rearing removes the basis on which parental right and duty rests, for once children attain the physical, psychological, and cultural maturity enabling them to participate independently in the institutions of freedom, parenting loses the object of its care. On the one hand, parents are freed of the obligation to nurture, support, and educate their former charges and, on the other hand, children are no longer obliged to follow the directives of their former guardians. In neither case is there any contract to withdraw from;[62] because the parent- child relation is an ethical association, once its unity dissolves, all its domestic rights and duties become supplanted by the entitlements parents and children alike now enjoy as persons, moral subjects, civilians, fellow citizens, and members of independent families.[63]

Consequently, parents have a right to demand that grown children live on their own and support themselves. The property and future income of parents, wed or unwed, is not something to which mature children have any claim. Because child-parent relations never entailed the joint ownership of family property that marriage establishes, once parents lose their responsibility for supporting grown children, the latter lose their right to any domestic property. Similarly, if adult "children" need care due to illness or social difficulties, their former guardians have no *domestic* obligation to give them aid. Parents may feel *morally* obliged to intervene, based upon the history of acts, intentions, and emotions linking them and their children. Strictly speaking, however, once children have grown up and established an independence of their own, the bond between them and their parents is no longer juridically a family relation, even if children continue to live in the family residence with the consent of their parents. In such cases where adult children and parents either continue or move back together, their common domicile is joined by an agreement between independent persons, rather than by membership in an ethical association.[64] Similarly, parents may employ otherwise permissible financial incentives[65] and emotional pressure to influence their grown children, but beyond such personal maneuvers, parents have no right any longer to curtail the latter's activity.[66]

Conversely, because child rearing is not a contractual exchange between parent and child, but an ethical responsibility, parents are not due compensation from their children for the costs of upbringing.[67] When children reach maturity and leave their parents for an independent life, they do not stand in any formal debt, no matter how much gratitude they rightly feel.

Nevertheless, the severance of domestic ethical community between adult children and their parents does not mean that they now owe each other no more consideration than what utter strangers deserve in their capacity as owners, moral subjects, civilians, and fellow citizens. Although a history of family association does not alter property entitlements, nor warrant any social or political privileges, it does have bearing upon moral relations to the degree that agents may owe others honor, respect, and gratitude for what has transpired between them. In this regard, purely moral considerations of benevolence and gratitude find an enduring application to parent-child relations, provided these conform to moral requirements. Although the subjection of children to their parents may be temporary, Locke is not off target in insisting that children owe their parents a perpetual respect and benevolence, provided one takes into account Locke's express qualification that this obligation be tempered according to the treatment parents have bestowed upon a child.[68] When that is done, the relation between parent and child has an abiding moral dimension that solely reflects the morally relevant factors that distinguish behavior toward strangers from conduct toward former intimates and benefactors. In each case, the difference in moral treatment of parents and strangers rests neither upon juridical duties of property right nor upon the ethical consideration of membership in a domestic association. Instead, any special deference to parents resides strictly in the moral consideration of the acts and intentions of former guardians. For this reason, Kant can duly claim that, after being raised, a child's only obligation to parents is a mere duty of virtue, the *moral* duty of gratitude.[69] Unlike ethical duty, such moral obligation remains caught in the subjectivity of conscience, where the absence of any binding common determination of good intentions and purposes leaves it to each agent to decide upon a universally valid course of action by means of a personal estimation.[70] Beyond what these edicts of conscience command, any further ties between parents and adult children are matters for "individual negotiation."[71]

Marriage and Parenting

Marriage might appear to drop out entirely of the ethics of parenting insofar as parent-child relations and marriage need not be linked and the imperatives of child rearing apply equally to single guardians, unwed cohabitants, and spouses.

Of course, the conjunction of marriage with parenting automatically serves to complement each element. In this respect, Hegel maintains that until spouses raise children, the love in which marital unity resides remains merely inward and subjective and separately manifest, dwelling in the heart and demonstrative initiatives of each partner; once child rearing commences, spouses face their love in the external, objective, unitary existence of their children.[72] Yet, be this as it may, it is far from clear that this objectification of marital love transforms either marriage or parent-child relations beyond combining them as they are independently given. Although Blustein argues that becoming parents engenders a strengthened, richer love between spouses, enhancing the psychological and moral development of children,[73] this is at best a possibility that could just as well be countered by heightened marital strife. By the same token, any effort to strengthen family relations by requiring that child rearing take place within marriage[74] might encourage some to marry, but without providing any guarantee that such marriages would endure, any enhancement of childless marriages, nor much rationale for depriving qualified unmarried singles and couples from enjoying the right to be parents.

Marriage does still entail qualifications of its own upon upbringing simply because spouses are obliged to comply with the norms of conjugal right while engaging in parenting, just as parental obligation serves to place limitations upon how exclusively spouses can attend to each other.

One obvious marital imperative is the sharing of child rearing duties. Like all domestic exertions in marriage, child rearing cannot become the burden of one spouse simply because of gender, tradition, or the unilateral decision of another spouse. Allowing such asymmetries to be imposed not only violates the marital right to codetermine household affairs, but impedes the social and political opportunities of the parent bearing the lion's share of child care. Moreover, if child care responsibilities are allotted by gender, this is likely to foster sexual stereotyping throughout all the spheres of right, engendering corresponding differences in how boys and girls are raised and educated, all contrary to the gender-neutral principles of each and every institution of freedom.[75] Any departure from equal child care responsibilities is only justifiable if the spouses are all agreeable, their agreement is not compromised by the illicit pressures of gender discrimination in other spheres, and the resulting arrangement does not conflict with exercising anyone's rights outside the home. In this connection, any reliance upon third party day care must be jointly authorized by spouses, except when so doing involves an impractical joint micromanagement of parenting. If disagreements arise among spouses on day care decisions, a resolution depends upon the same alternatives besetting any conjugal dispute: spouses must either compromise among themselves or submit to a recognized arbitrator, a predicament that once more sets in relief the limits of domestic right.

Any joint allocation of child care duties presupposes, of course, that spouses are equally responsible for the upbringing of their children. Three sets of circumstances might seem to cast such shared responsibility into question: first, situations where one spouse does not want to have the child that another has allowed to be born or adopted, second, polygamous families, and third, families with stepparents and stepchildren in varying degrees of custody.

Whereas unwed individuals do not have any automatic parental duties to offspring that they have unwillingly produced, can spouses evade parental duties for a child that their mate has unilaterally brought to term or unilaterally adopted? If the mere residence of a child in the home of spouses imposed parental duties upon them all, one might ask whether a pregnant woman can unilaterally give birth and retain custody of the child when that would impose child care responsibilities on an unwilling parent? Given that procreation is not a duty of marriage, a spouse certainly has no right to unilaterally demand that his or her mate give birth to a child. If, however, childbirth imposes parental duty upon every spouse, unwilling spouses might appear to have a right to demand that either an abortion be performed or the newborn child be given up for adoption, or, as a last resort, the unilateral decision to produce children be grounds for dissolving the marriage and freeing the unwilling party from unwanted child care duties. If, alternately, marriage does not entail sharing of child care obligations, then one spouse could unilaterally have a child without thereby forcing parental duties upon a recalcitrant partner.

Can, however, one spouse have parental duties that the other lacks without disrupting their conjugal unity of right and welfare? Certainly, the sharing of marital property makes any claims for child support a common liability. Moreover, the duty to care for one's spouse cannot shut itself off from aiding one's spouse in caring for dependents. To permit any such isolation of a private domain in the life of one spouse about which the other need not bother would inject an asymmetry disrupting the unity and reciprocity of right and welfare. This would be especially true for a relationship so intimate and taxing as parenting. Consequently, if one spouse becomes a parent through childbirth or adoption, parental duty must extend to all parties of the marriage. For just this very reason, spouses should not unilaterally take on parental responsibility. If they do and their reluctant mate cannot be persuaded to accept the unwanted parenthood, their marriage stands in jeopardy of breakdown.

It follows that polygamous marriages should not operate as if subgroups of spouses could take on and apportion parental responsibilities without the cooperation of the others. If such subdivisions occur, they undermine the unity of the polygamous household, transforming it into an extended family in which conjugal relations lose their reciprocity and independent privacy.

Similar consequences apply to step relations. Stepparents can hardly share property and interests with their spouse if they fail to share parental obligations for stepchildren. This holds true whether they have complete or partial custody of stepchildren, or only retain duties of support for stepchildren living entirely in the home of a former spouse. In each case, if stepparents could avoid parental responsibility, they and their spouse would be left with separate domestic spheres of interest compromising the unity of marriage. Consequently, stepparents have the same right as any other spouse to codetermine how their children are to be raised to autonomy. Once more, consanguinity has no automatic privilege. On the other hand, since parental right and duty rest upon an ethical commitment to raise children to mature autonomy, a commitment tied neither to marital status nor place of residence, the presence of stepparents does not deprive nonresident ex-spouses or ex-informal cohabitants of parental entitlements and obligations *if* their retention contributes to the welfare of the child. How these residual rights and duties get integrated with those of the custodial parent and stepparent is a matter that must be resolved either by the parties involved or by some higher authority.

Sibling Relations and Family Ethics

The parent-child relation provides the key for understanding the peripheral role of sibling relations in family ethics as well as the attraction of "fraternity" as an ideal for social and political institutions in which nepotism remains an injustice.

To begin with, because children are subject to parenting insofar as they lack the maturity to make them responsible agents, the inability of children to be strictly obliged to serve the interest and welfare of other family members applies to relations between minor siblings. Just as children have neither the right to codetermine family affairs (including the course of their own upbringing) nor the duty to care for the family welfare, so they have no right to preside over the rearing of their siblings nor any strict duty to make their siblings' welfare their own concern. Nevertheless, minor siblings are ethically connected insofar as they are raised by the same guardians. By belonging to the same household, siblings have an equal claim to parental care and can be required by their parents to perform services for each other and other family members that contribute to the imperatives of upbringing. These entitlements and requirements of obedience apply to children regardless of their relative age, gender, birth in or out of wedlock, biological ties to their parents, or any other factor irrelevant to their position as a child under parental care.[76] Like any childhood misconduct where immaturity undercuts full responsibility, misbehavior by and between siblings is subject to discipline for the sake of proper development rather than of retributive punishment. This applies to sexual relations that violate the incest restrictions compatible with family right.

At maturity, however, sibling relations lose their common subordination to parental authority and their common entitlement to parental care and support. Since they no longer have any claim to family property and income and never had the joint ownership and welfare that spouses enjoyed, siblings face one another as completely independent persons, free to form separate families of their own and exercise their social and political rights unimpeded by kinship relations. Adult siblings are neither entitled to share one another's property, nor to be cared for by one another when in need. Once they have entered civil society as independent agents, their well-being becomes the concern of impersonal and impartial organs of public welfare. At most, siblings' common childhood experiences may entail the special moral considerations that apply between adult children and parents in virtue of past actions and intentions. So long as their parents are deserving, siblings are joined in a purely moral relation of gratitude to and concern for their former guardians. Similarly, the character of their own intimacy as childhood companions inscribes their adult relations with a trove of common experiences and expectations that call for moral consideration, rather than for any further rights and duties rooted simply in kinship. As with parent-child relations following maturity, whatever special treatment morality may entail is a matter for conscience to determine, with all the perplexities and uncertainties that such subjective determination involves.

Accordingly, sibling relations have a certain luster: whereas they do not impede the impartiality of social and political freedom through domestic hierarchy and nepotism, they offer the promise of a personal moral consideration, which may temper the waning of traditional community.

CHAPTER VII

The Dissolution of the Family through Divorce, Death, and Disability

The just family is subject to several forms of dissolution, given the constitutive relations of domestic right: marriage and parenting.

As we have seen, the *ethical* relation of parenting eliminates itself through the completed upbringing of children, at which point parents and their adult progeny outgrow their correlative domestic rights and duties, retaining only moral ties and the social and political bonds that apply equally to strangers. Before this culmination, children may lose their domestic relation to a parent through the latter's death, mental or physical disabling, or failure to provide adequate care, be this due to external necessity, malice, or negligence.

By contrast, the ethical relation between spouses is subject to two main forms of dissolution: the destruction of the rational autonomy of a spouse through death or mental or physical harm, and the resolve of one or all spouses to withdraw from marriage by divorce. Both of these marriage breakdowns have ramifications for parental duty when children are involved. Yet since marriage need not involve parenting, the two forms of marriage dissolution must be conceived first solely with respect to how the rights and duties of spouses are affected and then secondly with respect to how parental obligations should be handled. Moreover, since the "natural" occurrences of death, disease, and injury that terminate

marriage have implications for any divorce settlements, it makes
sense to begin by conceiving how divorce should be determined.[1]

The Right to Divorce

At a time when divorce rates are in global ascendence, reaching
levels rendering lifetime marital vows a wishful relic,[2] family values appear no more decisively at issue than in the regulation of
divorce. The rise of civil society and self-government, simultaneously disengaging the economy from the household and political
power from kinship, has done much to put divorce at center stage
by freeing marriage from the pressures of economic and political
alliance and by providing social welfare institutions that make
single life a viable prospect for each spouse. Although the decline
in the political and economic importance of marriage and the correlative empowerment of individuals to choose their mates may
more closely found matrimony on personal love and intimacy, by
eliminating external pressures these same developments destabi-
lize the staying power of marriage.[3] Not surprisingly, modernity's
creation of conditions facilitating divorce[4] has fostered a renewed
debate over what terms should govern divorce, as well as over the
very legitimacy of marital separation. For even if the institutions
of social and political freedom remove key traditional obstacles to
divorce, they still leave open the basic question of whether domestic right is compatible with the elective dissolution of marriage.

If marriage were a contract, contractual freedom would sanction divorce only when both parties agreed to rescind their agreement or when the terms of the marriage agreement already contained escape clauses allowing unilateral withdrawal from matrimony under specified conditions. What those conditions should be
and what arrangements should follow upon divorce would be purely
arbitrary, depending upon the agreement of the marriage partners.[5] The ground rules of divorce cannot be so simple, however,
because marriage is not a contract, but an agreement to merge
private domains into a united domestic community, eliminating
the distance for contractual relations between spouses while conferring ethical rights beyond the pale of ownership.

For just this reason, the right to marry cannot be translated
into a duty to marry, as Puritan law once mandated. Insofar as the
rights and obligations of marriage are ethical norms, ingredient
in a form of community membership, they apply only to individuals
already belonging to a common family. Prospective spouses cannot

yet have any domestic duties to one another, but stand only under the same obligations that property, moral, social, and political relations impose upon strangers. Consequently, although individuals' status as persons and moral agents entitles them to marry, subject to legitimate incest and bigamy prohibitions, domestic right cannot oblige an agent to marry any particular individual, let alone anyone at all.

Yet, if the ethical character of marriage precludes an obligation to marry, it does not directly entail a parallel liberty to withdraw from marriage. The ethical community of law in civil society, for example, no more accommodates unilateral withdrawal from legal responsibility than the ethical community of the state permits citizens to relinquish their political obligations at will. Since membership in an ethical community subjects individuals to norms predicated upon existing institutions rather than solitary volitions, the right to unilateral disengagement cannot be assumed.

If divorce is to have legitimacy, this must accordingly derive not from the general ethical character of marriage, but from the particular type of ethical community that conjugal life involves.

On this score, Hegel suggests that divorce should be allowed because the ethical bond of marriage rests upon feeling, whose subjective, accidental character makes it inherently prey to contingency.[6] Certainly, feelings can always wax and wane, and feeling does play a determining role in the marriage decisions of spouses, whose resolve to marry one another cannot be deduced from any universal considerations. Indeed, if love provides the only basis for marriage that is not extraneous to the freedom to marry, is not, as Engels suggests, the only ethical marriage one in which love continues?[7] Yet can the emergence of a mere feeling to withdraw from marriage be sufficient grounds for dissolving conjugal life? Political obligations cannot be renounced on the basis of feeling, since the unity of the state rests upon law.[8] Why should the subjective discretion underlying the choice of marriage partners make the ensuing marriage vulnerable to a change of heart? Hegel himself is well aware that the ethical love characterizing the relation of spouses is not reducible to subjective feelings of attraction; the ethical love of spouses rather consists in a form of interaction in which they perform the roles of mutual caretakers of a common domestic good.[9] This performance may or may not correspond to the vicissitudes of romantic allure. Consequently, a mere change of feeling need not shatter the bond of marriage. What counts is rather the change of heart that accompanies a breakdown in conjugal conduct, where feelings of opposition and enmity undergird a failure to uphold the joint right and welfare of marriage. When relations reach this stage of marital alienation, where spouses no longer abide by the roles comprising marriage, but interact instead as estranged individuals trapped within a common home, domestic community has become a phantom that can hardly sustain the rights and duties defining the life of spouses. For this reason, Hegel recognizes that marriage retains rights against temporary feelings and opinions of feelings; the latter may not actually signal the total alienation constituting marital breakdown.[10] Accordingly, Hegel admits that divorce cannot simply follow from subjective feelings of marital dissatisfaction. An objective certification must be made to establish that conjugal alienation has in fact occurred, requiring the attestation of some authorized third party.[11]

These conclusions follow from the ethical character of marriage, whose obligations cannot be made contingent upon the arbitrary willing of one or more individuals since they are instead built into the existence of a form of community. Only if the association has collapsed do its constituent rights and duties fall into desuetude. Divorce upon demand, be it unilaterally or bi- or omnilaterally requested, would thus be precluded. At the very least, any such requests would have to be supplemented by an impartial inquiry into the condition of marriage, an inquiry that would result in divorce only when marriage breakdown could be certified.

Yet, even under such circumstances, the right to divorce might still be questioned if it were legitimate to require spouses to overcome their discord and uphold their marital obligations. Why should the vagaries of subjective feeling and individual behavior suspend an ethical relation when in other spheres of community, disharmony and lack of rectitude do not destroy the bonds of association?

Is compulsory marital rapprochement, however, really feasible? Impracticalities of enforcement might seem insurmountable, since compelling rectitude in conjugal relations requires policing the most private affairs of every marriage. Such difficulties are reflected in the crisis that beset fault divorce regimes when couples seeking divorce commonly fabricated stories of infidelity and spousal abuse, creating a climate of distrust from which no-fault divorce seemed the only escape.[12] Since the privacy of marriage makes discovery of the facts largely dependent upon the testimony of the spouses, any third-party investigation cannot be easy. Yet, analogous problems apply to remedying violations of parental or conjugal rights and duties in general, as well as any other wrong where third-party testimony is unavailable. Justice still requires that the facts be uncovered and that available testimony be weighed. In every case some balance must be struck between the feasibility and intrusiveness of surveillance and upholding the very rights that are being protected. Hence, pragmatic challenges do not settle the matter.

Nor, conversely, does the entitlement to divorce hang upon any pragmatic advantages for marriage that the option to divorce might be thought to provide. Hume suggests that liberty of divorce not only offers an escape from domestic antipathy and strife, but the best prophylactic against their outbreak, insofar as compulsory domestic confinement changes inclination and desire to aversion, robbing love of the freedom that alone can sustain conjugal romance[13] and preclude adultery.[14] Yet, as Hume himself admits, if predictions of domestic happiness are allowed to count, one can equally argue that a right to divorce is a license to destroy the happiness of children as well as that of spouses by removing the necessity of lifelong companionship that encourages the forgetting of frivolous quarrels and the withering of inclinations for new mates and separate interests.[15] Either way, the appeal to happiness rests upon contingent outcomes, for whom the testimony of experience can ensure no necessary future confirmations, even if illicit assumptions of psychological mechanisms are made. Whether freedom to divorce will end up promoting or undermining the happiness of children is just as devoid of any necessary, universal answer as whether divorce will make marital life a happier venture. Innumerable intervening factors may affect the outcome, including the surrounding social and political opportunities open to ex-spouses of different genders and sexual orientations, attitudes to divorce and sexual liberation, provisions for child care, and all the unforeseeable twists and turns of personal development.[16] Yet the indeterminability of prudential judgment is not the most crucial liability of any such pragmatic, utilitarian approach; what robs it of any legitimacy is its neglect of the exclusive normativity of self-determination, which can claim universal validity precisely by being undetermined by the external circumstances upon which happiness hinges.

More decisive for the right to divorce than any difficulties of enforcement or alleged effects upon marital happiness is the scope of conjugal community. Unlike the ethical bonds of civil society and of the state, those of marriage extend no farther than the spouses involved. Consequently, when spouses no longer fulfill their conjugal roles the results are qualitatively unlike those following from their failure to behave with social and political rectitude. In the latter case, their deviance does not undermine the existence of the institutions of civil society and the state, which continue to function so long as other individuals preponderantly perform their civil and political roles. By contrast, when spouses cease to observe their marital obligations, the activities in which marriage has its existence no longer occur, creating a situation analogous to social or political anarchy, where institutions collapse because individuals predominantly stop acting in conformity with the roles that animate their erstwhile social and political community. In effect, the moment spouses act with separate rights and welfare, their conjugal union falls into desuetude, canceling the current and future extension of their former marital rights and duties. A right to divorce is thereby entailed by the particular reach of the ethical bond of marriage.

Decisive for the parameters of this right is how the advent of marital breakdown is equivalent neither to feelings of dissatisfaction on the part of one or all[17] spouses nor to the opinion of one or all that the marriage has collapsed. Some impartial determination of marital breakdown must be made and the results must be made public since what lies at stake is the termination of a relation of domestic right that crucially affects how the parties involved may interact with others. Just as marriage must take a public form, with its own recognizable formalities, so too must the certification of marriage breakdown and the imposition of divorce.

Two questions now pose themselves, questions in response to which the different contemporary divorce regimes have distinguished themselves as competing solutions. First, what exactly constitutes the marital breakdown from which divorce should issue? Must fault be established, and if not, how can no-fault divorce avoid enabling personal feeling and opinion to annul an ethical relationship? And is marital breakdown dependent upon the willingness to divorce of one or all spouses? Secondly, to what extent does marital breakdown, publicly certified by an authorized third party, leave ex-spouses unencumbered by their former relationship? They may obtain the right to marry anew,[18] but what if any obligations carry over from the old marriage to the new? How is common property to be distributed? Are ex-spouses at all responsible for each other's future care, financially or otherwise? These groups of questions need to be resolved first in respect to spouses without dependent children and then with regard to spouses who are parents of minors.

Consent, Fault, and the Grounds for Divorce

The controversy over grounds for divorce properly proceeds in common recognition of three provisos: first, that spouses are entitled to divorce; secondly, that grounds of divorce, whatever they may be, must be impartially and publicly identified and applied to each individual candidate for divorce; and thirdly, that given the ethical character of marriage and the particular scope of conjugal relations, marital breakdown becomes the locus for identifying grounds of divorce. The question that therefore must first be answered is what comprises impartially and publicly certifiable evidence of marital breakdown.

The contemporary debate over divorce has tended to formulate the question in terms of two alternatives: fault and no-fault divorce, which may or may not be combined.[19] No-fault divorce allows divorce to proceed on the basis of the willingness of one or all spouses to withdraw from marriage, without need of any admission of violations of marital rights and duties by one or more spouses.[20] By contrast, fault divorce terminates marriage only on the condition that one or more spouses have demonstrably violated conjugal obligations. Historically, these alternatives have been weighed in terms of prevailing domestic and social conditions, where marriage is restricted to monogamous, heterosexual unions and where gender inequality within and without the home compounded by conflicts between household responsibilities and social and political opportunities have tended to leave wives disadvantaged by divorce settlements, especially when those settlements treat spouses as if they were in equal positions in starting single life anew.[21] Although such conditions must not be ignored in shaping divorce policy within a particular body politic, the principle determining the legitimate grounds of divorce must be established independently of unjust circumstances that violate the structures of household as well as social and political freedom.

Although the liberalization of divorce laws since the 1970s has generally moved to no-fault termination of marriage in opposition to the retention of fault grounds,[22] fault and no-fault divorce need not be mutually exclusive options. They can conceivably complement one another, especially if they have different ramifications for divorce settlements. Although fault and no-fault grounds for divorce may well entail different types of divorce settlements, what first must be determined is whether either or both comprise sufficient evidence of marital breakdown. Other drawbacks that might be attributed to either option are moot until this question is decided,[23] for the ethical character of marriage requires that nothing can count as a ground for divorce unless it is tied up with the dismantlement of conjugal community.

By itself, no-fault divorce treats the resolve to withdraw from marriage of one or more spouses to be a sufficient ground for ending marriage. This resolve may be certified as an enduring commitment by the addition of waiting periods and compulsory marriage counseling, but these qualifications still leave the consent to divorce of one or more parties the decisive factor. Insofar as marriage is an ethical union, the question on which no-fault divorce must hang is whether such consent comprises sufficient testimony to marital breakdown.

Whether consent by one or more parties is a necessary condition for divorce does not tilt the scale for one or the other alternative, since fault divorce could require consent in addition to fault, just as well as operate without any consent at all, as a compulsory outcome of a finding of marital breakdown.[24] Nevertheless, the role of consent in relation to marital breakdown must be determined, irrespective of how fault should enter into divorce.

It might appear that marital breakdown must always involve consent to divorce on the part of at least one spouse, since the union of marriage has not collapsed unless at least one spouse has willingly ceased to perform his or her conjugal duties. If a spouse has inadvertently ignored marital obligations the possibility of instruction lies open to remedy the nonmalicious wrong. But if a spouse has knowingly withdrawn from the common enterprise of married life, the marital union is shattered and the spouse responsible would be expected, as a coherent individual, to desire the formal separation that his or her conduct has prepared. In such a case, the opposition of the other spouse would not be sufficient to eliminate the breach in marriage. On the other hand, making *mutual* consent a *requirement* for divorce would both ignore incidences of marital breakdown and enable spouses committing marital misconduct to chain their partners to a relation the latter wish to flee, blocking a divorce warranted by fault simply by withholding consent.[25] Of course, if more than one spouse has withdrawn from the mutual care and codetermination of conjugal life, marriage has obviously become an empty fiction and both spouses could be expected to consent to the formal consummation of the estrangement they have chosen. In either situation of unilateral or mutual consent, the will to divorce would be a constitutive element in marital breakdown. Significantly, however, such consent would be accompanied by a corresponding pattern of behavior in which marital duties have been intentionally violated.[26]

By contrast, one or more spouses could desire divorce without having already ceased to perform their conjugal roles. In those circumstances permitting consent to mandate divorce would be tantamount to allowing mere feeling and opinion to annul the ethical union of marriage.[27] Such is the errant path sanctioned by many U.S. jurisdictions and followed most extremely by the Swedish Family Law Reform of 1973, which mandates that any spouse's will to dissolve marriage should always suffice to bring upon divorce, as if marriage were but an expression of a eudaemonistic individualism,[28] hardly distinguishable from the informal cohabitation that not accidentally figures so prominently in Sweden.[29]

Although the resolve to divorce by one or more parties is ingredient in marital breakdown, contrary to Swedish policy, unless that resolve is a firm, freely given commitment associated with estranged and/or derelict behavior, it does not suffice as evidence of a rupture of marriage.[30] Of course, if a spouse's determination to divorce is not an intermittent nadir of changing moods, but an unbending resolution, the road to actual estranged conduct is already under foot.

Alternately, if one or more spouses violate marital duty but none desire to withdraw from marriage, they retain a conjugal commitment that renders the violation merely a partial wrong of a union that still persists. Hence, although such violations call for some remedy, which may involve outside intervention running the gamut from counseling to punishment, divorce without the consent of either party would violate marital freedom, depriving spouses of conjugal entitlements that no one else has a right to put in forfeiture.[31]

Yet if consent of at least one spouse is a necessary, but not sufficient condition for the marital breakdown from which divorce should proceed, the establishment of fault is, for its part, hardly a sufficient supplement. The admission of marital misconduct, either with respect to the handling of common domestic property and earnings, or with respect to care for the well-being of conjugal partners, need not signify a general rupture of marriage. Nonmalicious or malicious misuse of joint property may represent only a passing or partial injury to conjugal trust, just as episodes of physical and mental cruelty,[32] of infidelity, or of inadvertent or express neglect may fail to disrupt abiding resolves to uphold the joint experience of matrimony.[33] In each case, the mere specification of the marital wrong leaves open whether it is simply a violation calling for remedy within the framework of a persisting marriage or the manifestation of an irreconcilable breach of conjugal harmony.[34] This is true even of desertion, which would ordinarily signal the most obvious breakdown of marriage[35] if it were not for the possibility that the separated parties may still seek reconciliation. Hence, desertion too must be placed in the context of the abiding resolve of the marriage partners before it figures as the fatal blow to matrimony. Desertion can accordingly figure as a punishable marital wrong, since conjugal duty has not yet fallen into desuetude when a spouse leaves another.

Although the absence of any will to divorce leaves marital misconduct a remedial wrong rather than a ground for divorce, the mere addition of consent does not tip the balance, no matter whether divorce is favored by all spouses or only one, be it victim or malefactor. Some divorce regimes prohibit an abusive spouse from suing for divorce from an unwilling victim, as if fault should affect whose consent may count.[36] Conditions of gender bias within and without the home certainly accentuate the plight of victims of such suits, whose special vulnerability makes them more likely to be abused in the first place. Yet, the question of grounds for divorce is a separate issue from how divorce settlements should be administered and how gender equality can be enforced in families, the economy, and the political arena. Determining that marriage may or may not have broken down when an abusive spouse seeks divorce depends upon the same scrutiny of marital behavior as a situation when the victim of abuse sues for divorce against an unwilling spouse. In each case, protecting the right and welfare of the most vulnerable spouse remains an imperative whether or not the marriage should be abandoned. If the will to divorce on the part of victim or abuser accompanies a situation where marital misconduct is not a peripheral, remedial lapse, but the emblem of a broken marriage, then sufficient grounds for divorce are present. Once again, what counts is not the current incidence of fault, or, for that matter of sex and/or romance, but whether conjugal roles are preponderantly fulfilled or abdicated.[37] The malicious violation of marital rights by one or more spouses may be a constituent in matrimonial collapse, but so may be the outbreak of nonmalicious, but irreconcilable disagreements over how conjugal sharing is to be squared with property, earnings, economic and political involvements, friendships, kin relations, and other personal affairs, including decisions to have children[38] or views on how to raise them.

The ramifications for the fault/no-fault divorce debate are therefore mixed. On the one hand, consent by at least one spouse is a necessary but not sufficient condition for divorce. On the other hand, fault, understood as marital misconduct, may or may not be part of the pattern of marital rupture that must supplement the resolve to divorce. Irreconcilable differences without fault may just as well supply the additional factor to consent allowing for divorce. Whether or not fault is present, in each and every case the resolve to divorce must be authenticated as not just subjective sentiment and opinion, but the reflection of a real marital breakdown.

Although family right must leave it to the legal process of civil society to deliver the judicial formalities of how divorce should be publicly filed, investigated, and decided, conjugal community does already mandate that the extremes of no-fault divorce on demand and exclusive fault divorce are equally impermissible. Some intermediary procedure must be followed where divorce with or without fault is accompanied by some impartial, public certification of marital breakdown. Hence, although neither divorce on demand nor divorce by joint registration is permissible, unilateral divorce and mutual consent divorce are legitimate, subject to the authoritative certification of the rupture of conjugal community.[39] By its very nature, the assessment of marital breakdown involves an evaluation of actions and intentions prey to not only the uncertainties of empirical observation but the subjective discretion required to subsume the observed facts under the categories of marital conduct. In addition, the practicalities of the expense and time consumed by judicial inquiry cannot be ignored when they end up infringing upon other structures of right.[40] What tests are to be relied upon cannot help but involve contingent elements. Whether the testimony of outsiders must supplement that of one or more spouses, or whether some waiting period and/or time of separate habitation need transpire to certify the enduring character of marital estrangement are questions that fall beyond the grasp of philosophical principle. With regard to such details of certifying grounds of divorce, judgment must enter where conceptual precision ends.[41]

What does, however, call for principled determination are the just terms of divorce, which then may be applied to particular cases. Although the authentication of marital breakdown suspends conjugal obligations henceforth between the new ex-spouses, their withdrawal from marriage should still pay heed to how the remnants of conjugal life ought to be dismantled.[42] These remnants issue from the two sides of matrimony subject to external regulation: joint property and mutual care for joint welfare.

Property Settlements and Alimony in the Divorce of Spouses without Dependents

The joint ownership proper to marriage has obvious implications for the divorce settlement. Since spouses unite into a joint domestic personhood with common property, they are entitled to an equal share of what they jointly own. In the case of spouses with no dependent children, joint ownership has been shown to extend to all property that spouses bring into marriage, as well as to all earnings accumulated during marriage. Consequently, the property settlement for divorce between spouses without dependent children would seem to have a simple form: a complete equal division of property and of earnings and employment benefits accumulated during marriage, with value equivalents provided for items that cannot be reasonably divided.

Strictly following such a property settlement principle would ignore differences in *future* income, employment and pension benefits,[43] the length of marriage, incidences of marital misconduct, and to what extent prior divisions of domestic duties during marriage unequally prejudice or enhance the future livelihood of the spouses. Alimony would also play no role, since a simple division of joint assets leaves ex-spouses as independent persons whose future livelihoods stand in no different a relation than that of strangers.[44] How their separate standards of living develop and how public welfare administrations provide guarantees for their health care, employment benefits, and retirement would be utterly unaffected by their past conjugal history, save for any effects of marriage upon their respective earning potentials.

Provided prior marriage relations have not unequally prejudiced the livelihoods of ex-spouses and issues of child care do not supervene, differences in future earnings would be no more a problem for *family* right than differences in pension benefits resulting from future employment. Such discrepancies could become issues for *social* justice, but then remedying resulting disadvantages would be a public concern, rather than the particular responsibility of the more affluent ex-spouse.[45] The equal division of marital assets would here have fulfilled all abiding conjugal obligations, leaving ex-spouses with no further special duties to share future income or provide other care.[46]

When, however, the arrangement of marital relations has left spouses with unequal earning potentials, including different levels of employment and pension benefits, the issue arises of whether the divorce settlement should remedy the impending inequity by transferring additional resources from the privileged to underprivileged spouses so as to equalize their separate livelihoods. Such transfers could include unequal divisions of marital property enhancing the position of the disadvantaged ex-spouse,[47] continued sharing of employment and pension benefits, and alimony payments garnished from the income of the more affluent partner to supplement the earnings or subsidize vocational training of the partner who earlier sacrificed career prospects for the sake of another spouse's future.[48] Whatever the mode of redress, the selected remedy would retain its legitimacy only so long as the marriage-related handicap remained operative. Once that handicap could be impartially and publicly certified to have been overcome, the livelihood of each ex-spouse would become a completely independent affair, subject only to the mercies of private charity and the guarantees of public welfare institutions.[49]

Given that divisions of conjugal roles are legitimately matters of codetermination by spouses, any inequalities in earning potential arising from marriage decisions should in principle be the responsibility of "victim" and "beneficiary" alike. Genuine coresponsibility, of course, can and has often been lacking due to domination by one spouse at home. Moreover, genuine coresponsibility can and has more and more pervasively been absent without direct domestic domination due to gender discrimination in society and state, as well as due to failures to accommodate child-rearing responsibilities in workplace and political activity. Both of these contingencies have given otherwise unbiased spouses "impartial" grounds for privileging the career of the husband. In such cases, where the voluntary character of marital decisions is suspect, the grounds for redress are evident. When, however, marital right is observed and social and political opportunities are not conditioned by gender differences and domestic responsibilities, the codetermination of marital roles might seem to absolve the "favored" ex-spouse from any duty to continue some form of support for the disadvantaged one. This would be true only if the ethical character of marriage were ignored and joint marriage decisions were viewed as contractual engagements, engendering duties extending no further than the terms of agreement. Since, however, marriage unites the interests of spouses, every agreement is subsumed to the end of furthering the common good of the marriage. When the dislocation of divorce severs the union of welfare, any disadvantage that hinges upon prior marital decisions should be handled in recognition of the end of mutual interest that underlay those decisions. Otherwise, divorce settlements will ignore the ethical commitments that must be acknowledged in order for the withdrawal from marriage to count as such. Consequently, even when spouses have acted in accord with marital right in a civil society and body politic that do not allow gender and family activities to disadvantage individuals, they will be responsible for ensuring that divorce will not disadvantage one another owing to their prior jointly decided marital roles. In effect, the career advantages of one spouse that have been fostered by the domestic sacrifices of another represent a jointly owned career asset, which should enter into the division of marital property in divorce, especially when it may represent the most economically important asset of marriage.[50]

Much contemporary practice has tended to ignore this imperative by repudiating alimony as a relic of an antiquated homemaker-breadwinner household ideology and by privileging equal property divisions as the proper vehicle for respecting the ideal of marriage as a partnership of equal individuals.[51] Yet some contemporary divorce regimes have recognized the persistence of postdivorce disadvantage rooted in prior marital arrangements and pursued different approaches to address the problem. In England, the 1984 amendments to the Matrimonial Proceedings and Property Act of 1970 empowered courts to impose divorce settlements placing the divorced parties as closely as possible in the same financial position they would have occupied if divorce had not occurred.[52] In West Germany, the 1976 reform law similarly calculated support according to the marital standard of living.[53] Due, however, to the added expenses of separate households and unequal custodial responsibilities, as well as to the contingencies of each ex-spouse's livelihood, such a strategy proves to be impractical.[54] Instead of maintaining past standards of living, what instead counts is removing the abiding disadvantage wrought by past sacrifices and dependencies, something that alimony or adequate compensatory payments can address.[55] Tailoring support agreements along these lines is the more fitting task.

Is the resulting responsibility for support, however, in any way conditioned by the brevity of a marriage? Should one ex-spouse be forever burdened with subsidizing the earnings of a less economically viable counterpart when their marriage has lasted only briefly? This question is, to a large degree, moot once one recognizes that the responsibility for continued support is contingent upon a disadvantage caused by life decisions made and endured during marriage. The shorter the marriage, the less impact such decisions are likely to have upon future earning potential. Hence, the length of marriage drops out as an independent qualifying factor.

Indifference to the length of marriage might seem less innocuous in property divisions, especially when there is a great disparity between the assets that each spouse brings into marriage.[56] Yet, if marriage is an ethical union in which individuals consolidate their right and welfare, why should it matter how long a marriage lasts? Have not both spouses relinquished their separate claims as the price of determining themselves as married partners? And why should a leveling of property not be a positive outcome of divorce?

Much of the debate over how marital property should be administered reflects concern for situations where gold diggers marry only to divorce and acquire half the assets of some dupe. This concern lacks the anachronistic injustice of efforts to limit joint marital ownership and divorce property settlements in order to preserve wealth within some bloodline, either promoting kin relations extending beyond the marital and parental ties of the just family or simply safeguarding inheritance of wealth by male issue. Whereas these latter concerns violate the prerogatives of domestic freedom, the problem of mercenary divorce strikes at the ethical core of marriage.

In so doing, mercenary divorce puts into focus several general issues revolving around property settlements. First, although the brevity of marriage might seem a significant indicator in gold-digging divorces, conditioning property divisions by the length of marriage would neglect the more decisive factor of fraudulent intent, which need not, of course, figure in marriages that suffer an early collapse. If malice is what instead matters, a more general question arises: should fault affect property settlements even if it is not the exclusive, let alone sufficient, condition for divorce?[57]

Secondly, although mercenary divorce may put at risk half of all the assets of its victim, the callousness of its appropriation raises the issue of whether certain property, such as family heirlooms and personal memorabilia, should be protected from property settlement divisions, either in all divorces or only where one spouse has victimized another. In addition, mercenary divorce raises anew the question of whether a domicile and its furnishings deserve special treatment in property divisions.

If fault were to affect the division of joint property among divorcees, the extra levied property would amount to compensation for the victim of marital misconduct.[58] Although punishment for marital wrong can and should be impartially meted out as soon as an authoritative inquiry and judgment have been made, only after divorce could compensation for marital misconduct be effected. During marriage the regime of joint property makes any compensation paid by malefactor to victim an empty gesture, since what is "transferred" is already co-owned by the "beneficiary." On the basis of family right,[59] property settlement in divorce provides the only opportunity for providing compensation to victims of marital misconduct.[60] Because the rights such wrong violates ought to be upheld, available remedies should not be ignored. Consequently, fault has a role to play in the property settlements of divorce, modifying the equal division of joint assets that would follow in the absence of either fault or disadvantage due to prior marital arrangements. Where marital misconduct has either squandered family wealth or caused injuries whose past or ongoing care imposes expenses upon the victim, the malefactor should make up the loss to the victim out of the former's remaining share of marital property, or, when that does not suffice, out of future earnings.

These imperatives of property settlement might appear unduly harsh, no matter how long a marriage has lasted, if they were to ignore the special attachments to certain elements of marital property due to their sentimental and personal nature. Provided the scope of such attachments is limited, there appears little reason why property settlements could not achieve an equitable division of family wealth in accord with the sentiments of the parties. Indeed, since right merely requires that joint property be equally divided with respect to its exchange value, there is no reason why the preferences of divorcees for particular household items should not be accommodated as much as conformity with equality of wealth permits. Since, however, sentiment can extend to each and any household article, and the exchange value of personal items can vary immeasurably, any strict rule becomes problematic. When the custody of children is not involved, the home itself becomes fair game for being put in the balance of dividable family goods, unless the prior disadvantage of one spouse makes retention of the home an important mainstay of that divorcee's livelihood. In the case where one spouse has a special need for the home and its furnishings, property settlements should respect this consideration where possible, adjusting the division of the remaining assets if equity requires it.[61]

Divorce Settlements of Spouses with Dependents

The grounds for divorce would only differ when prospective divorcees are parents of dependent children if the breakdown of marriage were incompatible with fulfillment of the duties of parenting. If that were true, married parents would find themselves in a conflict of right, where marital freedom would contradict the entitlement of children to be brought up to autonomy.[62] Divorce may often be a shattering experience for children, but so may life within a miserable marriage. In any event, the duties of parents extend to ensuring the happiness of their children only to the degree that happiness is a precondition for their development to maturity. The emotional upheaval of having one's parents divorce may be indelibly painful, but that does not make it so irrevocably damaging that it robs a child of the possibility of achieving rational autonomy. Divorcing parents have the right to hope that their decision to separate still leaves them able to bring their parenting to fruition. So long as this is true, the right to divorce does not conflict with the obligations of parenting.[63]

Accordingly, whereas divorce may formalize a marital breakdown, alienating spouses from one another, it entails neither an abandonment of parental duties nor a cessation of child-parent relations. Divorcees remain responsible for the upbringing of their children and it is the continued fulfillment of this responsibility that distinguishes the divorce settlements of parents from those of childless spouses.[64]

Insofar as divorce establishes independent private domains for each divorcee, parental relations of divorcees involve both direct custodial care and indirect child support, each of which can be distributed in varying arrangements. Whatever be the legitimate variations in custody and child support, the property settlement between parenting divorcees must achieve a division that facilitates those arrangements. For although children may have no separate claim in the division of joint marital property, each parent remains obliged to provide for their upbringing.

This obligation may be lightened by the external supplement of social assistance provided by the welfare institutions of civil society. Generous social benefits for disadvantaged and/or custodial ex-spouses may enable equity considerations to survive divorce policies emphasizing the independence and self-sufficiency of divorcees.[65] Extensive public subsidy of child care need not, however, relieve noncustodial parents of financial responsibility for child support, as historical experience in Germany and Sweden makes evident.[66] Alternately, as U.S. policy illustrates, an absence of universal child care assistance combined with private orderings of child support can leave postdivorce disadvantage a welfare problem, with the associated indignity and dependency falling wholly upon the custodial parent.[67] Whether the costs of divorce should be entirely transferred from ex-spouses to the public at large raises issues parallel to the question of whether tort litigation should be wholly preempted by no-fault social insurance. In each case, the costs of settlement can reach levels imposing hardships upon the very parties whose welfare should be preserved. Although public sharing can disperse these hardships, a complete elimination of personal responsibility can equally cast in doubt the autonomy of the parties, whose rights can hardly be recognized if the corresponding liabilities are ignored. From a systematic point of view, the interaction between the child-support obligations of divorcees and public assistance for child care, education, housing, clothing, medical care, pension guarantees, career training, etc. can only be addressed following the systematic determination of the parental obligations of ex-spouses apart from civil institutions and of what public assistance programs are mandated by social justice in civil society. Consequently, what here lies at issue is determining how parental obligations affect divorce settlements independently of any public assistance. Deciding how parental support obligations and public assistance should be balanced must await the conception of the relation of family and civil society.[68]

The determination of custodial rights and child support are themselves intertwined to the degree that custody arrangements can place differing burdens upon divorcees that affect their ability to support themselves and their dependents. Although parents have a right to oversee the upbringing of their children, this right is always conditional upon fulfilling the imperatives of child rearing. When parents divorce, the same qualification applies: any custody arrangement remains contingent upon its conformity with the demands of child rearing. So long as an arrangement meets those requirements, parents are entitled to exercise their prerogatives of parental responsibility to select between it and any other qualified options. Given the nature of parenting, the distinguishing of permissible arrangements depends upon factors that are relative both to the character of the divorcees and to independently given objective factors. If divorcees are equally capable and willing parents and their new living circumstances are equally amenable to child care, as well as within affordable reach of one another, some form of joint custody would be a viable option so long as it permitted a sufficient degree of continuity in the life of the children to facilitate their development. What schedule such joint custody follows can be left to the discretion of the parents provided it accords with the emotional and educational needs of the children. When the custody arrangement puts equal demands upon the parents in terms of time and expense, the custody arrangement need not be supplemented by any separate support agreements that would transfer property or income from one divorcee to another. If, however, the custody arrangement puts particular burdens upon one parent, the other is responsible for support to balance this inequity.[69] This support may involve not only the transfer of accumulated money and income, but, when applicable, ownership or occupation of the former family home.[70] In a society such as ours, where gendered roles within and without the family leave child custody overwhelmingly in the hands of women who have already suffered a retardation in their earning potential due to their prior domestic burdens, custodial women divorcees are ordinarily due a double support supplement, one part to compensate for the burdens of child custody and another part to compensate for underdeveloped career opportunities.[71]

Due to the joint intimacy of the home of each ex-spouse, the child cannot avoid sharing the standard of living of parents, as it becomes redefined in the aftermath of divorce through the combination of custody and support arrangements. Given, however, the added costs of separate domiciles and the added responsibilities of new families created through remarriage, family resources can provide no guarantee for maintaining the level of affluence that a child may have enjoyed before divorce. Moreover, since living conditions alter, custody and support arrangements must be subject to continual supervision so as to implement revisions addressing the particular circumstances of children and parents, such as changing health and educational needs, as well as general situations in society, such as variations in inflation.[72]

As an ethical relation, parenting is independent of gender, sexual orientation, ethnicity, and any other factors extraneous to the providing of care. The application of custody and support settlements should reflect solely the actual capabilities and circumstances of the parents in question, whatever be their other features. From this perspective, differences of personal behavior, health, or occupational demands may make divorcees unequally suited to retain custody of their children. Fault for marital, as well as parental misconduct, may here affect custody and corresponding support arrangements provided they bear upon the suitability of a parent for physical custody or for certain visitation arrangements.[73] When pertinent differences in parental ability are impartially and authoritatively established, divorce settlements must accordingly assign principal or exclusive custody to the more suitable parent, while arranging for sufficient child support from noncustodial parents to offset the burdens of custody. So long as contact with the noncustodial parent does no harm to the upbringing of the children involved, that parent has rights of visitation. Although other kin, such as grandparents, do not have any juridical rights as caretakers of related dependent children, the general interests of such children would ordinarily dictate rights of visitation for those relations with whom contact presents no harm.[74] As far as possible, all such arrangements should be made with the cooperation of the parents involved, since otherwise their parental responsibility would be usurped.

Needless to say, whether custody be joint or not, divorced parents may disagree on innumerable issues of child rearing, as well as violate custody and support agreements inadvertently or with malice. Disputes and other nonmalicious violations of custody rights and obligations call for adjudication and due compensation, whereas malicious violations call for an authoritative judgment and punishment. Unless some third party is authorized to adjudicate disputes and enforce child custody and support agreements, the welfare of children and their custodians will hang in the balance, awaiting the victory of force or compromise.[75] As with all situations where family right and duty require intervention by an external authority, the solution hinges upon the legal and welfare institutions of civil society, which themselves rest upon the workings of constitutional self-government.[76]

These imperatives of custody and support agreements become multiplied and interwoven when stepchildren and stepparents enter the equation, either as members of the household before divorce, or upon remarriage. Since each new coupling reshapes the conditions of child care and support, prior settlements should be susceptible of due revision to balance the provisos of marital separation and continuing parental responsibility. The extended network of step relations resulting from "serial polygamy" thereby resembles the complications divorce settlements confront within a context of polygamy, where defections or additions to the marital horde can always introduce new circumstances calling for alterations in existing custody and support agreements. Although the numbers of relations are increased, the principles remain the same.

Death in the Family and Inheritance

Like every other institution, the family is subject to the destruction of the rational agency of its members. This destruction can occur through death or through mental and/or physical harm that robs individuals of their capacity to think and will. Because of the narrow scope of domestic community, these misfortunes are calamities for the family, whether they befall childless spouses or married or divorced parents and their children. Nonetheless, the domestic ramifications are very different for conjugal and parent-child relations, given the joint nature of marital property and the limits of parental responsibility.

The case of death in the family is perhaps more clear-cut than that of mental and physical depersonalization. When a spouse dies, the ramifications for family property are straightforward, provided the joint property regime is duly observed. Since spouses should be joint owners of all property within the consolidated domesticity of marriage, the death of one leaves the other spouse sole owner of the abiding domestic property, or, in cases of polygamy, leaves the remaining spouses co-owners of the same household property that they shared before. This co-ownership extends to any insurance benefits that follow from the death of a spouse. The presence of dependent children does not affect this distribution, so long as they remain cared for by the surviving spouse or spouses. Since these children are minors, they cannot own property on their own without the cooperation of some trustee, and joint marital property never belongs to children, since all that children have a right to is the care sufficient to bring them up to be competent participants in the institutions of freedom. Although parents remain obliged to furnish support for such care, whether or not they are the actual custodial guardians, doing so is not equivalent to giving children ownership of some portion of marital property.

These imperatives of family right equally ensure that divorce settlement obligations maintain their hold beyond the grave. When an unmarried divorcee predeceases an ex-spouse to whom continuing support is due either as alimony or for child care, the estate of the former is responsible for maintaining those contributions insofar as no other competing claims have primacy.[77] When a spouse dies who is a remarried, noncustodial divorcee owing support payments to the family in which his or her children are raised, these obligations should still be met by drawing from the portion of the joint estate that would fall to that spouse if that spouse were to divorce again, allowance made for support of any dependents in the last marriage.[78] Drawing upon more than that portion could impinge upon the property right of the other spouse, who need have no abiding parental obligations to the noncustodial stepchildren.[79] In cases where the remaining property is insufficient to continue such support, family relations offer little solution and should be supplemented by further public guarantees that can only be implemented through the institutions of civil society.

By themselves, family relations offer little basis for any inheritance from parents to children. Grown children have no domestic claim to the property of their parents when one predeceases another, since the surviving spouse retains ownership to the estate that was formerly jointly owned, whereas autonomous, mature offspring have no right to support from their parents.[80] Even when adults lose all their parents, their kin relation gives them no right to the family estate. Because parents cease to have support obligations once their children have matured, the estate of parents who die together or die last is freely disposable according to either the testamentary will that civil institutions permit or according to the intestate regulations that accord with the imperatives of social and political equal opportunity.[81] The positive discretion of civil institutions must here provide guidance, since property right by itself cannot make explicable how the will of a person who has ceased to exist can still dispose over property; any testamentary right instead must issue from the recognized will of civil society, as stipulated in positive law.[82]

When dependent children survive the death of custodial parents, the situation is different, owing to the abiding demands of child care support. In this case, the children's right to be raised to autonomy mandates that they should be taken custody of either by an able noncustodial parent, some other qualified private adult or adults, or some public agency. Because the estate of the predeceasing parent or parents still remains connected to the welfare of the surviving children, the new guardian is entitled to draw upon that estate for child care expenses. Yet, insofar as surviving kin have no further claim upon the estate, any remainder should be left for the distribution conferred by testamentary freedom or intestate regulations.[83]

In all of these cases, distinctions between "legitimate" and "illegitimate" children possess no juridical significance. Whether a child is born within or without wedlock, whoever have assumed parental responsibility incur a financial duty that extends to their estate if they predecease their charge. The same principle applies to stepchildren. As long as a parent is responsible for the support of a child, that responsibility carries over to the parent's estate, irrespective of whether the children are cared for by an ex-spouse or were brought under the deceased's care through marriage.

Nonetheless, for just the reason that children have no claim upon any portion of marital property independent of their right to be provided the means for maturation, the death of a child leaves family property unaltered, save for any support arrangements for the deceased, which lose their reason for being and become defunct. The existence of any trusts in the name of the child is an unrelated matter, since they are not part of the family property. Because neither parents nor siblings have any domestic right to such property, the inheritance of trusts is determined by testamentary discretion or intestate regulations.

Since the only ethical domestic ties consist in conjugal and parental relations, family right gives siblings, grandparents, and other kin no claim to any share of the marital property that legitimately remains entirely within the ownership of the surviving spouse, with the qualification that dependent children (both custodial and noncustodial, as well as dependent stepchildren) be provided for upon its basis. Family right is therefore jeopardized by any testamentary conventions, such as the Roman freedom of testament, primogeniture, and marital estates of dower and courtesy[84] that allow endowing particular children, male blood lines, other more distant kin or unrelated beneficiaries at the expense of surviving spouses and their dependents.[85] Similarly, the succession rights of surviving spouses and their dependents are defeated by the toleration of *inter vivos* transfers that allow a predeceasing spouse to funnel marital property to someone else, as well as unilaterally squander family wealth.[86]

Although inheritance from husband to wife was exceptional prior to this century, the historical trend has since followed the right direction, increasingly giving due preference to surviving spouses over children and other kin, both in testate and intestate succession.[87] Simultaneously, however, the financial significance of inheritance has dwindled, partly through the liberation of economic and political relations from kinship, partly through civil society's social guarantees of livelihood, and partly through the rise of survivorship arrangements including life insurance and pension sharing.[88] To the extent that these developments reflect the emergence of the normative relations of civil society and democratic government, they validate the general decline in the importance of the family as a conduit of wealth.[89]

The Domestic Implications of Depersonalization

Once death in the family is considered in light of conjugal and parental right and duty, the implications for ownership and care follow clearly enough. Even doctrines of reincarnation and the immortality of the soul inject little ambiguity since the spirit of the deceased person must be recognizably embodied in order to retain any rights. The situation can appear more disturbingly clouded for family members who lose their rational capabilities, particularly given the gradations of such disabilities. Physical or mental debilitation may strike at spouses or children and deprive them of the actuality or potentiality of the rational agency without which they are unable to recognize the rights of others or exercise their own rights and duties. When these debilitations are temporary, the stricken individuals retain the potential to bear family right. Temporarily affected children remain in the same juridical position as before, since they are subject to parental authority only so long as they have the yet unrealized potential to be independent persons. Spouses who suffer temporary physical or mental conditions robbing them of their rational agency may lose the capacity to comanage household affairs and provide care for their counterparts, but their retention of the potential to return to active membership places them under the guardianship of their own spouses, who retain responsibility for their welfare, and therefore cannot dispossess them of the property they share. Under these conditions, any attempt by the caretaking spouse to divorce a stricken partner would have legitimacy only if a marital breakdown involving genuine estrangement can be impartially demonstrated and only if the divorce settlement not only follows the ordinary principles of property division, but ensures adequate care for the rejected invalid. That care remains the responsibility of the other divorcee insofar as the debilitated ex-spouse cannot care for him or herself and no one else has a particular ethical duty to be personally accountable for the latter's welfare. What alone can mitigate that responsibility is the public assistance that civil institutions can contribute.

When the rational agency of a spouse or child undergoes irreversible harm, reducing the victim to an animal or vegetable existence,[90] domestic relations cannot possibly retain their constitutive significance. An irremediably insane, severely mentally impaired, or comatose individual can hardly exercise any of the rights or observe any of the duties of marriage, nor have any potential to do so. As a consequence, the marriage ceases as a direct result of such calamity and any residual caretaking relation between one spouse and the stricken partner has a purely moral dimension that public intervention can relieve.[91] Since the annulment of marriage involves the removal of ethical rights and duties that must be generally recognized, some public, impartial certification of the state of affairs must be made, followed by some recognized formality of annulment.

In the case of irreversibly impaired children, parents retain personal responsibility for providing care, since no other individuals have any particular obligation to bear the burden of a caretaking without upbringing. Civil institutions, however, can relieve parents of their charge without violating any rights of the victim since the latter's status as a potential person has been obliterated. A systematic treatment of such intervention must await the conception of the relation between family and civil society.

CHAPTER VIII

The Family in Relation to Civil Society and the State

Ever since the rise of modernity, the relation between civil society and the state has been a focal point of conflict and controversy, encroaching upon every issue of social and political justice, however obscured by race, nationalism, and cultural parochialism. Yet, with the renewal of feminism and the emergence of the gay rights movement, the comparatively neglected relation of family and civil society has come to the fore of modernity's unfinished agenda of replacing traditional oppression with institutions of freedom. Like the link between civil society and state, that between family and civil society has a historical dimension reflecting the interwoven processes wherein the demarcation of political and social spheres has involved extricating the economy from the household and liberating the state from dynastic rule and nepotism. If modernity has witnessed parallel disengagements of family bonds from economic and political association, the emergence of a private household set apart from the public domains of society and state is not merely historically significant.[1] To the degree that these institutional spheres each realize a distinct form of autonomy, their integration into a compatible system of freedom becomes a matter of right. For unless the freedoms of family membership can coexist with those of social and political community, an insurmountable conflict between irreconcilable rights will ensue, rendering the tragedies of Antigone and Agamemnon an inescapable fate.

The suspicion of implacable incompatibility has haunted thinkers from Plato to Rawls,[2] who could find little to conciliate the
particular, partial attachments of the family with the universal
concerns of social and political justice. It seemed that either the
family would have to be sacrificed at the altar of public unity or
the common good would have to be fatally compromised by household favoritism. Whether that good be the political embodiment of
virtue, the maximization of individual happiness, or the realization of equal opportunity, the autonomy of the family presented a
deviant challenge.

Nevertheless, a solution becomes possible once the family, civil
society, and the state are conceived as institutions of ethical community,[3] where members exercise conventional roles whose defining
freedoms can only operate within an existing association reproduced by just those modes of self-determination. Here individuals
enjoy household, social, and political rights that are given neither
by nature nor in function of the self, but only by participating in
an association whose own character is determined by the concept
of self-determination rather than by the contingencies of historical
tradition. In these terms, rational agents each possess the political
freedom of a self-governing citizen solely by belonging to a representative democracy, just as they enjoy the right to satisfy self-
selected needs through occupations of their own choosing only
within a publicly regulated market where everyone's livelihood
depends upon facilitating the same economic freedom of others.
By the same token, individuals can exercise the right to codetermine their family life and the upbringing of their children only by
belonging to a household of free and equal spouses. When such
structures of family, social, and political freedom are examined, it
turns out that they have a systematic unity, where the rights of
each sphere can only be upheld if adjustments are made enabling
the other associations to realize their own freedoms at the same
time. For these reasons, these mutual adjustments are not restrictions upon the freedoms in question, but rather the conditions of
their very realization. Citizens, for example, can exercise their
political freedom only if their social and family rights are simultaneously respected, for otherwise oppressions in society and at home
undermine equal political opportunity, generating the type of deformations long bewailed under the rubrics of "bourgeois" and "sexist"
democracy. Conversely, unless civil society and the state organize
themselves to accommodate the family rights of their members,
individuals' household involvements will interfere with the exercise of their social and political freedoms, eliciting in turn unequal

divisions of roles within the family that undermine the autonomy of spouses and parents.

To comprehend these interconnections, which still bedevil the modern achievement of freedom, the relation of family and civil society must be treated first. Although politics presides over family and society, self-government presupposes the existence of free households and regulated markets. These not only can exist prior to and apart from democratic government, but they must already have supplanted the traditional family and social structures that impede political self-determination. Hence, before the self-governing state can be conceived in relation to household and social freedom, the interplay of family and civil society must be determined.

Although this interplay has a historical dimension essential for understanding the development of modern civilization, it equally has a conceptual character central for ethics insofar as the family and civil society attain normative validity once they are reconstructed as institutions of freedom. By becoming structures of self-determination, they overcome the juridical determination by external factors constitutively plaguing foundationalism. The key lesson bears repeating: Although foundationalism is commonly assumed to exhaust the possibilities of philosophical justification by advocates and detractors alike, its emblematic distinction between justifying factor and justified practice always leaves problematic the legitimacy of the privileged ground of normativity.[4] Whether the foundation of validity be construed as a highest good or a privileged procedure of ethical construction, its immediate givenness can never enjoy the normativity it confers upon conduct and institutions, whose validity consists in being derived from the special prior ground. Only if the ground of normativity is determined by itself can it satisfy its own standard of validity. Yet, to achieve this satisfaction, the foundation must relinquish its given priority and become self-determined, so that what determines validity and what is determined as valid are one and the same. Then normativity and freedom are united and foundationalism is overcome.

Consequently, so long as the family and civil society comprise associations of self-determination, their interplay concerns normatively valid institutions possessing an ethical universality or practical necessity susceptible of philosophical conception. By contrast, normatively neutral descriptions of household and social formations are purely empirical in character insofar as they address a domain of conventional arbitrariness that takes on a universal and necessary character only when ethical standards are realized. This is reflected in how all the great philosophers from

Plato through Hegel have properly restricted themselves to conceiving normatively valid institutions, allowing conceptions of unjust institutions to enter in only in relation to the genesis or dissolution of their paragon counterpart.[5] In so doing, such philosophers have preceded their ethics with nothing more than what can be conceived a priori about nature and rational agency, which together provide sufficient enabling conditions[6] for determining normatively valid institutions. Further claims about what families, societies, or states must invariably be are idle speculations transgressing the limits of empirical investigation.

Consequently, from a philosophical point of view, the relation between family and civil society cannot help but concern the ethical relation between the nonempirical, purely conceptual determinations of the structures of family and social freedom.

The Elementary Normative Structure of Family and Civil Society

Reconstituted as an institution of freedom, the family has no place for master-slave relations or extended kinship bonds. Instead, as the preceding argument has established, the household becomes restricted to two constitutive relations that may or may not be combined: the relation of spouses and that of parent and child. Each can figure as a structure of self-determination provided it is no longer defined in terms of the natural factors of gender and procreation that traditionally determine household roles. Individuals interact as spouses by freely forging a unitary private domain recognized as such by others, joining their property and welfare independently of any restrictions imposed by natural and otherwise extraneous factors of sexual difference and orientation, procreative capacities, race, ethnicity, birth, social rank, parental arrangement, or anything else unrelated to the capacity of the prospective spouses to honor their duties and exercise their rights as codeterminers of their common home. Accordingly, in a free family, spouses can be of any gender and sexual orientation (as well as include imaginable rational agents who asexually reproduce), need not have children, stand unbeholden to the will of elder kin (as in traditional extended families), and enjoy the right and duty to comanage family property and to care and be cared for by one another without allowing household roles to be assigned independently of spouses' codetermination.

By contrast, the parent-child relation comprises a structure of freedom to the degree that parental responsibility is assumed as a recognized ethical commitment revolving around providing children with the care needed to enable them to grow up into autonomous individuals, capable of exercising the rights of owner, moral subject, family member, and ultimately, social agent and citizen. Although parent and child may be biologically related, such a natural tie is not constitutive of their family bond, which, as an ethical relation, can apply just as well between an adopted child and a parent of any sexual orientation, or, for that matter, require depriving abusive, uncaring mothers or fathers of their offspring. Whatever the case, the relation of parent and child eliminates its own right and duty when the child becomes an autonomous adult, freed of the tutelage of parental authority, and freeing the parent of the duty of support.

In contrast to the particular and all-inclusive ethical unity of the family, civil society comprises a framework of interrelated self-determinations that is universal in scope, extending as far as individuals can be found who pursue self-selected particular ends that can only be realized by serving as a means for others to do the same.[7] The market provides the rudimentary structure of civil association, enabling its participants to exercise a specifically economic freedom of choosing what commodities to acquire and what earning activities to practice in interdependence with others. Although the market is the indispensable institution for enabling need and occupation to be self-determined, the economic right it makes possible remains beyond the exercise of all members of civil society if commodity relations are left to their own. The contingencies of exchange and production, which continually generate unequal development, inequalities in wealth, and threats to the health and safety of society, create their own barriers to the exercise of economic freedom. Accordingly, civil society is obliged to foster three further institutions of social freedom to uphold the prepolitical rights of its members: social interest groups, civil legal institutions, and public welfare agencies. In forming social interest groups, individuals unite around shared particular civil interests, utilizing a common bargaining front to facilitate market transactions in their favor. Yet, because social interest groups still remain dependent upon the acquiescence of other market participants, they can never be counted upon to secure the social welfare of their own members, let alone that of others, nor enforce their members' rights against malicious and nonmalicious wrongs. Accordingly, legal institutions must enter in to stipulate objectively the civil rights of all, provide an authoritative adjudication of disputes and infractions, impose appropriate compensation and punishment, and guarantee access to the legal process. Nevertheless, because the courts restrict themselves to righting particular wrongs, leaving economic disadvantage otherwise intact, an additional public intervention must be made to overcome the inequities of the market to the degree that they impede equal economic opportunity.

Given these structural divisions, the normative relation between the family and civil society revolves around determining how the rights and duties of spouses, on the one hand, and of parent and child, on the other, can be upheld in consonance with the operation of market freedom, social interest group activity, the civil administration of law, and the public administration of welfare. These connections themselves have two sides: first, the way in which the normative relations among spouses and parent and child affect the various dimensions of civil freedom, and secondly, how the institutions of civil society impact upon the realization of family freedom.

The Effect of Family Freedom upon Civil Society

The effect of the free family upon civil society has two seemingly contradictory dimensions. On the one hand, the reconstruction of the family as an institution of freedom is a precondition for the universal realization of each of the four spheres of civil society. On the other hand, the particular unity of family property and welfare appears to threaten equal economic opportunity and the efforts of social interest groups, legal institutions, and public welfare administrations to guarantee the conditions allowing all members of civil society to exercise their social autonomy.

To begin with, the elimination of the yokes of external restrictions upon the choice of marriage partners, domination by other members of extended kin groups, and gender privilege enables spouses to interact within the household with the respected freedom and equality that first allows the family no longer to impede the participation of each and every spouse in market transactions, social interest group activity, legal proceedings, and public welfare involvements.[8] In other words, only when spouses codetermine household affairs, exercising equal authority over the management of family property, the upbringing of children, and the representation of the family welfare outside the home can the civil roles of market participant, social interest advocate, legal subject, and public welfare client apply universally to all adult rational agents.

In this respect, the free family is a precondition of civil society and political democracy independently of its role in upbringing, which Okin, largely following Rawls, emphasizes in identifying the gender-neutral family as the school of justice comprising the essential foundation of a just society.[9] As the need for public education indicates, the free family is not the only, nor the sufficient, school for justice, and household autonomy itself presupposes the self-determination of property owners and moral subjects. Moreover, it is a mistake to root the institutions of right at any level in psychological attitudes.[10] Because rights are structures of interaction and not monologically determined phenomena, it is a category mistake to think that the psychological reaction of children to the conduct of parents has any constitutive relation to participation in and the structuring of relations of right.[11] Indeed, the recognition at play in exercising one's civil autonomy in respect of that of others can be accompanied by an indeterminate variety of emotions and attitudes.[12]

Transcending any psychological confines with the intersubjectivity of recognized rights, the free family's achievement of universal access to social freedom appears nonetheless to be undercut by the household limit of the particular welfare to which family members are joined. As beneficiaries of one another, spouses would seem to enjoy a right to be cared for above and beyond the anonymous social benefits that civil law and public welfare organs distribute to each individual in respect to merely personal right and need. Not only does this disadvantage single adults, but it would seem to exacerbate inequalities in economic assets insofar as spouses benefit from the added opportunities of combined resources. Moreover, the varying degrees of resources and care that parents provide for their children inject further differentiations in the social opportunities of individuals. Finally, through inheritance, the family becomes a channel for widening stratifications of wealth, undercutting equal economic opportunity still more.

For liberal thinkers such as Rawls and Fishkin,[13] these ramifications render family autonomy irreconcilably at odds with social justice. Yet the conflict persists only if civil society ignores the impact of the family upon social opportunity and fails to employ the correctives that fall within its power and that social right makes obligatory. First, whatever economic advantages accrue to spouses in virtue of joint household property and mutual care can be mitigated by providing single individuals with the equivalent of the benefit they lack and by means of the same progressive taxation of wealth and income that can minimize unequal economic opportunity among

individuals. Hence, although the joint ownership of family property entitles the surviving spouse to retain what had been wealth
enough for two or more, equitable taxation policies can reduce resultant advantages within the limits dictated by social justice. The
same remedy applies to the channeling of wealth to children
through inheritance. Although family right entitles minors to benefit from that share of the household wealth required to ensure
their proper upbringing, family right does not itself entail a right
of inheritance for adult children who have left the tutelage of parents and for whose support their parents are no longer responsible. Consequently, any inheritance of adults from their deceased
parents depends upon the positive law of civil society, whose toleration of such testamentary transfers of wealth can cohere with
equal economic opportunity so long as subsequent taxation (be it
in the form of a special inheritance tax or simply a wealth tax)
eliminates the economic advantage of family ties.

The effects upon social opportunity of differential child rearing among families might appear to be less amenable to remedy.
Of course, if this were an intractable problem, the remedy would
not require dismantling the family, since marriage could be retained so long as child rearing were detached from parenting.[14]
Certainly differences in family wealth, education, care, and love
can strongly influence how well children are able to exercise their
social freedom. Differences in family wealth and education can, of
course, be counteracted by public measures to minimize the formation of such inequalities in the first place. Yet, public guarantees
of decent livelihoods and affordable education still do not compel
parents to provide their children with comparable formative experiences and opportunities. Public institutions can offer supplements
to those in need, but this would require a potentially unwieldy
and intrusive system of monitoring. Such supervision can be circumvented by public institutions, such as universally affordable
day care centers and schools, that ensure that all children are provided sufficient cultural exposures to enter society without significant disadvantage.[15]

Nonetheless, public monitoring of upbringing cannot be dispensed with to address the consequences for equal social opportunity of the psychological impact of differing levels of parental love
and care. This problem applies not only between children of different families, but among children of the same household. Whether
or not personality formation is to be attributed primarily to emotive relations to parents, variance in parental care and affection

can certainly reach such extremes as to impede the autonomous development of children and hamper the subsequent exercise of their rights in civil society. Such cases border on those situations where parents' failure to provide an adequate upbringing for their children calls either for compulsory external aid or puts in forfeiture their guardianship and mandates adoption by more suitable parents. Then, public intervention is just as feasible and obligatory as in cases of "ordinary" child abuse, for which the difficulties of monitoring parental conduct pose no more of an insurmountable obstacle. Although less extreme cases of psychological "maladjustment" will occur,[16] it is questionable whether they can qualify as unequivocal social handicaps. Personality differences among independent agents are neither equatable with differences of ethical character nor with degrees of property, moral, family, or civil self-determination.

Needless to say, any alternate scheme of public upbringing would be susceptible to the very same differences in treatment that children can experience in families. Facilities might vary from institution to institution, and even if measures were taken to reduce such differences, caretakers could always favor or disfavor their various charges, conceivably producing the same array of psychological effects that occur in family child rearing.[17] In any event, the public provision of services that families cannot provide, such as education, health care, legal protection, and other social benefits, will engender a mixed arrangement, where children receive care from public and private strangers in addition to the primary upbringing of their parents. This combination will itself play a role in reducing the inequalities produced by the differentials in parental care.

For all these reasons, the alleged contradiction between family autonomy and equal social opportunity is far from intractable. Social justice does require public regulation of family life, but not removing child rearing from the home and instituting a system of collectivized upbringing.

The Impact of Civil Society upon Family Right

If the free family is a precondition of civil society, whose social rights household relations need not disrupt, the domestic rights of family members cannot themselves be enduringly realized without the contribution and accommodation of civil institutions.

To begin with, if a civil society is absent, signifying that individuals are not at liberty to associate in terms of self-selected particular interests, this may well entail that privileged differences of race, ethnicity, hereditary rank, age, and kinship relations fix occupations and political roles, intertwining social privilege and political role.[18] Such distinctly premodern conditions undermine the ability of individuals to marry whom they will, codetermine their households as free and equal spouses and independently raise children to autonomy.[19] Analogous impositions on family freedom occur under modern totalitarian conditions where the independence of civil institutions is suppressed and political authority directly administers prepolitical affairs.[20] Either way, unless a society has arisen that has demarcated itself from both kinship and political rule, the family cannot gain its own autonomy.

Yet, civil society upholds family right not simply by removing incompatible social formations. Civil society also plays an active role in sustaining the rights and duties of family members.

This is most evident in connection with civil legality. Like property and economic rights, family rights must be stipulated publicly as civil law in order to become universally knowable in an objective form to the agents upon whose recognition depends the realization of these rights.[21] Similarly, marriages, adoptions, and divorces ought to be authoritatively executed and registered in accord with legally specified formalities. Moreover, violations of family rights should obtain an objective adjudication and remedy that only public courts and penal systems can provide. Left to their own resources, spouses can no more ensure that their rights and duties are upheld by one another than parents and children can themselves guarantee that the entitlements and correlative duties of child rearing are observed. In either case, family rights can be violated either nonmaliciously or maliciously. Spouses can disagree in good faith over the comanagement of household property and income, the provision of mutual care, and the upbringing of children, creating disputes that only an external objectively recognized authority can resolve. Similarly, spouses, parents, and children can inadvertently violate the rights of one another, calling for an objective adjudication and remedy in which compensation, but not punishment, can figure, at least to the degree that the joint ownership of family property allows. By contrast, when family members maliciously or negligently[22] transgress their household duties, law and the courts must respectively stipulate the appropriate punishment and apply it to certified violations, including cases where spouses refuse to share household resources and responsibilities.[23] Analogous needs for legal remedy apply to the regulation of divorce and to the enforcement of divorce property divisions, support settlements, and custody arrangements. In every case, the legal system must ensure access to legal expertise in and outside of litigation to family members irrespective of their private resources and regardless of whether malicious or nonmalicious wrongs are at stake.[24]

These measures completely parallel the treatment of wrongs of single individuals by the legal process. Family relations, however, inject a further normative proviso: that the legal process be so organized as not to disadvantage legal subjects who are family members. This disadvantage occurs whenever participation in legal institutions involves no provision for family members to have their household duties simultaneously fulfilled. In order for the legal process to avoid interfering with the very family rights it is otherwise committed to uphold, civil society must ensure that litigation, as well as out of court legal consultation, poses no domestic hardships for participating or other nonparticipating family members. When flexible scheduling cannot alone suffice, provision should be made for child care, either in kind or through reimbursement, as well as for any domestic services that spouses require while legal matters transpire.

Such accommodations in the legal system are indicative of how every other sphere of civil society must undergo adjustment to avoid conflicting with family right.

The market is the key, being the basic structure of civil freedom that all other civil institutions presuppose. Historically, markets may incorporate slavery and discriminatory practices privileging a particular gender, sexual orientation, ethnicity, religion, political affiliation, or other factor extraneous to the exercise of economic freedom. Such deformations have obvious effects upon the family whenever its members come from both discriminated and nondiscriminated groups. For whenever one spouse's economic opportunities are limited through discrimination, the family will have an economic incentive to favor the economic career of the privileged spouse and to increase the domestic burdens of the discriminated partner. In just this way, current gendered labor markets undercut the formal equality of spouses by fostering a gendered division of domestic activity even where spouses have overcome traditional heterosexist prejudices on household roles.[25] Similarly, current or merely past market discrimination that affects all members of families fosters situations where the resultant economic disadvantage of the victimized group, reflected in greater unemployment, poverty, and lack of education and training, restricts the availability of economically viable marriage partners, favoring the growth of single-parent households. This intensifies women's bondage to child rearing, given the gendered division of household roles and the dearth of jobs and affordable day care.[26]

Although these examples indicate how the market can incorporate practices at odds with right to the detriment of family freedom, they do not signify that commodity relations are inherently tied to gender or any other discrimination of individuals through factors independent of the exercise of economic freedom. On the contrary, the market, as well as the dynamic of capital accumulation it entails, is indifferent to all such factors, relating individuals to one another simply in function of self-selected needs for the commodities of one another. Independently of any special concern for family right, economic right makes imperative that the legal system prohibit and punish all such market discrimination, whose malicious intent renders it not simply a tort requiring compensation, to which current American enforcement erroneously restricts itself, but a crime deserving punishment.

Since such discriminations are historical contingencies just as extraneous to civil society as bisexually reproducing individuals are to the free family, the *necessary* impact of markets upon family right must be sought where incidental natural and cultural differences play no role. The resulting normative principles can then be applied to the terrestrial contingencies of our own gendered tradition.

In markets governed strictly by economic concerns, family members face incipient disadvantages in function of the two primary dimensions of domestic right, matrimonial and parent-child relations. Because spouses are obliged to care for one another and to restrict their use of the family property in accord with the demands of codetermination and the joint domestic welfare, their economic options are limited in ways not hampering single adults. Spouses either fulfill their matrimonial obligations and forego certain economic opportunities or they permit the demands of the market to compromise their honoring of their spouse's rights. A similar dilemma applies to parent-child relations, with the additional difficulty that minor children are less likely to reciprocate in providing financial support and care for parents than spouses do for one another.[27] By being responsible for child care, parents of any gender and sexual orientation are subject to financial burdens and time constraints that prejudice their economic options in ways that childless individuals, be they married or not, can escape.

Needless to say, the same factors that make family relations an economic disadvantage hinder the participation of spouses and parents in social interest groups, comparatively handicapping joint advocacy of the special economic needs of family members as well.

When these generic difficulties are compounded by contingent discrimination on the basis of gender, sexual orientation, race, ethnicity, and other extraneous factors, the outlook for family right and the economic welfare of affected spouses, parents, and children becomes all the more grim.

If civil society is to uphold the economic opportunity of all its members, without prejudice to their domestic situation, market activity and social interest group advocacy must be subject to a public regulation specifically resolving the tension between economic and family freedom. Given the existence of families, it is not enough for the public administration of welfare to effect the measures necessary to realize the equal opportunity of single individuals. Guaranteeing full employment at a wage above poverty, making available affordable food, clothing, shelter, health care, and legal counsel, ensuring a conventional standard of living for those unable to work due to age or mental and physical disabilities, limiting child labor to enable the young to be educated and duly raised, ensuring access to affordable education and occupational training at all levels, and levying graduated wealth and income taxation sufficient to make differences of wealth compatible with equal economic opportunity may all be fundamental imperatives of right in civil society, still awaiting sufficient implementation in most corners of the world. And, admittedly, only when these measures have sufficiently reduced economic inequality and freed the welfare of individuals from dependence upon family wealth can the choice of marriage partner escape the economic compulsions that led Engels to regard the full freedom of marriage to await the abolition of capitalist production.[28] Nevertheless, by themselves these universal public guarantees of the conditions for exercising economic autonomy still do not address the difficulties peculiar to the interplay of markets and family membership.[29] Moreover, their implementation can further aggravate the conflict between the exercise of economic freedom and the well-being of the free family. Such is the case, for example, when employment, income supplements, health care, and child care benefits are made conditional upon the separation of spouses or of parents and children.[30]

To uphold domestic right and duty without undermining economic opportunity, further measures must be taken both within and without the workplace. First of all, no-marriage or no-child rearing clauses in employment contracts must be prohibited since they blatantly sacrifice family right at the altar of economic expediency.[31] Further, the schedules of the market activity and social interest advocacy of family members must be adjusted to allow them to care for spouses and children without prejudice to their economic welfare. This involves publicly guaranteeing limited[32] and flexible work, shopping, advocacy, and welfare administration hours, with no detrimental effect upon income, related occupational benefits, and prices. Flexible schedules, however, still leave unaccounted for how family members are to be cared for during economic and social interest group activity. Consequently, civil society must publicly ensure the availability of affordable care for children and other family members at hours and locations compatible with every occupational situation.[33] Moreover, to cope with particular periods where children and other family members require extended attention, public authority must guarantee *paid* family leave with security of renewed employment without prejudice to occupational advancement.[34] Needless to say, if, following current U.S. federal law, family leave is provided without pay, family members are still disadvantaged by their domestic responsibilities. In this regard, sufficient *paid* parental leave must be extended to childbearing parents and their custodial partners to prevent the periods of pregnancy, childbirth, and its aftermath from posing any disadvantage for either parent's participation in the institutions of civil society.[35] Finally, to prevent the added costs of child rearing from being an impediment to economic freedom, parents should be publicly assured family allowances that give them equal economic opportunity with childless adults.[36] To avoid social stigma and work disincentives, such family allowances should be universal entitlements, given independently of employment, wealth, and income levels.[37] All these measures should be so constructed as to take into account the specific hardships of family members of separated and divorced households as well.

Family and State

Although these imperatives of social justice apply exclusively to the relation of family and civil society, it is not hard to conceive how similar accommodations in political activity must be implemented to prevent family relations from impeding the political freedom of citizens. Just as work, shopping, courts, social advocacy, and welfare agencies must be scheduled to enable individuals to fulfill their family duties without suffering social disadvantage, so each facet of political life must be organized so that family responsibilities do not conflict with equal political opportunity.

As with equal economic opportunity, the required adjustments in political arrangements are not external restrictions. The measures enabling citizens to engage in politics without neglecting their household obligations are necessary to the realization of democracy simply because political self-determination cannot occur without the achievement of family freedom. If spouses are not free and equal codeterminers of their household affairs, the subjection of one to another in the home will make any political involvement by the dominated members contingent upon the authorization of their household masters. Moreover, since political action presupposes a liberation from social dependence achieved through education, training, and economic opportunity, any impediment that family life imposes upon its members' social activities presents a further barrier to political autonomy. Under such conditions, the extension of universal suffrage and universal access to political office provide a merely formal political equality, where the identity of ruler and ruled is subverted by the hierarchy in family relations.

What prevents family freedom from simultaneously undermining political sovereignty by subordinating the aims of the state to the parochial concerns of each particular household is the demarcation of household and state. Together with the separation of civil society and state, this disengagement of kinship from rule enables each sphere of ethical community to retain its own integrity.

Admittedly, kinship could seemingly accord with self-government so long as the state extends no further than the consanguine borders of clan, phratry, or tribe. Because such a situation precludes a plurality of different families, broadly understood, it is virtually equivalent to the universal kinship that Plato relies upon to eliminate the conflict between nepotism and the common good of the state.[38] Once, however, political community incorporates unrelated individuals and a plurality of gens, self-government can only be achieved if political power becomes something wielded by individuals independently of their family membership. So long as families are particular and kinship remains connected to rule, the body politic bifurcates into a privileged clan of rulers and a class of subject strangers. For this reason, the emergence of a body politic defined by territory rather than by kinship allows for a first flowering of political freedom by establishing a citizenry with political privileges and protections given separately from tribal membership.[39] As the Athenian state demonstrates, however, the overthrow of a gentile constitution still allows for division of the citizenry by social station, where the failure to separate society and state casts nobles, peasants, and artisans into distinct political ranks preventing rule from being a self-reflexive exercise of freedom.[40] Only when social as well as kinship groups are divested of political power can citizenship become an agency of self-rule, where the will that governs derives from those who are governed.

Hence, only by virtue of a double reform of family ties, establishing domestic freedom within the home and removing kinship from the social and political arenas, can political self-determination become a possibility.

Although these complementary developments might be regarded as preceding the workings of self-government both temporally and structurally, the political organs of democracy must themselves take two parallel initiatives to uphold the integrity of household freedom, as well as the domestic conditions for political freedom. These initiatives involve, on the one hand, the political authorization and enforcement of family right and duty, and, on the other hand, the politically controlled coordination of political and household activities such that neither mode of freedom conflicts with the other.

Both measures emanate from the sovereignty of politics by which the exercise of political freedom determines the whole body politic, including the relation of the different spheres of right. Although the institutions of civil society already provide a legal stipulation and enforcement of the prepolitical rights of ownership, family membership, economic opportunity, and due process,[41] political freedom incorporates civil legality within the framework of constitutional self-government. This allows the public institutions of civil society and the law they promulgate and enforce to have constitutional legitimacy as well as the imprimatur of issuing from the legislative, authorizing,[42] and executive organs of self-government. Already, the legalization of right in civil society carries with it a transformation of content, giving right a certified universal specification involving legally enforceable formalities.[43] With the exercise of political freedom, laws that had been stipulated through such prepolitical civil devices as common law tradition, judicial review, and codification by recognized legal authorities, now become determined through the statutes of a political legislature in conformity with constitutional law. This brings with it a further modification of content, first insofar as political self-legislation draws a distinction between citizens and noncitizens, a distinction lacking in the global reach of civil society, and secondly insofar as law must now regulate political affairs as well as ensure the conformity of nonpolitical practices with the exercise of self-government.

The latter task is as manifold as the parallel endeavor of making family freedom compatible with the civil entitlements of economic opportunity, social advocacy, and legal right. Once more the availability of time and resources is of the essence. The particular burdens, financial and otherwise, of caring for spouses and children must be publicly alleviated if family members are not to be disadvantaged in their political life. To engage in politics on a par with their fellow citizens, spouses and parents must not only be assured the resources to meet their domestic obligations; they must equally be furnished with flexible and limited hours at work, school, and child care facilities, as well as with compatible scheduling at government functions, elections, and other political events. Then alone can family members find comparable time to participate in extra-parliamentary political agitation, party work, electoral campaigning, voting, or office-holding without having to neglect their family affairs.

To the degree that family right involves universal principles that should not be violated with impunity, constitutional law should extend to family relations and specify the inalienable household rights and duties of spouses, parents, and children, leaving the contingent dimensions of these entitlements and obligations to the corrigible labors of positive legislation. The failure to provide such constitutional enactment represents one of the major shortcomings in the U.S. Constitution and many of its modern successors.[44] Attempts to circumvent the gap by appealing to an implicit "right to privacy" have proven to be sorry substitutes insofar as they simply offer negative prohibitions excluding external interference in household affairs or extol the personal liberty of an unencumbered self.[45] Either way, the positive rights and duties specific to the ethical community of the family are ignored. That the U.S. Constitution equally neglects the social rights of civil society only compounds the problem.

Some remedy might be sought in international conventions, such as the Universal Declaration of Human Rights (1948), the Convention on the Elimination of All Forms of Discrimination against Women (1979), and the Convention on the Rights of the Child (1989), which have begun to articulate principles of certain aspects of family right.[46] Yet, like all treaties, such agreements remain contingent upon the choice of individual states, whose assent may only be window dressing, concealing an actual constitutional order in which household freedom remains abused.

When, however, democracy secures its own preconditions by upholding the property, household, and social rights of citizens in conformity with equal political opportunity, the family becomes a pillar of political freedom, not only excluding the domestic domination that subverts political equality, but joining family members in recognition of the unity of the good of the home with the good of the state. Only then can self-government cast off its residual deformations and bring freedom to totality.

Notes

Introduction

1. These factors are "natural" in the sense of being given, rather than being determined by the will of the individuals to whom they apply. Although their privileging is a matter of convention, they themselves are not artificial products of conduct.

2. The rise of demarcated social and political domains has occurred by overthrowing the feudal relations exemplified in estates where individuals' roles in society are tied to political privileges and where both are tied to birthright. Admittedly, such feudal relations could be eliminated without separating civil society and the state by means of a totalitarian solution where government directly administers the economy.

3. In this vein Aristotle claims that the family is an association rooted in nature from which all others follow (see Aristotle, *Politics,* I, 1252b10–30), Rousseau maintains that the family is the earliest and only natural society (see Jean-Jacques Rousseau, *The Social Contract and Discourse on the Origin of Inequality*, edited with an introduction by Lester G. Crocker [New York: Washington Square Press, 1967], "On Social Contract," chapter II, 8), and Locke proclaims conjugal relations the first society, from which relations of parents and children and then master and servant follow (John Locke, *The Second Treatise of Government* [Indianapolis: Bobbs-Merrill, 1952], chapter VII, 44).

4. Allan Bloom is one who argues that justice does not apply to the family since nature imposes a hierarchy and gendered division of labor upon household organization. See Susan Moller Okin, *Justice, Gender, and the Family* (New York: Basic Books, 1989), 26, 36–37, for a critical discussion of Bloom's position.

5. Mark Poster argues analogously that Freudian psychoanalytic theory provides an accurate portrayal of the dynamics of the bourgeois family, but not a conception applicable to other historical family formations where a nuclear patriarchal household is not encountered. See Mark Poster, *Critical Theory of the Family* (New York: Continuum, 1988). Similarly, Okin

points out that psychoanalytic and other psychological theories of personality development have taken gendered parenting as the locus for personality development and have therein examined how gender is reproduced. See Okin, *Justice, Gender, and The Family*, 131. Freeing psychological theory from such assumptions about gendered parenting would still, however, retain the assumption of the disengaged nuclear family.

6. Poster makes this claim, mistakenly assuming that it provides an adequate handle for developing a critical theory of the family. See Poster, *Critical Theory of the Family*, 143–44. Although Poster admits that a theory of the family must not privilege any particular historical form, he assumes that the family is always the context within which transpire the oral, anal and genital stages in experience in which personality development is allegedly rooted (150). This assumption, however, can well be questioned.

7. Hegel raises these issues in his introductory critique of past theories of the family. See G. W. F. Hegel, *Vorlesungen über Rechtsphilosophie*, Edition Ilting (Stuttgart-Bad Cannstatt: Frommann-Holzboog, 1974), IV, 425–29.

8. Michael Walzer, *Spheres of Justice: A Defense of Pluralism and Equality* (New York: Basic Books, 1983), 238.

9. Gary Stanley Becker's *A Treatise on the Family* (Cambridge: Harvard University Press, 1991) provides a classic example of an acclaimed effort to measure the family by the calculus of atomistic self-interest, a calculus that abstracts from the substantial unity of shared right and welfare that distinguishes family association from market relations. Richard A. Posner's dissection of sexuality, *Sex and Reason* (Cambridge: Harvard University Press, 1992) applies the same narrow vision to sex and love, as if all intimacy were merely for the sake of maximizing pleasure.

10. Conceiving the family in contractual terms might seem to meet an insurmountable obstacle in that children have no choice about into which family they are born or adopted. Yet, liberal theorists since Locke have set aside this apparent difficulty by arguing that children do not yet have an independent capacity of choice and that the purpose of upbringing is to provide them with the conditions for becoming an autonomous individual, capable of owning property and entering into contract.

11. Immanuel Kant, *The Metaphysics of Morals*, trans. Mary Gregor (New York: Cambridge University Press, 1991), secs. 22–23, AK 276–77.

12. Immanuel Kant, *Lectures on Ethics*, trans. Louis Infield (New York: Harper Torchbooks, 1963), 167.

13. Walzer follows in Kant's footsteps by incoherently claiming that the family is just like the market, except that in domestic affairs the commodities own themselves, as shown in the "gift of self" and the "voluntary exchange of selves" supposedly characterizing parental care and marriage. See Walzer, *Spheres of Justice*, 238.

14. Derrida makes this point in his commentary on Hegel's account of marriage in Jacques Derrida, *Glas*, trans. John P. Leavey Jr. and Richard Rand (Lincoln: University of Nebraska Press, 1986), 195.

15. Admittedly, as Barbara Herman emphasizes, Kant does inject into marriage obligations of care and support accompanying the exchange of bodies.(See Herman, "Could It Be Worth Thinking About Kant on Sex and Marriage?" in *A Mind of One's Own: Feminist Essays on Reason and Objectivity*, ed. Louise M. Antony and Charlotte Witt [Boulder, Colo.: Westview, 1993], 63.) These duties, however, are not, as Herman herself notes, compatible with the freedom of contract (61). Although Herman suggests that marital care can fit the parameters of the "institution-based right" of Kantian justice (63), the partiality of conjugal duty requires grounding in something extending beyond the formal limits of Kant's principle of external right, which only connects the actions of individuals under universal rules. That something is ethical community, which, as we shall see, can confer rights and duties of group membership that distinguish between insiders and outsiders.

16. Hegel, *Vorlesungen über Rechtsphilosophie*, IV, 422.

17. Okin, *Justice, Gender, and the Family*, 121.

18. Walzer, *Spheres of Justice*, 227–28.

19. Social contract theory does this by starting with individuals in a condition antecedent to the enactment of normatively valid institutions, as if the predicament of choice available to them in that "natural" context should somehow mandate how to construct the type of community they should inhabit. Needless to say, this strategy completely abstracts from the framework of ethical community, in which the norms of valid conduct are predicated upon membership in an existing community *already* embodying those norms.

20. Significantly, when Rawls grudgingly identifies the participants of the original position as heads of families, his rationale is that their family membership allows for consideration of the rights of future generations, which will allegedly ground his just savings principle.(See John Rawls, *A Theory of Justice* [Cambridge: Harvard University Press, 1971], 128–29.) Attending to the rights of future generations, however, is by no means identical with parents' concerns for their *own* children. Moreover, the production and rearing of children need not depend upon the family, as schemes for collective rearing since Plato reflect, nor need the family have children in order to involve the special rights and duties that correspond to what distinguishes domestic association from other forms of community. When Rawls elsewhere brings the family into his theory of justice in any positive way, it is only as a primary school of moral tutelage, that is, as an instrument for achieving independently determined normative aims, an instrument whose own structure is taken for granted (ibid., 463, 467ff.).

21. Michael J. Sandel, *Liberalism and the Limits of Justice* (New York: Cambridge University Press, 1982), 33–34.

22. Cited by Okin in *Justice, Gender, and the Family*, 27.

23. Okin observes that the overcoming of distributive justice in the family historically originated in the circumstance that women relinquished their legal personality upon marriage, with all rights to control household property and income passing to the husband (ibid., 30.) Yet with the

eventual acknowledgment of both spouses' right to codetermine household affairs, the absence of distributive justice takes on a different character. Moreover, that household property, income, career qualifications and other socially relevant "goods" are still unevenly distributed between husband and wife (as Okin powerfully documents, see ibid., 31ff.) does not mean that household community is reducible to the same considerations that apply to social justice.

24. Consequently, Okin is misguided in thinking that the mere opposition of aims and hopes between spouses and parents makes justice, as defined in liberal theory, a crucial virtue in family life (ibid., 32). The resolution of family conflict involves norms of a different character.

25. Walzer notes this, without, however, offering any justification other than an appeal to "our" shared conventions. See Walzer, *Spheres of Justice*, 227, 229.

26. Okin, *Justice, Gender, and The Family*, 174.

27. Nozick raises this point. See Robert Nozick, *Anarchy, State, and Utopia* (New York: Basic Books, 1974), 167.

28. For a critique of reflective equilibrium in Rawls's historicization of Kantian ethics, see Richard Dien Winfield, *Reason and Justice* (Albany: State University of New York Press, 1988), 105–16.

29. Walzer, *Spheres of Justice*, 238.

30. Okin claims that the circumstances of justice do apply within the family because the family is part of the basic structure of society and thereby affects the opportunities of individuals in society (Okin, *Justice, Gender, and the Family*, 27). Yet whereas the family may well have an effect upon individuals' social and political opportunities, this only signifies that the family falls within the circumstances of justice, e.g., that the family is a presupposition of social and political justice, but not that the same circumstances of justice fall *within* the family itself.

31. Rawls, *Theory of Justice*, 74, 105, 301.

32. James S. Fishkin, *Justice, Equal Opportunity, and the Family* (New Haven: Yale University Press, 1983).

33. Similarly, Nozick observes that families conflict with patterned distributional principles since the favoritism of family behavior incurs transfers within families that upset the favored distributional pattern. Nozick, *Anarchy, State, and Utopia*, 167.

34. Although morality has come to be used loosely as a general term for normative conduct, reflecting certain subjectivizations of ethics, morality has its own specificity as the particular mode of self-determination where agents hold each other accountable for acting with good aims and good motives, where what counts as good must equally be decided by each agent's own conscience.

35. Jeffrey Blustein suggests that the family "lays the foundation for that 'subjective freedom' and interiority characteristic of a moral agent" by reinforcing "in children a sense of their own particularity" (Jeffrey Blustein, *Parents and Children: The Ethics of the Family* [New York: Oxford University Press, 1982], 94). Although parental care is certainly di-

rected at the particular welfare of the parent's child, and the *presumed* love is addressed to the individuality of the child, none of this attention is specifically directed at the moral accountability of the child, which centers around the normative significance of an agent's purposes, intentions, and conscience. It instead concerns the role of the child within the *ethical* community of the family, which may presuppose the potential personhood and moral subjectivity of the child, but adds the special consideration that the parent child relation involves. The particularity of the child here has an *ethical*, and not just *moral* standing.

36. Hobbes and Rousseau both tend in this direction. Hobbes describes the family as a little monarchy (Hobbes, Thomas, *Leviathan*, edited with an introduction by C. B. Macpherson [Harmondsworth, UK: Penguin Books, 1986], 257) whose rights and consequences are allegedly the same as those of a sovereign by institution, and for the same reasons (Hobbes, *Leviathan*, 256), whereas Rousseau characterizes the family as the primitive model of political societies, where the chief of state is like the father and the people correspond to the children (Rousseau, *Social Contract*, chap. II, 8).

37. Okin, *Justice, Gender, and the Family*, 126–31.

38. David Archard ignores this specificity of political power when he suggests that the existence of structures of power in the family makes the distinction "between 'private' family and 'public' State . . . fundamentally mistaken and dangerously misleading" (David Archard, *Children: Rights and Childhood* [New York: Routledge, 1993], 113). For this reason, he cannot comprehend how a *"form* of family whose members enjoy equal status, share all significant familial tasks and which functions within an egalitarian society" could have a "sphere of existence . . . dramatically distinct and set apart from the 'public' domain" (116). Archard ignores how equality within the family need not conflict with the exclusive partiality of the household's own private domain, which does set such a family fundamentally apart from the dual public domains of civil society and the state.

39. Hannah Arendt, *The Human Condition* (Chicago: University of Chicago Press, 1958), 58.

40. Aristotle redeems the family's right to exist from Plato's critique only on this latter basis, as an enabling condition for participation in politics. See Aristotle's *Politics*, book I.

41. Alex Shoumatoff, *The Mountain of Names: A History of the Human Family* (New York: Simon and Schuster, 1985), 183, 188, 190.

42. When Sandel suggests that a family ethic must appeal to the human goods that household association realizes instead of to the autonomy that that association reflects, he suggests that the good of an ethical community consists of something other than the mode of freedom that that community makes possible and that the family cannot realize a freedom of its own, as if the unencumbered autonomy of property right and morality were exhaustive of self-determination (Michael J. Sandel, *Democracy's Discontent* [Cambridge: Harvard University Press, 1996], 104). If the good

realized by the family, like that of civil society and the state, is the form of freedom in which its community consists, that good will escape the foundational dilemmas of norms grounded in nature or tradition.

43. Walzer, *Spheres of Justice*, 231.

44. Okin attempts to challenge the communitarian appeal to tradition by questioning both whether a consensus on family values actually exists and whether any prevailing consensus should be granted authority under conditions of social domination (Okin, *Justice, Gender, and the Family*, 43, 67, 72). Although some postmodernists (Rorty and Foucault among them) appeal to a democratic antiauthoritarianism as an underlying justification for their embrace of "pluralism," the postmodern conditioning of reason and conduct by pragmatic factors undercuts any privileging of a resistance to domination. Accordingly, Okin's objection can be brushed aside by a soberly resolute postmodernist, just as Nietzsche can repudiate the modern agenda of democracy and social justice. Yet this still leaves postmodernism vulnerable to the charge that it incoherently privileges its own diagnosis of the fate of reason and conduct, a charge that Nietzsche and his latter day followers may ignore, but cannot deflect.

45. Richard Rorty is a prime perpetrator of this wishful thinking. See Richard Rorty, *Contingency, Irony, and Solidarity* (New York: Cambridge University Press, 1989), 44–69.

46. This is the stumbling block of Nietzsche's affirmation of a new aristocracy, as well as of the fascist ideologues who follow in his footsteps.

47. Juridical dependence signifies how the validity, rather than the existence, of something is conditioned. For example, although knowledge claims could not be made without a host of biological, psychological, and linguistic conditions, these factors cannot be juridical conditions to the degree that they make possible right as well as wrong beliefs. Because juridical conditions instead determine how valid and invalid claims should be distinguished, the conditions of consciousness and language cannot serve the epistemological (juridical) mission that transcendental philosophy has assigned them.

48. Harry Frankfurt is a prime example of a theorist of action who reduces autonomy to the second order desire of the capacity of choice.

Chapter I. Ethical Community as the Framework for Family Ethics

1. Although Kant gives procedural ethics its classic formulation with his categorical imperative, which makes the sheer lawfulness of the principle of choice the basis of its normativity, the formal principle of willing privileged by a procedural ethics may conceivably vary without affecting the logical limits of the whole approach. However the privileged choice procedure be defined, it ends up promoting liberty as a right insofar as a type of willing is sanctioned not by being bound to given ends but by choosing whatever ends it may in a form that all agents should adopt, a form

that therefore can be followed by all (e.g. a form of discretion that is universalizable).

2. F. H. Bradley, *Ethical Studies* (Oxford: Oxford University Press, 1988); Alasdair MacIntyre, *After Virtue* (Notre Dame, Ind.: University of Notre Dame Press, 1981); Sandel, *Liberalism and the Limits of Justice*; Charles Taylor, *Sources of the Self: The Making of the Modern Identity* (Cambridge: Harvard University Press, 1989); Walzer, *Spheres of Justice*.

3. Ludwig Wittgenstein, *Philosophical Investigations*, trans. G. E. M. Anscombe, 3d ed. (New York: Macmillan, 1968), paras. 202ff., 243ff., 268, 272, 288, 293.

4. Wittgenstein and his followers fail to realize that the contingency of language games undermines the authority of the Wittgensteinian position. If the claim that language games underlie meaning and truth is itself rooted in a contingent language game, its universal applicability collapses, whereas if the claim applies to discourse as such, it contradicts the very theory it advances. For a further development of this critique, see "The Ordeal of Self-Critical Critical Philosophy: Reflections on Husserl and Wittgenstein," in Richard Dien Winfield, *Freedom and Modernity* (Albany: State University of New York Press, 1991), 15–18.

5. Bradley, *Ethical Studies*, 190–92.

6. Hegel's oft cited slogan that "the real is rational and the rational is real" does not support the universal necessity of history because Hegel distinguishes the "real" from mere existence, ascribing to the former a self-grounded character that anticipates the structure of conceptual determination. Hegel systematically develops the contrast between existence and reality in section 2 (Appearance) and section 3 (Actuality) of book 2, The Doctrine of Essence, in his *Science of Logic* (see G. W. F. Hegel, *Science of Logic*, trans. A. V. Miller [New York: Humanities Press, 1969], 479ff.). In this connection, it is worth noting how Hegel conceives objectivity in contrast to existence, treating objectivity within the Logic of the Concept as a conceptually determined domain. See the *Science of Logic*, 705ff.

7. See William Maker's *Philosophy Without Foundations: Rethinking Hegel* (Albany: State University of New York Press, 1994) for a dissection of postmodernism's blindness to a foundation-free philosophy and ethics.

8. For a fuller treatment of how self-determination is the locus of normativity, see Winfield, *Reason and Justice*, part 3.

9. Although consenting to conventions may satisfy the natural liberty of the choosing will and the liberal theories that privilege this form of volition, consenting to a regime is different from participating in institutions in which one exercises self-determination, be it as codetermining spouse enjoying one's family freedom, market agent enjoying economic autonomy, or democratic citizen practicing self-government. For this reason, the right of a people to self-determination is a completely empty notion unless it is tied to the erection of a democratic state presiding over a

civil society in which families are organized as associations of freedom and the property rights and moral autonomy of all agents are duly respected.

10. For this reason, Hegel rightly claims that if one conceives ethical community as the primary topic of ethics, instead of first developing its preconditions, property and morality, one commences with the assurance of a unity grounded in nothing at all. See Hegel, *Vorlesungen über Rechtsphilosophie*, III, 480.

11. For a further discussion of this point, see Richard Dien Winfield, "The Limits of Morality," in *Overcoming Foundations: Studies in Systematic Philosophy* (New York: Columbia University Press, 1989), 135–70, and idem, "Morality Without Community," in *Freedom and Modernity*, 61–75.

12. A person's body is inalienable property since the will cannot have any entitled expression if it loses that ownership. The enslaved individual still retains the natural will, i.e., the capacity of choice, but even if slaves can make decisions, whatever slaves may do still counts as the responsibility of their master, whose will they juridically express. The distinction between the property-owning will of the person, who determines him- or herself as such through the recognition process of ownership, and the capacity of choice, which is given by nature, is what allows for the body to be something external to the will that has title to it. Any attempt to identify ownership with alienability or property with the commodity ignores the inalienable character of ownership of one's body and how all other forms of property presuppose it.

13. For this reason, it makes no sense to argue that property entitlements presuppose distributive justice. Although the ethical associations of family, society, and state may mandate adjustments in property relations in conformity with their own constitutive rights and duties, the normative claims of these distributive regulations all depend upon the prior recognition of personhood, without which participation in their associations is rendered impossible.

14. Jeffrey Blustein claims that "Hegel's philosophy of the family is intended primarily as *meta*-philosophy" (Blustein, *Parents and Children*, 95). Like many commentators, Blustein draws upon sections of Hegel's *Phenomenology of Spirit*, where Hegel is indeed not developing a positive philosophical doctrine, but observing the structure of consciousness as it examines its own truth claims in the different configurations of its foundational knowing. In the *Philosophy of Right*, however, Hegel is presenting a doctrine of right, conceiving the reality of self-determination, rather than conceiving different theories of ethics.

15. G. W. F. Hegel, *Elements of the Philosophy of Right*, ed. Allen W. Wood, trans. H. B. Nisbet (Cambridge: Cambridge University Press, 1991), § 165, p. 206.

16. Ibid., § 166, p. 206.

17. Ibid., § 202–5, pp. 234–37.

18. Ibid., § 280, 300–314, pp. 321, 339–50.

19. Ibid., § 157, pp. 197–98.

20. Kenley Dove alternately interprets Hegel to differentiate the three basic modes of self-determination—Abstract Right, Morality, and Ethical Community—in terms of the logic of being, essence, and the concept, or of given determinacy, determined determinacy, and self-determined determinacy, respectively. Dove points to these logical relations in order to support the view that Hegel distinguishes the three modes of ethical community by the three constitutive aspects of the logic of the concept: universality (family), particularity (civil society), and individuality (state). See Kenley R. Dove, "Phenomenology and Systematic Philosophy," in *Method and Speculation in Hegel's Phenomenology*, ed. Merold Westphal (Atlantic Highlands, N.J.: Humanities Press, 1982), 36–37.

21. This point, which Hegel emphasizes, is discussed by Derrida in his commentary on Hegel's analysis of marriage in Derrida, *Glas*, 195.

22. Hegel, *Vorlesungen über Rechtsphilosophie*, IV, 419.

23. Prenuptial agreements may impose partial limits to the sharing of property between spouses, but these figure only as marginal arrangements alongside a common home, in which resides the unity distinguishing the family from contractual alliances. This common home need not be a physically unitary dwelling, but rather signifies a united private domain, which may include spouses who share ownership and welfare while maintaining separate residences for longer or shorter periods.

24. As will be argued, the unity of conjugal property cannot include the bodies of each spouse since relinquishing ownership of one's one body deprives one of any possibility of embodying one's freedom in a recognizable fashion. For this reason, using force upon one's spouse's body remains a crime.

25. Hegel, *Elements of the Philosophy of Right*, § 184, p. 221.

26. Admittedly, the scope of political association may be universal only relative to the particular boundaries of domestic territory. Yet political association need not be bounded by a plurality of individual states since global political unity is not inconceivable.

27. A further strategy for certifying the completeness of Hegel's threefold division of ethical community is provided by Kenley Dove's interpretation, which ascribes universality to the ethical self of the family, particularity to the ethical self of civil society, and individuality to the ethical self of the state (Dove, "Phenomenology and Systematic Philosophy," 36–37), exhausting the three aspects of the logic of the concept, as Hegel develops it. Dove ascribes universality to the family on two accounts. First, "the family is One Person" (36), whereby presumably the member simply counts as drawn into the family unity, independently of any particular interests or any individuality consisting in the joining of universal principles to a particular group. Secondly, the family "member is a member through an immediate sentiment, the unity of *love*" (36). How this second aspect entails universality is hardly self-evident. Dove ascribes particularity to civil society insofar as its members determine themselves through particular interests that operate in terms of "a structure of interaction

(e.g., the world market) that extends in principle to *all* other ethical selves" (36), rendering each bourgeois an instance of a common unity. By contrast, Dove maintains, the political self is individual by belonging to a community that upholds "*universal* principles of justice (the constitution) within the territory and traditions of a *particular* people" (37). Universality can plausibly be ascribed to an association based on the sentiment of love insofar as that sentiment is not constitutively mediated by any particular interests or by the imposition of a distinguishable universal law to a particular domain.

28. For an attempt to reconstruct in detail the freedoms of civil society, see Richard Dien Winfield, *The Just Economy* (New York: Routledge, 1988), and idem, *Law in Civil Society* (Lawrence: University Press of Kansas, 1995). For a reconstruction of family and state, see Winfield, *Reason and Justice*, part 3.

Chapter II. Nature, Psychology, and the Normativity of the Family

1. Transsexual operations might also, one day, have implications for reproduction, even without the gradations between male and female.

2. Poster, *Critical Theory of the Family*, 15.

3. Poster observes, for instance, how among the Sioux, infants were fed not just by their mothers, but by any lactating women. See ibid., 149.

4. Shoumatoff mistakenly suggests that female lactation makes the mother-child unit universal. See Shoumatoff, *Mountain of Names*, 15.

5. Carol Gilligan, *In a Different Voice: Psychological Theory and Women's Development* (Cambridge: Harvard University Press, 1982).

6. Okin makes the latter point in critiquing Gilligan et al. See Okin, *Justice, Gender, and the Family*, 15.

7. Reay Tannahill distinguishes them as the biological and the social, using the term "social" in the commonly undifferentiated manner of modern social theory that tends to privilege society and reduce all other spheres of community to social interaction. See Reay Tannahill, *Sex in History* (New York: Stein and Day, 1982), 24. Hence, I have made the differentiation in reference to convention in general, leaving open within which sphere paternity is recognized.

8. Shoumatoff suggests that this is why Jews initiated a matrilineal succession of Jewishness in the Middle Ages, when rape of Jewish women was widespread and paternity became more uncertain than ever. See Shoumatoff, *Mountain of Names*, 37.

9. Tannahill, *Sex in History*, 24.

10. Shoumatoff recounts how Owen Lovejoy argues that the extended neotony of humans demands that men be more involved as parents, that this requires men to be certain who their children are, and finally, that this certainty requires monogamy and punishment for adultery. But, as Shoumatoff observes, the child's survival does not depend upon the continued presence of its biological father since others can care for it, espe-

cially under conditions of extended families. See Shoumatoff, *Mountain of Names*, 25, 27.

11. Nevertheless, as Tannahill points out, it would be a mistake to confuse matrilinearity (identifying descent through the mother's line) with matriarchy (conferring power to the mother), especially when a mother's closest male kin have historically tended to exercise the real power in matrilinear societies. See Tannahill, *Sex in History*, 353.

12. Shoumatoff argues that knowledge of ancestry was unimportant as long as people were hunter-gatherers and collectively decided matters affecting their community. When, however, differences in wealth and power arose and these differences were made hereditary, largely spurred on by the development of agriculture and its creation of durable wealth in land and produce, genealogy became vital (Shoumatoff, *Mountain of Names*, 62–63). This transformation in the significance of pedigree is not, however, automatically produced by the technological shift from hunter-gatherer subsistence to agriculture, since kinship ties can just as readily determine the distribution of the bounty of hunter-gathers as that of the harvest of farmers, just as ancestry may or may not be the decisive factor in determining who rules the community under either circumstance.

13. Whether kinship relations can avoid interfering with equal opportunity in other spheres is, of course, a matter of debate, especially for liberals like Fishkin and Rawls, for whom no valid normative principles stand opposed to distributive justice other than those of moral reflection.

14. Where upbringing occurs is tied to what role children are allotted in domains outside the family. Rybczynski observes that in medieval Europe, children were commonly sent away from home at age seven to begin work and apprenticeship to trade or court. Parents in Europe would subsequently see their own children growing up only with the rise of the bourgeoisie in the sixteenth century, who substituted formal schooling for apprenticeship, permitting a reunion of family and childhood. See Witold Rybczynski, *Home: A Short History of An Idea* (New York: Penguin Books, 1987), 48, 60. Of course, the history of slavery is rife with examples of children being snatched from their parents and raised elsewhere.

15. Walzer is one who makes this claim. See Walzer, *Spheres of Justice*, 239.

16. Poster points out how the assumption that personality is formed in childhood, together with the assumption of the bourgeois nuclear family, underlies the Freudian claim that family history is the key to the individual psyche. See Poster, *Critical Theory of the Family*, 2–3.

17. Max Horkheimer, *Traditionelle und kritische Theorie: Vier Aufsätze* (Frankfurt am Main: Fischer Taschenbuch Verlag, 1972), 206.

18. Poster describes these specific features of the "bourgeois family." See Poster, *Critical Theory of the Family*, xii.

19. Okin points out how in a gender-structured society where females are usually the primary nurturers, personality is subject to a sexually differentiated development of the sort uncritically universalized in psychoanalytic and most other contemporary psychological theories. See Okin,

Justice, Gender, and the Family, 131. Poster analogously observes that Freud's Oedipus complex would have no applicability in those eras where childhood masturbation is not forbidden and where parents are not disturbed by their children's overt sexual behavior. See Poster, *Critical Theory of the Family*, 8.

20. Once this historical contingency is recognized, Freud becomes, as Poster aptly phrases it, the "Adam Smith of the family" (Poster, *Critical Theory of the Family*, 24), who treats the personality formation specific to the modern nuclear family as if it were universally given by nature.

21. Locke, for instance, maintains that because the female commonly becomes pregnant before earlier children cease to be dependent upon her support, the father is obliged to remain married to the same woman longer than other animals whose young become self-subsistent before the next round of reproduction (see Locke, *Second Treatise of Government*, chap. VII, 45). Locke's argument rests upon the questionable assumptions that 1) nurturing occurs within the family of the biological parents of offspring, 2) that the family is heterosexual and monogamous, and 3) that nurturing within the family cannot be maintained unless parents remain married throughout the childhood of their offspring.

22. Poster, *Critical Theory of The Family*, 149.

23. Friedrich Engels, *The Origin of the Family, Private Property and the State* (London: Penguin Books, 1986), 35–36.

24. For a critique of Marxist base/superstructure schemas, see Winfield, *Just Economy*, 59–60, and idem, *Freedom and Modernity*, 142–44.

25. Tannahill suggests this rationale for family organizations incorporating incest taboos and intertribal marriage. See Tannahill, *Sex in History*, 28–29.

26. Although this would still allow for some coexistence of family forms of varying degrees of consanguinity, it would presumably result in the progressive triumph of those whose incest taboos were more exclusive. This could follow the ordering Engels portrays in his account of the genesis of the modern family, where incest taboos first only prohibit relations between parent and children, entailing a consanguine family whose spouses are siblings, followed by a "punaluan" family where incest also excludes intercourse between siblings, introducing a distinct category of cousins and nephews and nieces, and succeeded by the rise of gens, phratry, and tribe wherein marriage becomes prohibited among an ever-extending circle of blood relations. See Engels, *Origin of The Family, Private Property and the State*, 66–72, 128–29.

27. Shoumatoff, *Mountain of Names*, 18.

28. Poster argues that Freud's universalization of the Oedipus complex is challenged by Lévi-Strauss's advance of the incest taboo as the original factor establishing human society. Poster claims that the Oedipus complex is missing when incest taboos structure society by kinship relations, where authority emanates from the tribe, rather than from the parents (Poster, *Critical Theory of the Family*, 25). Yet, even if the social

group lays down the law, parents could still be the authority facing children in their immediate family. In other words, a society of households interrelated through incest taboos could still contain nuclear families in which the dynamics of the Oedipus complex are operative.

29. Shoumatoff, *Mountain of Names*, 18.

30. Shoumatoff points this out. See ibid., 14.

31. Shoumatoff discusses the extended functions of kinship in traditional societies. See ibid., 39–40.

32. As Shoumatoff suggests, the use of "brother" and "sister" appellations in unions, religious orders, and ethnic organizations is representative of lingering acceptance of premodern merging of kinship with social relations. See ibid., 40.

Chapter III. Friendship Morals versus Family Ethics

1. For an informative study of how contemporary Western legal systems have grappled with the issue, see Mary Ann Glendon, *The Transformation of Family Law: State, Law, and Family in the United States and Western Europe* (Chicago: University of Chicago Press, 1989), 252–90.

2. Plato, *Lysis* 215A, 215D.

3. Edward Halper discusses these contrasts between the "contradictory" requirements of friendship and the conditions of exchange relations in *Form and Reason: Essays in Metaphysics* (Albany: SUNY Press, 1993), 38–39. In the *Lysis*, as Halper points out, Plato does not directly provide a positive account of how reciprocity and benefit are reconciled in friendship, but rather indirectly indicates a solution by showing the untenability of other alternatives.

4. Given the dialectical character of the dialogue, which ends without seemingly endorsing any satisfactory account of friendship, the *Lysis* only obliquely suggests the above conclusion, first by identifying the possession of knowledge as the basis for being sought after as a friend (210D), then maintaining that friendship must involve mutual loving (212D), and later proposing that the true friend is sought after for his own sake (220B). The *Symposium* adds weight to the above interpretation in such passages as 183e and 184c-e (where valid love consists in helping the loved becoming wise and good), and 200e and 204b (where love is associated with love of wisdom).

5. Aristotle, *Nicomachean Ethics* 1156b7–10.

6. Halper, *Form and Reason*, 44, 47.

7. In line with the implied consolidation of private domains, Aristotle maintains that by nature complete friendship is directed at only one individual (*Nicomachean Ethics* 1158a10–15). Yet he qualifies this restriction, arguing that the limit to the number of friends consists simply in the largest number with whom one can live together (1171a3–7), a number that shrinks to one when an excess of friendship, passionate erotic love, is at

issue (1171a12–14). Given how Aristotle conflates friendship with the free family, his arguments bear upon whether monogamy is the only legitimate form of marriage.

8. *Nicomachean Ethics* 1155a27–28.

9. *Nicomachean Ethics* 1155a18–19, 1158b10–15, 1161a10–30, 1161b17–19, 1162a16–30.

10. *Nicomachean Ethics* 1156a16–1156b5.

11. *Nicomachean Ethics* 1156b7–1157b33, 1171b32–34.

12. *Nicomachean Ethics* 1161b12–13.

13. *Nicomachean Ethics* 1160b29, 1161b18–19.

14. *Nicomachean Ethics* 1160b33, 1161a2–3.

15. *Nicomachean Ethics* 1161a32–35, 1161b9–10.

16. *Nicomachean Ethics* 1161a3, 1161b30–1162a1, 1162a10.

17. See Plato, *Republic,* book V, 457d et seq.

18. Winfield, *Just Economy*, 13–16.

19. Kant, *Metaphysics of Morals*, #46, Ak. 469.

20. Ibid., part 2, chapter 1, section 1, #25, Ak. 449–50.

21. Ibid., #46, Ak. 469. Kant later does retract this denial, claiming that merely moral friendship does actually exist in its perfection. See ibid., #47, Ak. 472.

22. Ibid., #46, Ak. 470.

23. Ibid., #46, Ak. 471. Of course, this problem would be eliminated if friends all reciprocated in furnishing aid. Yet doubts as to the benevolence and respect of one's friends could still always linger.

24. Although palimony might seem to reduce the difference between friendship and marriage, the legitimation of palimony is open to question, especially if it applies to informal unions that are not equivalent to "common law marriages."

25. Walzer, in this connection, notes how private affairs, unlike family relations, require a "license for abandonment." See Walzer, *Spheres of Justice*, 238.

26. That the rearing of children in the family is contingent does not alter that if it does occur, it enables family membership to proceed without the mutual experience and attraction from which friendship is born.

Chapter IV. Marriage

1. For further discussion of the logic of systematic immanence, see Winfield, *Freedom and Modernity*, 3–13.

2. For a detailed account of these moves, see Winfield, *Reason and Justice*, part 3.

3. See chapter 1, sec. 5.

4. Moral subjects remain, however, liable, if not punishable, for compensating nonmalicious wrongs to the property rights of other persons.

5. The bonds of the family are less amenable to incorporating cases of human vegetables who can never escape comatose life, of individuals

who permanently lack the ability to use language, reason, and exercise rights and observe duties, and of incurably insane individuals. Individuals may be born into families with the two former limitations or be victim of disease or accidents leading to all three conditions at any point in life and family history. Yet once individuals lose the potentiality, as well as the actuality, of autonomous conduct, any residual incorporation in structures of right becomes a purely formal gesture.

6. Once marriage and divorce become recognized as a right, the Puritan requirement that all individuals enter conjugal union, once upheld in colonial New England (see Diana Tietjens Meyers, Kenneth Kipnis, and Cornelius F. Murphy Jr., eds., *Kindred Matters: Rethinking the Philosophy of the Family* [Ithaca, N.Y.: Cornell University Press, 1993], 236), can no longer be accepted.

7. Informal unions, where unmarried individuals live together with or without children, need not figure into the equation at this time, since it remains debatable whether they go beyond the limits of friendship. Once the nature of marriage gets further determined, the status of informal unions can be better assessed.

8. Of course, when an adult relative, such as an aunt, uncle, or grandparent, cares for a child, the bond fits the mold of parent/child relations in general.

9. This will include relations of "affinity" that arise from marriage, such as step- and in-law ties,

10. Among historical thinkers, Hegel most clearly recognizes the confusions in these misconceptions, even if he never succeeds in freeing his own conception of marriage from all traces of natural determination (as patently evident in his retention of exclusive heterosexuality and a gendered division of roles within the household). See Hegel, *Vorlesungen Über Rechtsphilosophie*, IV, 425ff.

11. Bertrand Russell, *Marriage and Morals* (New York: Bantam Books, 1959), 113.

12. The latter capacity for recognizing and being recognized involves separate considerations of physical commensurability and proximity, e.g., that agents have physical constitutions and spatiotemporal locations enabling them to voluntarily affect one another and to perceive and understand their respective acts of will.

13. If contract is considered by itself, independently of other institutions of freedom, which all presuppose person and property, the rights warranting respect have no other identity than that of property rights.

14. Kant, *Metaphysics of Morals*, #28, Ak. 280.

15. Locke, *Second Treatise of Government*, chapter VII, 44–45.

16. Ibid.

17. Kant, *Metaphysics of Morals*, #22, Ak. 276.

18. Okin, *Justice, Gender, and the Family*, 122.

19. In this connection, Hume remarks in his essay, "Of Polygamy and Divorces," that particular marriages would be as different as contracts of any other kind if human laws did not restrain natural liberty. For Hume,

the two governing restraints are that marriage be in accord with the conditions of consent and promote propagation of the species. See David Hume, *Essays: Moral, Political, and Literary*, ed. Eugene F. Miller, rev. ed. (Indianapolis: Liberty Classics, 1987), 181–82. Here as elsewhere, Hume ignores the normativity of ethical community.

20. Okin, *Justice, Gender, and the Family*, 122.

21. Ibid., 122, 130.

22. Ibid., 123.

23. Hegel, *Vorlesungen über Rechtsphilosophie*, IV, 438; idem, *Elements of the Philosophy of Right*, ¶164.

24. Derrida, *Glas*, 195.

25. "Marriage is a contract, a contract to pass out of the sphere of contract; and this is possible only because the contracting parties are already beyond and above the sphere of mere contract" (Bradley, *Ethical Studies*, 174).

26. Hegel, *Vorlesungen über Rechtsphilosophie*, IV, 430.

27. Ibid.

28. Hegel, *Elements of the Philosophy of Right*, remark to ¶163.

29. Derrida, *Glas*, 124, 194–95.

30. Hegel, *Vorlesungen über Rechtsphilosophie*, I, 299; III, 513–14.

31. Nonetheless, crimes violating the body and external property of a spouse deserve a distinct treatment, for the injury to property right is here inseparable from a corresponding violation of marital right as well. Hence crimes against one's spouse can warrant greater punishment than crimes against strangers.

32. Okin proposes this strategy. See Okin, *Justice, Gender, and the Family*, 121.

33. Hegel, *Vorlesungen Über Rechtsphilosophie*, IV 431–32.

34. See Nozick, *Anarchy, State, and Utopia*, 168, 237.

35. Søren Kierkegaard, *Either/Or*, Part II, ed. and trans. Howard V. Hong and Edna H. Hong (Princeton: Princeton University Press, 1990), 63.

36. As Glendon points out, this toleration can reflect the attenuated connection between sexual intercourse and reproduction, as well as the welfare state's supplanting of inheritance and marital property as key fixtures of economic security. See Glendon, *Transformation of Family Law*, 285–86.

37. George Wright points out in one of his many helpful comments upon this text that romance does have a reflective character, involving processes of judgment employing select criteria that constrain the choice of romantic partner. That this is often, perhaps always, true does not preclude the presence of feeling as a constitutive element of romantic love. In any event, a distinction must be drawn between the conduct of a romance, which involves reflection and decision, and the romantic passion that enters as a part of the relation.

38. Kierkegaard, *Either/Or*, Part II, 28.

39. Kierkegaard describes the contribution of marriage in these terms

(ibid., 23), although it must be admitted that the eternity in question is limited by the lifetimes of the spouses and the absence of divorce.

40. Kierkegaard coins this expression to describe this extension of romantic love. See ibid.

41. Ibid.

42. Lasch describes such marriage as embodying a therapeutic attitude, reinforcing American individualism and its utilitarian orientation towards the maximization of personal interests. See Christopher Lasch, *Haven in a Heartless World: The Family Besieged*, (New York: W. W. Norton, 1995), 102, 104, 107–8.

43. Bellah et al. describe the prevailing conception of marriage in contemporary America in these terms. See Robert N. Bellah, Richard Madsen, William M. Sullivan, Ann Swidler, and Steven M. Tipton, *Habits of the Heart: Individualism and Commitment in American Life* (New York: Harper and Row, 1986), 85, 89.

44. Ibid.

45. Kierkegaard dismisses this alternative as both immoral and unaesthetic in *Either/Or*, Part II, 27.

46. Kierkegaard, following Hegel, describes love in these terms as a unity of universal and particular, and of freedom and necessity. See ibid., 43, 45.

47. For an extended discussion of how modern legal systems in Western Europe and the United States treat informal unions, see Glendon, *Transformation of Family Law*, 253–90.

48. Hegel, *Vorlesungen über Rechtsphilosophie*, IV 423.

49. Accordingly, Bertrand Russell can observe that, "To say that it is your duty to love so-and-so is the surest way to cause you to hate him or her" (Russell, *Marriage and Morals*, 95).

50. Kierkegaard, *Either/Or*, Part II, 150.

51. Ibid., 67–68.

52. Judge William's implicit assumption of the conjugal obligation of spouses to be strictly open with one another has plausibility if it is understood, broadly speaking, as the mutual accountability of spouses for their common welfare and property.

53. Kierkegaard, *Either/Or*, Part II, 71, 83, 85.

54. In this sense, Kierkegaard is not off the mark in having Judge William describe marriage as an immediacy that contains mediation. See ibid., 94.

55. Ibid., 138, 141.

56. Ibid., 146.

57. Kierkegaard suggests that it is immediacy's "angel of death," even while equally judging marriage to be the true expression of love. See Søren Kierkegaard, *Stages On Life's Way*, ed. and trans. Howard V. Hong and Edna H. Hong (Princeton: Princeton University Press, 1988), 126, 157.

58. Russell is correct in observing that "the view that romantic love is essential to marriage is too anarchic" (*Marriage and Morals*, 52), but he is wrong to connect this conclusion to the position "that children are what

make marriage" (52). Rather, what gives marriage an ethical validity independent of romantic love is the domestic rights it enables individuals to enjoy as spouses.

59. Ibid., 51. In *Stages On Life's Way*, Kierkegaard observes that it is only timely to marry when one is in love; one is too young or too old at any other moment. See Kierkegaard, *Stages On Life's Way*, 147.

60. Engels argues that not until the abolition of capitalism has eliminated the role of economic considerations in the selection of marriage partners will individuals obtain full freedom to marry whom they choose, leaving nothing but mutual inclination as the remaining motive deciding the choice of spouses (Engels, *Origin of the Family, Private Property and the State*, 113). Since, however, socialism does not automatically remove social inequality and the public regulation of markets allows for significant enforcement of equal economic opportunity, the issue is not the abolition of capitalism, but whether civil society is sufficiently regulated so as to prevent economic inequalities from undermining family freedom.

61. Walzer, *Spheres of Justice*, 235–36.

62. Kierkegaard suggests this in *Stages On Life's Way* (108–9), observing that whereas resolution is not the result of the immediacy of erotic love, marriage, being an act of freedom, is not something immediate, but actualized only through a resolution.

63. As Engels notes, contrasting the situation in England (where the young could marry without parental consent, but parents retained the power to disinherit them) to that in France and Germany (where marriage required parental consent, but parents could not disinherit their children), liberating marital choice from the chains of parental consent does not remove the role of parental influence over marriage unless spouses are economically independent. See, Engels, *Origin of the Family, Private Property and the State*, 104. See also Glendon, *Transformation of Family Law*, 46.

64. Glendon, *Transformation of Family Law*, 35–36.

65. Whether spouses are entitled to demand sex from one another is a question that falls within the determination of the norms of conjugal life.

66. Glendon notes that the West German Constitutional Court (in 1978) and one state court in the United States (in 1976) ruled in opposition to the English and French prohibitions against marriage of transsexuals to individuals of the same former sex. See Glendon, *Transformation of Family Law*, 51.

67. Lévi-Strauss emphasizes this point in identifying the incest taboo as the factor instituting society by preventing the family from remaining an isolated self-contained unit. See Poster's discussion of Lévi-Strauss's position in Poster, *Critical Theory of the Family*, 25.

68. See Poster, *Critical Theory of the Family*, 99, 107.

69. Belliotti makes analogous arguments against the "tribalism" objection to incest. See Raymond A. Belliotti, *Good Sex: Perspectives on Sexual Ethics* (Lawrence: University Press of Kansas, 1993), 245.

70. Ibid., 244–45. As Belliotti points out (245), the "self-development

claim" by which psychoanalytic theory provides a rationale for incest taboos applies only to one type of incest: that of an adult guardian abusing a vulnerable child. It thus does not provide grounds for excluding marriage between siblings or cousins, anymore than between consenting adults of any kin relation.

71. Glendon, *Transformation of Family Law*, 55.

72. Shoumatoff, *Mountain of Names*, 232, 243.

73. Hegel, *Vorlesungen über Rechtsphilosophie*, IV, 448.

74. Shoumatoff, *Mountain of Names*, 231.

75. Ibid., 231, 244.

76. Glendon, *Transformation of Family Law*, 55.

77. Ibid.

78. For an account of these divergent policies, see ibid., 55–57.

79. As Reay Tannahill observes, whereas inbred populations offer natural selection little genetic option, outbred populations provide diverse genetic materials allowing natural selection to provide adaptations required for survival (Tannahill, *Sex in History*, 28). This would provide an evolutionary argument for incest taboos only if marriage were *restricted* to narrow inbreeding. If, on the other hand, inbreeding were one option among many, genetic diversity would still be available.

80. Inherited disorders, such as hemophilia, that do not prevent victims from exercising their rights and duties as owners, moral subjects, family members, social agents, and citizens, are not relevant to right, except in connection with how the extra costs they may entail affect the ability of society to uphold the rights of its members.

81. For an argument that negligence can be a victimless crime, see Winfield, *Law in Civil Society*, 48–49.

82. Glendon, *Transformation of Family Law*, 57.

83. Germany today follows this policy, whereas France approximates it by allowing dispensation for marriage between aunts and nephews or uncle and niece, while retaining a firm prohibition of marriage between grandparents and their children. See ibid., 55–56.

84. Glendon points this out. See ibid., 57.

85. Ibid.

86. Ibid.

87. Belliotti argues against the family breakdown claim as if it had to depend upon adverse reactions of other family members, which may not be forthcoming. See Belliotti, *Good Sex*, 243.

88. In discussing what incest taboos warrant application to marriage eligibility, Hegel maintains that a determinate limit in respect to closeness of relation cannot be given, and that different legal systems have drawn the line differently (Hegel, *Vorlesungen über Rechtsphilosophie*, IV, 449). Hegel's own criterion of exclusion consists in whether prospective spouses belong to the same domestic unity, into which they have relinquished their independent personhood. If they do, then they cannot engage in marriage, which is the *outcome* of freely relinquishing one's separate personality into the joint privacy of domestic association (Hegel,

Elements of the Philosophy of Right, ¶168; idem, *Vorlesungen über Rechts-philosophie,* I, 301; IV, 448). Hegel's argument has little application to adult relatives who are not already spouses, since as soon as children are recognized to have reached maturity, they attain an independent personality both with respect to their parents as well as toward their siblings and any kin who do not belong to the nuclear family. Accordingly, they enjoy the personal autonomy from which marriage can be entered and can satisfy the requirement that marriage should forge a unity of different persons (*Vorlesungen über Rechtsphilosophie,* III, 536–58.)

89. Belliotti suspects that incest among mutually consenting adults is not automatically unethical, but he does not provide the above demonstration. See Belliotti, *Good Sex,* 246.

90. Engels, *Origin of the Family, Private Property and the State,* 91.

91. Reference to social and political position is here used very broadly so as to include communities in which distinct spheres of family, society, and state have not emerged.

92. Tannahill, *Sex in History,* 47.

93. Engels claims that monogamy arises in order to produce children of undisputed paternity who can then become suitable natural heirs to their father's property (Engels, *Origin of the Family, Private Property and the State,* 92). Undisputed paternity, however, is no less and no more secured by polygyny.

94. In the essay "Of Polygamy and Divorce," Hume follows this route after first airing the pro-polygamy argument that men only retain the rule of reason over passion by employing polygamy to divide and conquer, escaping enslavement to any individual woman, sating sexual appetite, and regaining sovereignty within and without the home. In addition to transforming the intimacy and equality of spouses into a male tyranny, polygamy, Hume finally concludes, also undermines friendship (for fear of friends becoming a potential lover of the harem women), and makes a father a stranger to his horde of children. See Hume, *Essays,* 184–87.

95. Engels, *Origin of the Family, Private Property and the State,* 113.

96. Kant, *Metaphysics of Morals,* #26, Ak. 278; Hegel, *Vorlesungen über Rechtsphilosophie,* I, 301; III, 533–35; IV, 446–47; G. W. F. Hegel, *Grundlinien der Philosophie des Rechts,* vol. 7 in *Werke in zwanzig Bänden* (Frankfurt am Main: Suhrkamp Verlag, 1970), ¶167, p. 320; idem, *Enzyklopädie der philosophischen Wissenschaften III,* vol. 10 in *Werke in zwanzig Bänden,* ¶519, p. 320.

97. A full consideration of this possibility requires determining the norms of marital conduct, the upbringing of children by parents, and the modalities of divorce. The chapters that follow will provide the resources for more completely settling the possibility of a polygamous marriage in conformity with domestic right.

98. Hegel, *Vorlesungen über Rechtsphilosophie,* I, 301; III, 533–35; IV, 446–47. Hegel, *Grundlinien,* ¶167, p. 320; Hegel, *Enzyklopädie,* ¶519, p. 320.

99. Further testimony for psychological possibility is provided by cer-

tain "countercultural" communes that might qualify as reconstructed polygamous families.

100. Hume argues that polygamy leaves fathers hardly acquainted with their children.(Hume, *Essays,* 185.) If polygamy were purged of heterosexual male domination, the argument still could be made that all spouses, whatever their gender and sexual orientation, would endure attenuated relations to their children, who might then suffer psychological difficulties from the relative lack of intimacy with parents. Conversely, it could be argued, as Poster does (Poster, *Critical Theory of the Family*), that the intense isolated intimacy of early childhood in the nuclear monogamous family is precisely the cause of the psychological disorders that become paradigmatic for Freud's psychoanalytic theory of personality development. In the absence of any rigorous demonstration of the necessary psychological consequences of either form of marriage, it can be surmised, as Kant would argue, that such psychological reactions are inherently contingent.

101. Although Sir Charles Dilke found Mormon polygamy a bulwark against the concentration of wealth through inheritance (Shoumatoff, *Mountain of Names*, 144), the relation of polygamy to inheritance depends as much upon the social regulation of wealth as does the impact of monogamy upon inheritance. Primogeniture, for example, can operate or be excluded under either form of marriage. Analogously, when Wilhelm Reich advocates the abolition of monogamy as the key to liberating women, children and sexuality (Poster, *Critical Theory of the Family*, 49), he ignores how public regulation can prevent both monogamy and polygamy from remaining instruments of male economic domination.

102. Hegel makes this point regarding the monogamous family (to which he ascribes exclusive legitimacy). See Hegel, *Vorlesungen über Rechtsphilosophie*, III, 545.

103. This latter minimal procedure is, as Glendon notes, followed by the United States Uniform Marriage and Divorce Act, as well as by most states, even though the United States lacks identity cards, permits citizens to freely change names, and prevents private individuals from obtaining information on the civil status of others. Although social security numbers are recorded on marriage license applications in the Uniform Act, it should come as no surprise that the United States has a comparatively poor record in enforcing marriage law and support obligations from deserting spouses. See Glendon, *Transformation of Family Law*, 65–66.

104. Ibid., 62.

105. Ibid., 60, 62–63.

106. Ibid., 64–66.

107. Ibid.

108. Ibid., 67.

109. In the case of legitimate polygamy, this latitude would be conditioned by the agreement of the other spouses.

110. In this vein, Engels remarks that the full freedom to marry is undermined as much in countries with English law, in which parental consent

to marry is not compulsory but parents are free to disinherit children, as in countries with French law, where parental consent is mandatory, but parents are required to pass on a portion of their wealth to their children(Engels, *The Origin of The Family, Private Property and The State*, 104).

111. Engels falsely maintains that such economic considerations will render the freedom to marry a formal liberty as long as capitalist production persists (Engels, *Origin of the Family, Private Property and the State*, 107, 113). He fails to consider how public regulation of markets can ameliorate economic inequality under capitalism. See Winfield, *Just Economy*, part 2, for a discussion of how capitalism and economic justice need not be incompatible.

112. An opposite extreme is followed by naming policy in France, which forbids voluntary change of name, prohibiting marriage or divorce from having any legal effect upon a spouse's name, and retaining the birth certificate name as the abiding legal name of an individual (see Glendon, *Transformation of Family Law*, 106). Since, however, birth certificate name ordinarily represents a patrilineal appellation, the French rigidity does not reflect the equality of spouses nor is it necessitated by the practicalities of identifying marriage status, to which it provides no contribution. By contrast, the British and American policy, which permits individuals to use any name they wish, with exception made for fraudulent name changes, conforms to the equality of spouses but risks compromising the publicity of marital status unless alternate forms of personal identification (such as social security numbers) and marriage registration are rigorously maintained. See ibid., 104, 106.

113. To achieve this end in conformity with the equality of spouses, an ultimately rejected reform proposal in Germany advocated permitting spouses to choose between either the wife's or husband's birth name or the double name of both, with the restriction that no family name can contain more than two appellations. Although such a policy leaves open whether spouses whose names are not chosen have any rights to using their birth name for their children, an analogous policy could be applied to this further round of family naming. See ibid., 108–9.

Chapter V. The Conduct of Married Life

1. Spouses may agree to unequally divide their roles, but this does not involve a relinquishment of their abiding right to codetermine all dimensions of household affairs.

2. For this reason, Hegel points out that joint household property is not something immediate, like the ownership of a single person, which depends directly upon the existence of the person (unless civil law stipulates further testamentary rights), but rather something enduring, reflecting its role as the lasting security for the welfare of the family. See Hegel, *Grundlinien*, 323, ¶170.

3. Ibid.; Hegel, *Vorlesungen Über Rechtsphilosophie*, IV, 450.

4. Although Hegel makes the mistake of restricting marriage to monogamous, heterosexual couples in which the husband is the head of the household, exclusively representing the family outside the home, he nevertheless correctly emphasizes these two cardinal features of marital property, emphasizing how, in marriage, property is held in common as something serving not single satisfactions of one person, but the enduring welfare of the whole family. See Hegel, *Vorlesungen über Rechtsphilosophie*, I, 304; III, 539–41.

5. Glendon, *Transformation of Family Law*, 111.

6. Since, strictly speaking, the nuclear family restricts itself to relations between spouses and between parent and child, both monogamous and polygamous households can qualify as nuclear in distinction to the wider kinship webs of extended families.

7. Early efforts are marred by holdovers of male privilege. For example, the French Civil Code of 1804 simultaneously obliges spouses to provide fidelity, support, and assistance, but qualifies the reciprocity of right and duty by obliging the wife to be obedient to her husband and obliging the husband to protect his wife. Not until 1938 were these asymmetries removed and not until 1970 were husbands deprived of the title of head of the family. See Glendon, *Transformation of Family Law*, 89.

8. As the following discussion makes manifest, it is debatable whether these alternatives are all truly compatible with domestic right.

9. Glendon, *Transformation of Family Law*, 118.

10. Wright makes these comments in his annotations to this text.

11. Glendon maintains that prenuptial agreements virtually always safeguard the property of the economically stronger spouse since that strength provides a stronger bargaining position. See Glendon, *Transformation of Family Law*, 139.

12. As Glendon points out, this right was finally given to French women in 1956. See ibid., 113.

13. Ibid., 111.

14. Ibid., 119–20, 122.

15. The community property regime does, however, leave room for punishment of criminal, that is, malicious, mismanagement of marital property.

16. Hegel describes this situation as endemic to family relations, effectively granting exclusive legitimacy to community property by arguing that family members have no right, in the form of property right, against one another, because they have no property in distinction from one another. See Hegel, *Vorlesungen über Rechtsphilosophie*, IV, 452.

17. Glendon, *Transformation of Family Law*, 121.

18. Glendon cites this case in this connection. See ibid., 122.

19. Ibid., 118.

20. Ibid., 132–33.

21. Ibid., 124.

22. Ibid., 125.

23. Ibid., 130.

24. Ibid., 127.

25. Ibid., 137.

26. Ibid., 134.

27. Ibid., 134–35.

28. A further objection to these regimes lies in the argument made in the United Kingdom to justify voiding prenuptial agreements protecting against the effects of divorce. As Glendon reports, it is there maintained that divorce is encouraged by such agreements (See ibid., 137). More generally, it can equally be argued that the separate assets regime tends to reconstrue marriage in terms of atomistic liberty, transforming the ethical community of marriage into a union of convenience. Although such views may accompany that regime, it is not impossible to offer separate assets arrangements as a means of redeeming the ethical association of marriage from the alleged limitations of community property. Whether separate assets regimes offer an improvement is another matter.

29. Hegel seems to ignore this possibility in arguing that, although each spouse has a right to the family property, the contingency of feeling and nature in the immediate unity of marriage gives spouses licence to enter marriage pacts for their own security. See Hegel, *Vorlesungen über Rechtsphilosophie*, III, 542, 546; and Hegel, *Grundlinien*, 324–25, remark to ¶172.

30. Okin suggests these measures to counter male domination in heterosexual marriage. See Okin, *Justice, Gender, and the Family*, 152, 181–83.

31. Where gender privilege still persists, same sex spouses will more likely fulfill the ideal of a genuinely sharing, equal, and codetermined marriage, unless gender privilege has infected gay and lesbian relations, leading same sex spouses to divide their domestic roles in imitation of traditional heterosexual hierarchy. The commonplace, but contingent, association of effeminacy with homosexuality and masculinity with lesbianism reflects such infection.

32. For a systematic account of this public provision of welfare, see Winfield, *Just Economy*, 183–229.

33. This autonomy of welfare is recognized in the German Civil Code, which empowers spouses to determine what their marital community of life shall mean. See Glendon, *Transformation of Family Law*, 95.

34. Nevertheless, French divorce law tends to impose upon spouses a duty to love one another by making the failure to express affection a ground for divorce. See ibid., 96–97.

35. This is recognized in the concept of consortium in the United Kingdom, which specifies the right of spouses to mutual companionship and assistance without precluding separate residences. See ibid., 95.

36. Okin gives a vivid description of how such social injustices affect the division of tasks within the household. See Okin, *Justice, Gender, and the Family*, 146ff.

37. Okin details the dynamics of how unequal divisions of housework

entail unequal vulnerability to the consequences of marriage breakdown. See ibid., 137–46.

38. Ibid., 152–54.

39. Okin makes this claim, consonant with her tendency to make the division of tasks within the household the predominant cause of gender discrimination at large. See ibid., 116.

40. As would be expected, the Anglo-American separation of assets and the German deferred community regimes violate this imperative of domestic property right by holding spouses liable only for their own transactions, with exception made in some cases for debts directly related to household upkeep and child rearing (Glendon, *Transformation of Family Law*, 140–41).

41. The imperative to treat spouses as jointly taxable leaves undetermined how taxation of married individuals should compare to that of single persons. Joint taxation no more entails tax rates prejudicial to married individuals, such as encourage "tax divorces" and lead to the Swedish policy of taxing spouses separately on a par with single persons, than do tax policies favoring married couples, as in England, France, Germany, and the United States (ibid., 142–43). The determination of a proper rate is predicated upon an investigation of the relation of the family and civil society.

42. Strictly speaking, this point presupposes civil society and the state.

43. Glendon, *Transformation of Family Law*, 142.

44. Ibid.

45. As Glendon reports, one state court in the United States declared unconstitutional any tort of adultery on the ground that it would violate the right of privacy of individuals to engage in consensual sex (ibid.). This and other famous appeals to the mysterious right of privacy reflect the failure of the United States Constitution to have any articles guaranteeing specific family rights. The same failure applies to social rights, which only get a hearing if such tortured vehicles as the interstate commerce clause can be brought into play.

46. Mike Martin argues in this vein by claiming that "faithfulness is a virtue when it supports good through imperfect relationships" (Mike W. Martin, *Love's Virtues* [Lawrence: University Press of Kansas, 1996], 70). Since he fails to identify a good specific to marriage, his "virtue" of faithfulness remains at the level of morality, oblivious to the *ethical* rights and duties inherent in membership in marriage.

47. For a canonical presentation of the problems internal to a *moral* judgment of adultery, see Richard Wasserstrom, "Is Adultery Immoral?" *Philosophical Forum* 5, no. 4 (summer 1974): 513–28.

48. Glendon, *Transformation of Family Law*, 286.

49. Although modern states have not yet liberated their marriage law from restriction to heterosexual matrimony, laws criminalizing adultery have generally fallen into desuetude, while adultery has generally ceased to be recognized as an independent ground either for divorce or for civil action against a third party accused of disrupting a marriage. As Glendon

observes, these developments reflect the increasing public toleration of nonmarital sexual relations, the attenuation of the tie between sex and procreation, and the shift from inheritance to job benefits, pensions, and other public welfare guarantees as the basis for personal security in modern society. See ibid., 286.

50. Ibid..

51. Lasch bewails this denouement. See Lasch, *Haven in a Heartless World*, 11–12, 138–39, 144.

52. Although Wasserstrom observes that "a commitment to sexual exclusivity is neither a necessary nor a sufficient condition for the existence of a marriage" (Wasserstrom, "Is Adultery Immoral?," 524), he offers the instrumental argument that prohibiting extramarital sex helps sustain marriage at least during the period of life when spouses enjoy sexual pleasure (526). As Wasserstrom admits (527–28), such an argument takes for granted the normative desirability of marriage, which he, for one, has no justification to offer. Yet even given the justification of marriage, it could equally be argued, as Russell does, that tolerating adultery can serve to preserve marriage in face of the fickle vagaries of sexual appetite.

53. Hegel grounds the possibilities of marital wrong in the contingency of the feeling that underlies marriage as a *natural* ethical community (see Hegel, *Vorlesungen über Rechtsphilosophie*, III, 543). That arbitrariness, selfishness, and neglect can take the place of conjugal care, however, requires no reference to any natural factor other than the natural will: the faculty of choice that enables agents to will in opposition to each and every of their rights and duties.

54. For a discussion of why negligence is a form of crime, to which punishment and not just compensation applies, see Winfield, *Law in Civil Society*, 48–49.

Chapter VI. The Ethics of Parenting

1. Blustein, following Feinberg, suggests that the natural needs of children "are deserving of consideration simply as such" (Blustein, *Parents and Children*, 116). Given the exclusive normativity of self-determination, life does not have unconditioned value. The natural needs of an individual become matters of right only insofar as their satisfaction is either a precondition for the exercise of freedom or a factor in a certain form of self-determination. Survival needs, for instance, are basic matters of right since an agent cannot enjoy personhood, the most minimal agency of self-determination, without surviving. On the other hand, survival needs may also figure as factors in economic freedom if natural necessities take the form of commodities.

2. Blustein argues that parents have a duty to promote not just the self-determination of children, but their children's self-fulfillment as well, arguing that the achievement of autonomy need not include personal well-being (ibid., 199). Because self-determination and the achievement of per-

sonal happiness are indeed two different matters, the exclusive normativity of freedom deprives individuals of any right to self-fulfillment or happiness that is independent of exercising the different modes of self-determination comprising property, moral, family, civil, and political right. Self-fulfillment and happiness *may* conform to the exercise of these rights, but given the arbitrariness of desire, they equally may not.

3. For a discussion of the relation of universal, particular, and individual and how it bears upon ethics, see Winfield, *Freedom and Modernity*, 51–58.

4. While sharing Rawls's concerns about the incompatibility of the family with equal opportunity, Blustein attempts to secure a place for the family by arguing that child rearing in the family fosters a morally superior conception of self with a greater capacity for love than other arrangements can achieve (Blustein, *Parents and Children*, 201, 217–23). Besides relying on psychological assumptions that have no necessity, this argument offers little support for marriage before, after, or without child rearing.

5. Lasch discusses her position. See Lasch, *Haven in a Heartless World*, 123.

6. See Lasch for a discussion of Mead's view. Ibid., 72–73.

7. See Lasch for a discussion of Benedict's view. Ibid., 71.

8. Poster, *Critical Theory of the Family*, 204–5.

9. Lasch, *Haven in a Heartless World*, 123–24.

10. Strictly speaking, such an argument provides no particular legitimation for marriage, since parenting can be done by a single individual or by cohabiting lovers or friends, whereas marriage need not involve parenting. Even if the desired psychological development of a child depended upon care by parents who love one another, this would still not entail that they be married.

11. Blustein, *Parents and Children*, 218–21.

12. These consequences apply to Rawls's claim that a child's sense of self-worth is fostered by experiencing the love of parents (see Rawls, *Theory of Justice*, 464). Whatever truth this claim may have, it neither guarantees that nuclear families play a privileged role in providing such love, nor that individuals are incapable of attaining elsewhere sufficient self-respect to affirm their own rights and recognize those of others. In this connection, Rawls assumes the psychological principle that the child comes to love parents only if they first manifestly love him or her (463), a principle that is hardly self-evident.

13. Although Blustein attempts to give the family a legitimate place in liberal theory by claiming that the intimacy of the parent-child relation is a prerequisite for the autonomous development of individuals, he admits that whether parental or group upbringing will better serve the needs of child rearing is an empirical question, thereby lacking any universal or necessary resolution. See Blustein, *Parents and Children*, 160.

14. Blustein draws this distinction between exclusive and primary responsibility. Ibid., 140.

15. Rybczynski, *Home,* 48. Rybczynski does not here discuss the connection between a consistently developed civil society and the abolition of child labor, which provides the correlative condition for a universal public education of children.

16. Such antecedent assignment of custody to others might be due to a lack of parental qualifications on the part of the biological parents or to a voluntary agreement to produce a child for custodians who desire to be parents. The latter arrangement would be valid only if the transfer of custody was not detrimental to the child. Alternately, any involuntary transfer of custodial authority from qualified parents would be a violation of their parental rights.

17. Even when children are inadvertently produced by a couple who has intercourse using all available birth control precautions, those persons incur parental responsibility both by having intercourse and by bringing the pregnancy to term.

18. Blustein, *Parents and Children,* 147–48.

19. Ibid., 145.

20. Hobbes, *Leviathan,* 253–54.

21. Kant argues in this vein that because procreation should be viewed as an act whereby parents take the initiative of bringing a person into being without his consent, they are obliged to care for their child until it is independent. See Kant, *Metaphysics of Morals,* #28, Ak. 281.

22. A social welfare system that provides subsidies enabling minors to raise their offspring independently clearly violates the imperatives of child rearing, which require competent adults as guardians.

23. Hegel ties this formation of feeling in the child to parental love and thereby identifies the family as the chief place for the cultivation of the ethical in the heart of children. See Hegel, *Vorlesungen über Rechtsphilosophie,* I, 306–7; IV, 459. To the degree that such love is tied to the imperatives of upbringing, it comprises a spontaneous form of parental care, rather than a subjective feeling mired in receptivity and detached from conduct. Such an active parental love can thus be a matter of obligation to the degree that it forms a necessary part of successful child care.

24. Blustein, *Parents and Children,* 240.

25. Ibid., 241.

26. Ibid. Blustein also presumes that spouses should not raise children if the stability of their marriage is open to question. Yet, as will be argued below, if divorce does not prevent parents from fulfilling their parental responsibilities, Blustein's proposal for requiring spouses to undergo a trial period of marriage before becoming parents (242) would not be warranted.

27. This principle is generally observed by modern legal systems, which no longer allow illegitimacy to disadvantage children from a legal point of view. As Glendon observes, although modern legal systems distinguish between legal marriage and cohabitation, parent-child relations are recognized to involve the same rights and duties irrespective of the marital status of parents. See Glendon, *Transformation of Family Law,* 290.

28. Blustein argues in this vein that "marriage intended to be of indefinite duration is . . . more favorable to the healthy growth of the child's personality" (Blustein, *Parents and Children*, 238).

29. Ibid., 248.

30. In other words, parents have the right to offer offspring for adoption under the condition that the adoption will not be to the detriment of the child.

31. Religious beliefs can only disqualify an individual from becoming a child's guardian if those beliefs are tied to practices that violate the child's right to be brought up to autonomy. That children have previously been exposed to a particular religious upbringing does not automatically bar adults of different religious views from adopting them.

32. In this connection, the objection of the child to a prospective parent on such ground should not count. Any talk of providing children with the right to choose their own guardians must confront the possibility that the preferences of children conflict with their own best interests. Since children are not fully autonomous it is not incoherent to tie the normative validity of interest with freedom and yet make the current guardian of a child or public authorities the legitimate determiner of the child's best interest. Child liberationists, such as Richard Farson, tend to ignore this defining predicament of childhood, as does David Archard, when he suggests that even if children have no right to select their guardians, it is still important to give children as wide a choice as possible. See Archard, *Children*, 167. The same considerations apply to suggestions, such as that of John Holt (John Holt, *Escape from Childhood* [New York: Ballantine, 1974], 157), that children should have the right to select secondary guardians to supplement the care of their primary parents. This "right" also ignores the significance of the basic immaturity of minor children. Blustein points out that any such schemes of private choice of custodians present obstacles to equal opportunity (Blustein, *Parents and Children*, 210).

33. As Blustein observes, prohibiting or limiting childbearing by the disadvantaged only exacerbates the stigma of poverty (Blustein, *Parents and Children*, 137). The same could be said of simply tolerating levels of social inequality that rob the underprivileged of equal opportunity for parenthood.

34. As George Wright points out in his notes to this text, not all biological parents qualify as responsible. In the case of raped minors as well as adults lacking sufficient intelligence and sanity to act as responsible agents, public birth registration would serve more to identify children in need of adoption than to identify the custodial duties of biological parents.

35. Shoumatoff points out how issues of hereditary medical information bear upon the opposition between parents' right to privacy and children's search for knowledge about their biological parents. See Shoumatoff, *Mountain of Names*, 149.

36. "Civilian" here signifies bourgeois in distinction from citizen, i.e., a member of civil society in distinction from a participant in self-government.

37. See Blustein, *Parents and Children*, 127, for a discussion of how a child's knowledge and respect for his or her own rights is connected to knowledge and respect for the rights of others.

38. Since domestic relations are not political, parents need not be citizens in the nation in which they live, nor share citizenship with their children. Statelessness, however, is a political wrong insofar as it deprives individuals of self-government, a mode of freedom to which they are entitled.

39. See Blustein, *Parents and Children*, 119. Similarly, contrary to Blustein (119), duties of respect do not occupy a less central place in a theory of parenthood than duties of need-fulfillment, since respecting the right to self-determination of children entails fulfilling their need for physical health, emotional development, and education.

40. See Rawls, *Theory of Justice*, 92.

41. For this reason, Blustein is wrong in tending to identify children's needs in terms of primary goods. See Blustein, *Parents and Children*, 121.

42. See Jean-Jacques Rousseau, *Emile or On Education*, trans. Allan Bloom (New York: Basic Books, 1979).

43. Compensation is possible, both because the property of a parent need not all stand at the disposal of children (as will be discussed below) and because a parent can remain liable for compensation for injuries requiring continuing care by those who may take over custody.

44. Locke ties parental authority to the period of minority during which children cannot manage their property, with property understood to include their person as well as their goods (Locke, *Second Treatise of Government*, 98–99). What he does not explain is how, in conformity with his labor theory of property, children can have ownership of either, or, for that matter, how adults can come to own their own bodies.

45. As Hegel points out, since children are not yet persons, they cannot be subject to punishment proper; when they are disciplined, the aim is not the righting of wrong so much as advancing their education and maturation toward freedom. See Hegel, *Elements of the Philosophy of Right*, ¶174; Hegel, *Grundlinien*, 326; Hegel, *Vorlesungen über Rechtsphilosophie*, I, 305.

46. Hence, corporal punishment that does not debilitate physically or emotionally is not automatically beyond parental prerogative.

47. Hegel describes these two sides of obedience, arguing that they preclude reliance upon play as the chief form of upbringing, since that strategy gives free reign to the personal preferences of children, which stand in need of an external regulation. See Hegel, *Elements of the Philosophy of Right*, remark to ¶175; Hegel, *Grundlinien*, 328; Hegel, *Vorlesungen Über Rechtsphilosophie*, III, 551, 553.

48. Moreover, since retribution is directed against the malefactor's willing against right, the proper form of punishment is confinement, which duly restricts the will, in contrast to infliction of pain and mutilation, which improperly directs itself against feeling.

49. Hegel argues that parents have the right to make their children

perform household service, provided it is based upon and limited to family care (Hegel, *Elements of the Philosophy of Right*, ¶174; Hegel, *Grundlinien*, 326; Hegel, *Vorlesungen über Rechtsphilosophie*, I, 305). Since, however, children lack the independence to be held fully responsible for caring for others, such service is only legitimate if it serves the purposes of upbringing. Hegel himself acknowledges this when he observes that children have household services to perform as determined in accord with the demands of education (Hegel, *Vorlesungen über Rechtsphilosophie*, III, 551).

50. Kant, *Metaphysics of Morals*, #28, Ak. 282.

51. As Hegel puts it, because children are implicitly free, they cannot belong as property to parents or anyone else. See Hegel, *Elements of the Philosophy of Right*, ¶175; Hegel, *Grundlinien*, 327.

52. As Locke puts it, lunatics and idiots are never set free from their parents. See Locke, *Second Treatise On Government*, 34.

53. In this regard, David Archard suggests, without providing *any* details, that parents should make the family a site where children can participate in limited self-government to contribute to their education in democracy(Archard, *Children,* 164). Since, however, all parents can therein offer children is limited participation in *household* self-management, the training is not really an education in self-government, where the universal ends of the state are at issue. A similar conflation of political with nonpolitical activity underlies the argument for workplace self-management made by Carole Pateman, who claims that such economic self-management serves as a training ground for political self-determination. See Carole Pateman, *Participation and Democratic Theory* (New York: Cambridge University Press, 1970), 110.

54. Hobbes, *Leviathan*, 253–54.

55. Kant argues that parents' right over children is not alienable because a child is not property (*Metaphysics of Morals*, #28, Ak. 282). Yet, Kant equally maintains that children belong to their parents since they can be brought back like a thing to their parents even against their will (#28, Ak. 282).

56. Hobbes, *Leviathan*, 254.

57. Locke, *Second Treatise of Government*, chapter VI, 30.

58. Ibid., 32.

59. Ibid., 33, 36.

60. A right to give up children for adoption does not reduce child care to an object of alienable property, provided the right is duly limited by concern for the welfare of the child. In that case, parental responsibility retains its ethical character, imposing limits upon contractual agreement.

61. For the justification of good Samaritan duties at all levels of right, see Winfield, *Law in Civil Society*, 49–50, 101–2.

62. Accordingly, Kant observes that merely by attaining the ability to be independent, children become emancipated from parental control, doing so without having to withdraw from any contract. See Kant, *Metaphysics of Morals*, #30, Ak. 282.

63. Jane English argues that grown children owe their parents nothing on the grounds that the parent-child relation is akin to friendship, which, in contrast to favors and contractual relations, creates no debts, but instead involves mutual expressions of affection so long as love persists (see Jane English, "What Do Grown Parents Owe Their Parents?" in *Having Children: Philosophical and Legal Reflections on Parenthood*, edited by Onora O'Neill and William Ruddick [New York: Oxford University Press, 1979], 351–56). Although mature children may well have the same moral responsibilities to their parents as do friends to one another, this is only due to the *cessation* of the ethical relation between parent and child, a relation that lacks both the equality and disengaged autonomy specific to moral agents in their interaction with friends and strangers alike. Parents and other adults may equally give care for a child motivated by love, but only parents do so with the special custodial rights and duties that family membership alone confers. Furthermore, when parents do care for their immature children, the ensuing custodial relation hardly possesses the mutuality characterizing friendship. English's account ignores these salient features.

64. Rousseau attempts to capture this transformation in the terms of social contract, arguing that as soon as children's self-preservation no longer depends upon parental care, the natural bond between parent and child dissolves, leaving any further joint living a voluntary arrangement sustained merely by convention. See Rousseau, *Social Contract,* chapter II, 8. Rousseau fails to recognize that what distinguishes the two successive arrangements is not a contrast between nature and convention, but a distinction between different forms of freedom, one involving an ethical domesticity, the other a relation between individuals in their capacities as persons and moral subjects.

65. Testamentary gifts can play a major role in such manipulations, provided civil society has not curtailed testamentary privileges. Engels points to such pressures in describing how in England parents can still exert control over the marriage decisions of their children by threatening to disinherit them, an option prohibited elsewhere in the Europe of his day. See Engels, *Origin of the Family, Private Property and the State*, 104.

66. Walzer makes this point. See Walzer, *Spheres of Justice*, 235.

67. Kant analogously observes that when a child has completed his education and become emancipated from childhood, parents renounce their right to govern him and all claims to be compensated for their child care (Kant, *Metaphysics of Morals*, #29, Ak. 281; #30, Ak. 283). Although Kant distinguishes morality only from legality, ignoring ethical community, he appropriately concludes that the only obligation a grown child owes its parents is a duty of virtue, the *moral* duty of gratitude (#29, Ak. 282).

68. Locke, *Second Treatise of Government*, 38, 40.

69. Kant, *Metaphysics of Morals*, #29, Ak. 282.

70. For an analysis of the subjective limits of morality, in distinction from property right and ethical community, see Winfield, *Overcoming Foundations*, 135–70; and idem, *Freedom and Modernity*, 61–75.

71. See Bellah, *Habits of the Heart*, 89.

72. See Hegel, *Elements of the Philosophy of Right*, ¶173, Hegel, *Grund-linien*, 325; Hegel, *Vorlesungen über Rechtsphilosophie*, III, 547–48; IV, 455.

73. Blustein, *Parents and Children*, 247.

74. Blustein suggests such a policy. See ibid., 250.

75. Okin describes the all too familiar form these consequences have taken. See Okin, *Justice, Gender, and the Family*, 116.

76. The right of siblings thus corresponds to what de Tocqueville describes as the democratic family, where children are completely equal and therefore independent, in contrast to the aristocratic family, where the age and gender of siblings stamps each with a certain rank and corresponding prerogatives. Consequently, siblings in the democratic family, de Tocqueville maintains, can enjoy an intimacy lacking in their aristocratic counterparts, just as parents and children can enjoy an openness and affection when parents no longer follow aristocratic prerogatives of imposing custom and tradition upon their grown children, deciding marriage and career plans for them. See Tocqueville, Alexis de, *De la démocratie en Amérique,* books 1 and 2 (Paris: Garnier-Flammarion, 1981), 2:241–44.

Chapter VII. The Dissolution of the Family through Divorce, Death, and Disability

1. The dissolution of marriage involving no parent-child relations can, systematically speaking, be determined directly following the account of marital conduct. Since, however, what pertains to such dissolutions gets incorporated into the dissolution of marriage of parents, it is more convenient to analyze the two sets of marriage dissolution one after the other, following the analysis of parent-child relations.

2. Shoumatoff observes that the combination of rising divorce rates and high rates of remarriage has created a pattern of serial monogamy, making a form of polygamy widely available to women, as well as generating a complex of step family relations whose frictions and rivalries resemble those of polygamous households (Shoumatoff, *Mountain of Names*, 162, 166, 167). It is questionable whether serial monogamy has any literal resemblance to polygamy, since the only specifically domestic bonds that connect ex-spouses are postdivorce support arrangements of either each other or dependent children. As Shoumatoff suggests (165, 167), the pattern of divorce and remarriage may, however, shake the confidence and commitment of individuals entering into marriage, encourage an explosion of "prenuptial agreements," and make the entanglements of steprelations a central feature of domestic life.

3. Glendon, *Transformation of Family Law*, 195.

4. Another factor contributing to the rate of divorce is the great extension in life span fostered by modern social welfare initiatives in public

health and education. As Glendon reports, from the sixteenth through the nineteenth centuries, death dissolved marriage as often as divorce does today (ibid., 194). Combined with modernity's diminution of the role of kinship in determining individuals' status and economic position (194–95), increased longevity extends the opportunities for voluntary dissolution of marriage, both by extending marriage beyond child-rearing ages when parenting may be the glue of matrimonial endurance and by providing time for multiple remarriages.

5. As Glendon recounts, the French Revolution's repudiation of ecclesiastic marriage in the name of individual liberty entailed that marriage be viewed as a civil contract, terminable by mutual consent, as well as a restraint upon individual freedom that either spouse should be able to throw off unilaterally. These implications were reflected in the 1792 divorce law, which made divorce available by mutual consent and incompatibility of temperament. See ibid., 159–60.

6. Hegel, *Elements of the Philosophy of Right*, ¶176, p. 329ff.; Hegel, *Vorlesungen über Rechtsphilosophie*, I, 299; III, 554.

7. Engels, *The Origin of The Family, Private Property and the State*, 114.

8. Hegel, *Vorlesungen über Rechtsphilosophie*, III, 554.

9. Hegel, *Elements of the Philosophy of Right*, ¶163, p. 202.

10. Ibid., ¶176, p. 329.

11. Ibid.

12. For an account of how this widespread fabrication paved the way, at least in part, for no-fault divorce, see Glendon, *Transformation of Family Law*, 191.

13. Hume, "Of Polygamy and Divorces," in *Essays,* 188. Hume here further intimates that if polygamy is prohibited, divorce is all the more necessary to provide the variety that so enhances love.

14. Russell observes that in Protestant countries, where divorce is readily available, in part as a prophylactic against adultery, adultery is strongly condemned, whereas in Catholic nations, where divorce is prohibited, adultery is tolerated, at least when perpetrated by men. See Russell, *Marriage and Morals*, 151–52.

15. Hume, "Of Polygamy and Divorces," 189.

16. Shoumatoff reports that the Kanuri of Nigeria have a 100 percent rate of divorce, yet retain an otherwise stable domestic life (Shoumatoff, *Mountain of Names*, 162). Although divorce is particularly unsettling for the modern nuclear household, Shoumatoff observes that the modern step family resulting from divorce generates an extended domestic network lessening the isolation of the nuclear family (166–67).

17. For the time being, the issues at stake apply equally to monogamous marriages and to polygamous unions that have been reconstructed in accord with conjugal freedom, reciprocity, and equality. Matters become further complicated when one spouse in a polygamous arrangement seeks divorce from just one other, from whom the remaining spouses may not be alienated. Such disagreement may, of course, alienate the divorce

initiator from every other spouse, leading to a simplified opposition that approximates the parameters of monogamous divorce. In any event, when relations between different sets of members of a polygamous household become fractured from one another, establishing parallel enclaves that may or may not overlap, the unity of the entire marriage is in jeopardy, posing the possibility of a divorce of all concerned, conceivably followed by new marriage arrangements.

18. As Glendon points out, divorce's legal dissolution of marriage has a double function: it releases spouses from the consequences of marriage and enables them to remarry. See Glendon, *Transformation of Family Law*, 149.

19. Russell somewhat analogously divides the desirable grounds of divorce into two types: defects of one partner (such as insanity, alcoholism, and criminality) and relations between spouses. He allows them to complement one another by adding the qualification that no other ground beyond mutual consent need be required except a defect in a spouse (Russell, *Marriage and Morals*, 156–57). Although this seems to suggest that Russell disallows divorce based upon unilateral consent without fault, he acknowledges that when one spouse finds life with the other intolerable because of incompatibility or a new attachment to someone else, the absence of fault does not preclude this signifying a breakdown of marriage warranting divorce. See ibid., 157.

20. Misfortune might be added as an additional no-fault ground of divorce, but it only serves as an independent basis for the termination of marriage if the misfortune makes it impossible for the spouses to resolve to continue their marriage. Only then does the termination of marriage truly issue from something other than the will of one or both to separate. That is the case in situations where the misfortune undermines the personhood of one spouse, destroying the basis for any marital *interaction* whatsoever. In such cases, the marriage termination is an annulment and not a divorce, properly speaking, insofar as divorce can only proceed between individuals who retain personhood.

21. See Okin for a discussion of the injustice that results from treating unequal spouses in a gendered society as if they were equals. Okin, *Justice, Gender, and the Family*, 160ff.

22. For a comparative discussion of this liberalization, see Glendon, *Transformation of Family Law*, 148ff.

23. Among the common objections to fault divorce that are advanced to tip the balance towards no-fault divorce are 1) that fault divorce deepens and perpetuates hostility between spouses, 2) that fault divorce fosters collusive divorces where perjured testimony about marital misconduct shakes respect for the legal system, and 3) that fault divorce serves no public interest by prohibiting the legal termination of moribund marriages in which fault does not figure, as well as the remarriage that could follow (ibid., 191). The first objection is largely moot given how fault can still figure in determining the financial and custody arrangements in divorce settlements and in how considerations of future feelings between

ex-spouses have no juridical claim. Secondly, the problem of perjury in fault divorce becomes diminished when fault is properly treated as only an element in the establishment of marital breakdown, which must be supplemented by other evidence. Moreover, the ease of collusion need not undermine the entire legal system when other spheres of legality escape such difficulties. The third objection has more clout, once it is recognized that marital breakdown can occur without fault, in which cases retaining the empty shell of a decayed marriage does strike at the public interest of upholding domestic right.

24. A perverted example of such a scenario can be found in the recent decision of Cairo's Court of Cassation to divorce unwilling spouses on the grounds of the husband's alleged blasphemy. See the *New York Times*, National Edition, 6 August 1996, A4.

25. See Glendon, *Transformation of Family Law*, 152.

26. That unilateral divorce, i.e. a divorce by repudiation, might tend under contemporary conditions to be a tragedy for the wife that divorce law should prevent need not imply the compromise of the 1975 French Reform Law, which sanctioned divorce by mutual consent, but restricted unilateral divorce to cases where fault figures and the interests of both spouses are protected (ibid., 162). The remedy for the above tragedy is to be found not in restricting the grounds of divorce, but in molding the terms of divorce settlements to guarantee the welfare of the disadvantaged spouse.

27. Among the modern divorce regimes that have widened the availability of no-fault divorce, the retention of restraining hardship clauses (as in the divorce statutes of England, France, and Germany) and mandatory separation periods indicate that even no-fault divorce must meet standards that render it more than an exercise of individual caprice (see ibid., 192).

28. See ibid., 184–85. The Swedish Family Law Reform of 1973 at least has the virtue of consistency: in making unilateral divorce an unqualified right, it eliminates all fault grounds, requires no statement of reasons for divorce nor admissions of marital breakdown, institutes no investigation of the predivorce situation, makes no attempt to reconcile the antagonists through mediation or counseling, and imposes no waiting period unless one spouse is opposed or has custody of children, in which case a six-month waiting period intervenes after which divorce must be granted if either spouse persists with that request (187).

29. Glendon suggests that in the Swedish context, the enactment of unilateral divorce figures as a rescue effort to redeem legal marriage in the eyes of those for whom the liberty of informal union is the height of domestic freedom (ibid.). When divorce on demand is combined with separate property regimes, any such rescue is a very Pyrrhic victory.

30. The German Marriage and Family Law Reform of 1976 reflects this proviso by mandating the foundering of marriage as the sole no-fault ground of divorce, without requiring any actual separation period (ibid., 178–79). The latter allowance is appropriate, for although separation may

serve as testimony to the foundering of marriage, it is hardly a necessary condition for marital breakdown.

31. For this reason, the decision of the Egyptian court of cassation, cited above, is a violation of family right.

32. When "cruelty" is taken as a self-sufficient ground for divorce, the way is open for such absurdities as the case cited by Russell of an eminent film star whose spouse sued for divorce on the basis of having to endure discussions on Kant (Russell, *Marriage and Morals*, 157). Russell concludes that the only way to avoid such situations is to permit divorce by mutual consent without fault and to restrict divorce by unilateral consent to those cases in which some specific evident ground, such as insanity, has been demonstrated (158). Another possibility, which Russell himself admits, is to allow unilateral divorce when marital breakdown has been confirmed owing to general incompatibility or a passion for some one else (157).

33. In this vein, Russell argues that adultery should not count by itself as a ground of divorce since infidelity may just as well be an intermittent and not uncommon impulse that does not eliminate spouses' ardent desire to remain married. Only when adultery represents a preference for another on the whole does it constitute a real breach of marriage. See ibid., 157–58.

34. Although recent French divorce law has avoided embracing perfunctory consensual divorce, it has equally ceased to treat adultery as a fault ground automatically entitling the victim to divorce and preventing the malefactor from a divorce by repudiation (Glendon, *Transformation of Family Law*, 168). This conforms to the proviso that fault qualify as a ground for divorce only when it is a constituent of a condition of marital breakdown.

35. Russell maintains that genuine desertion comprises a ground for divorce since it comprises the end of marriage, while warning that allowing it to so figure encourages desertion (Russell, *Marriage and Morals*, 154). Yet if a spouse is willing to resort to desertion to facilitate divorce, the conditions of marital breakdown would seem to be manifest.

36. A somewhat mixed example is the French 1975 Reform Law, which curtails the freedom of divorce by repudiation in the case of mistreated spouses who are likely to suffer the consequences, while allowing for unilateral divorce in cases of prolonged separation or mental illness(Glendon, *Transformation of Family Law*, 162–66). Although the latter allowance contradicts a literal interpretation of the traditional vow that spouses "take each other for better or worse, in sickness and in health," it accords with the ethical character of marriage, whose conjugal community collapses when a spouse loses rational autonomy or when life together ceases.

37. Kojève points out that the disappearance of love is never the juridical cause of divorce, which is why legal systems that allow for divorce on the basis of mutual or unilateral consent characterize such divorce as one without cause (e.g. without fault). Love cannot itself be a cause, for what matters is not the feelings of spouses, but the compatibility of their

actions with their being as spouses. See Alexandre Kojève, *Esquisse d'une phénoménologie du droit* (Paris: Éditions Gallimard, 1981), 509 n. 2.

38. Postwar German divorce legislation duly eliminated divorce on the ground of "unreasonable refusal to beget offspring," a fixture of the Nazi 1938 Divorce Law (Glendon, *Transformation of Family Law*, 176). Although the lack of any obligation of spouses to rear children makes such a provision at odds with domestic right, conflicts over whether to have children can certainly figure as an important element in marital breakdown once they harden into an irreconcilable difference.

39. As Glendon describes, recent French divorce law has established such a regime of unilateral and mutual consent divorce without divorce on demand or divorce by registration. See ibid., 173.

40. When the report of the Archbishop of Canterbury's Group, *Putting Asunder* (1966), correctly made the breakdown of marriage the exclusive ground for divorce, and then required that courts not take the spouses' own word as reliable, but make their own inquest, the objection was made that such inquiry would take too much time and money to be feasible. A period of separation was suggested as a practical alternative to a judicial inquiry. See Glendon, *Transformation of Family Law*, 151–52.

41. Wilkinson argues that because no strict determination of how fully spouses fulfill their marital obligations can be made, public authorities cannot judge when marriage has failed and must leave it to one or more spouses to judge that the marriage should be terminated (James H. Wilkinson, "A Theory of the Family: Critical Appropriations of Hegel and Aristotle," *Owl of Minerva* 24, no. 1 [fall 1992]: 29). This justification of no-fault divorce without objective scrutiny asks for too much; that no strict determination can be made does not preclude that some third party impartial judgment can be rendered.

42. Although U.S. divorce law tends toward the Swedish deformation by allowing (in at least forty-one jurisdictions) unilateral divorce without fault or formal delay, many states at least recognize that divorce must incorporate a due settlement of financial and custody issues by making the granting of divorce contingent upon the completion of settlement agreements (Glendon, *Transformation of Family Law*, 189–90). As Glendon observes, however, this effort is often defeated when interstate divorces terminate marriage while property and children fall outside the jurisdiction of the court (190).

43. Swedish divorce law treats pensions as a privileged property of individuals that is not divisible in divorce settlements (ibid., 225). This would make sense if a real distinction can be drawn between benefits secured but not yet enjoyed during marriage and assets currently at the disposal of spouses. By contrast, in German and, since the 1970s, United States divorce law, pension-sharing is considered a property, rather than a support issue. The West German reform law of 1976 accordingly restricts itself to dividing the pension rights accumulated by spouses *during* marriage. Nonetheless, a major impetus between pension sharing is the impending inequality of livelihoods awaiting housewives who have no

employment benefits or women whose pension benefits are inferior due to treating their careers as secondary to those of their husbands. In these cases, support issues intervene. See ibid., 217–18, 229.

44. As Glendon observes, the contemporary shift in divorce law to treat ex-spouses as independent equals for whom alimony has no place tends to reduce the difference between informal family and postmarital support obligations, especially when long-standing cohabitations are granted legal consequences not given to short-lived marriages (ibid., 290). In both cases, what is ignored is the qualifying factor of how much marital roles affect the livelihood of ex-spouses.

45. Paragraph 1569 of the West German 1976 reform law mandates the blanket principle that "If a spouse cannot take care of his support after divorce by himself, he has a claim for support against the other spouse" (cited in Glendon, *Transformation of Family Law*, 219). Yet, if the inability to be economically independent is not conditioned by prior marriage arrangements, why should an ex-spouse be personally responsible for further care and support? The right to have one's economic welfare secured is a public responsibility falling to the institutions of civil society. When such institutions are either not present or negligent, providing care to the indigent becomes a moral responsibility extending to whoever is in a position to help. That the past intimacy of the ex-spouse may entail special moral obligations is similar to the situation of adult children and their parents, between whom domestic rights and duties no longer strictly apply.

46. Okin analogously lists as conditions for equal division of property that spouses have equally shared paid and unpaid labor during marriage and that no spouse's career has taken priority at the expense of the other (Okin, *Justice, Gender, and the Family*, 166). Strictly speaking, however, each of these conditions should count only to the degree that it translates into earning inequalities. One spouse, for example, might have followed a lucrative career solely so that the other can pursue unmarketable artistic pursuits, with the result that upon divorce, the beneficiary is insolvent and the benefactor is more affluent than ever.

47. Swedish law, for example, awards the family home and its basic furnishings to the divorcee who "needs it most," usually, but not always, by being the custodian of minor children (Glendon, *Transformation of Family Law*, 224).

48. As Glendon points out, alimony will provide the chief instrument for such compensation among all those individuals who own little valuable property and consume most of what they earn (ibid., 229).

49. Although, as Okin documents, no-fault divorce laws have historically reduced the ability of women to receive a division of marital assets compensating for the unequal earning potential that gendered conjugal roles have imposed (see Okin, *Justice, Gender, and the Family*, 162ff.), the determination of grounds of divorce need not influence the imperatives of equitable property settlements, which could follow the above compensatory norms with or without no-fault divorce.

50. See ibid., 163.

51. See Glendon, *Transformation of Family Law*, 233ff.

52. Ibid., 199–200.

53. Ibid., 221.

54. Ibid., 200–201.

55. With the 1975 law on divorce settlements, France has turned away from alimony and embraced compensatory payment, foreshadowing the notion of "severance payment" for homemaking labors that has gained currency in Sweden, Germany and certain jurisdictions in the United States (ibid., 208, 211). Although such compensation may be thought to better respect the equality of spouses without ignoring the disadvantages resulting from household divisions of labor, many, if not most "breadwinners" may be hard pressed to furnish lump sum payments adequate to redress the disparities in livelihood.

56. The new Swedish Marriage Code embodies this concern by enabling courts to deviate from the rule of equal division of marital assets when inequity would result owing to the brevity of marriage and the inequality in property holdings prior to marriage (ibid., 225).

57. Modern legal systems have tended to limit the role of marital misconduct in divorce property settlements, restricting its application to alimony payment, whose own place has faded with the move to no-fault divorce and the promotion of the equality of spouses. See ibid., 198–99. Where divorce on demand has been restricted, fault has influenced property and child support settlements largely through the indirect pressures of victimized spouses, who can bargain for desired financial arrangements by withholding agreement to a fault divorce (199).

58. Support payments based on fault would not comprise a punitive fine since the payment is rendered the victim, rather than the public. Whereas the particular wrong of crime (where there is a victim) consists in the injury to the right of the victim, the universal wrong of crime lies in the malicious willing against right itself, a wrong that can only be removed by constraining that will by public authority. In the cases (such as in corporate crime) where monetary fine is an applicable punishment, the payment should be rendered to the public, rather than to the victim, since the victim's wrong is already remedied by compensation. Needless to say, much contemporary tort law ignores this imperative.

59. Within civil society, the judicial system is obliged to provide publicly subsidized compensation to victims of wrong when the malefactors are either unable or cannot be compelled to provide due compensation. A system of comprehensive social insurance can be relied upon to achieve this righting of wrong once some certification has been made that compensation is not forthcoming from the malefactor.

60. A variation on such compensation is provided under French tort law, which allows a divorcing spouse to sue for civil damages for violations of marital duty such as adultery, defamation, and assault and battery (Glendon, *Transformation of Family Law*, 214). The unity of marital property precludes such suits between spouses who are not yet terminating their marriage.

61. Although the family home and its furnishings tend to receive special treatment in divorce settlements in many countries, only in Sweden does the law mandate that the marital domicile and its contents be awarded to the spouse "who needs it most" (ibid., 234).

62. Russell maintains that spouses should commit themselves to remain married at least for the duration of the upbringing of their children, reflecting Russell's view that marriage has its justification in child rearing since childless matrimony adds nothing of ethical significance to romance (Russell, *Marriage and Morals*, 158). Unless there is grave cause, parents will therefore violate their parental obligations by divorcing. To prevent this from occurring, Russell proposes that spouses recognize the paramount claims of their children by relaxing the strictures of marital fidelity while banishing the scourge of marital jealousy (160–61). Russell here assumes that the interests of children are at odds with divorce without grave fault, but compatible with a loveless marriage in which infidelity is indifferently accepted. This assumption largely derives from Russell's accompanying assumptions that marriage and child rearing involve solely heterosexual unions and that divorce results in exclusive maternal custody, with a resulting alienation of the children from their father. Only on that basis can he describe a regime of easy divorce as a transition from the biparental to the purely maternal family (160).

63. Consequently, Blustein's call for a special form of marriage committed to child rearing, with divorce permitted only under conditions of exceptional hardship, would lose its rationale. See Blustein, *Parents and Children*, 241–42.

64. Blustein suggests that in our society, the presumption that a woman's husband is her "child's natural father . . . renders it unnecessary for the state to determine paternity every time the woman makes a claim for child support upon divorce" (ibid., 239). The obligation for child support, however, does not rest upon consanguinity, but rather upon the recognized ethical commitment that makes a spouse a responsible parent. For this reason, the divorce of custodial parents imposes child-support obligations without need for any determination of biological paternity.

65. As Glendon observes, whereas divorce policy in the United States tends to promote spousal independence and self-sufficiency without providing sufficient public benefits for disadvantaged spouses and custodial parents, the Nordic countries at least combine a commitment to such independence with family subsidies that reduce the injustice of treating unequals as equals (Glendon, *Transformation of Family Law*, 236).

66. Ibid., 224.

67. Ibid., 232–33.

68. For this reason, any evaluation of the arrangements of divorce settlements in a particular nation must take into account the social welfare policies that coexist with family law.

69. Okin maintains that when the incomes of noncustodial and custodial ex-spouses are equal, the standard of living of the two households should be equalized by transferring income from the noncustodial to the

custodial parent (Okin, *Justice, Gender, and the Family*, 179). This principle is another form of the proviso that the added expenses of physical custody be compensated. If, however, one were to make the more blanket demand that ex-spouses always be subject to income and asset transfers ensuring equal standards of living, this would impose support obligations illicitly extending beyond the burdens of physical custody and those of disadvantageous marital roles.

70. Swedish divorce policy follows the imperative of awarding the family dwelling and its chief furnishings to the custodian of minor children, provided that spouse is most in need of such occupancy (Glendon, *Transformation of Family Law*, 224).

71. This double burden reflects a further disadvantage that Okin points to: that ex-wives with children are less likely to remarry due to the social "drawbacks" of child custody and lower income, a predicament that only exacerbates the gulf in welfare between themselves and their ex-husbands (Okin, *Justice, Gender, and the Family*, 166). All of these inequities in the outcome of divorce only intensify the vulnerability of women within marriage, especially when little escape from domination and abuse is available short of separation (see ibid., 167).

72. Child support, not to mention alimony, should thus be indexed to inflation, as is done, for example, in Sweden (Glendon, *Transformation of Family Law*, 226).

73. As with property and support settlements providing compensation for marital misconduct, fault here plays a decisive role even when the grounds of divorce do not reside in fault. As Glendon observes, because fault still bears upon the issues of custody and financial settlements that commonly figure at the center of disputes between divorcing spouses, fault remains a crucial matter within no-fault divorce regimes. See ibid., 155.

74. In the United States, the vast majority of states duly guarantee visitation rights to grandparents in the event of a parent's death or divorce. See Shoumatoff, *Mountain of Names*, 173.

75. A public intervention should not wait until support delinquents have been apprehended, prosecuted, and penalized to attend to the welfare of victims; instead, the Swedish example should be followed where dependents of a delinquent or defaulting support debtor are paid a "maintenance advance," while public authorities pursue collection (see Glendon, *Transformation of Family Law*, 227).

76. A factor compounding the ease of divorce in the United States is the notorious laxity of American enforcement of support payments for compensation or custody obligations. As Glendon observes, this breakdown in family law enforcement benefits the economically stronger spouse (ibid., 190), who, given the equally notorious failure of American civil society to provide sufficient child care and maternity benefits at home and at the workplace, tends to end up being the noncustodial ex-husband.

77. The 1975 French divorce law, for example, duly makes the heirs of deceased spouses responsible for alimony until the death of the beneficiary (ibid., 213).

78. In systems, such as that of the United States, that favor surviving spouses in inheritance, provisions are still made to bequest a portion of the estate of a remarried divorcee to children of a previous marriage (ibid., 243–44). Although such measures may end up meeting the support obligations incurred by that estate, it is those obligations that deserve attention, an attention readily satisfied by continued payments, rather than a single transfer of property.

79. The surviving spouse, might, however, have taken on noncustodial support responsibilities, provided such polyparental relations are acceptable to the custodial parent/s.

80. Hegel, *Vorlesungen über Rechtsphilosophie*, IV, 465.

81. Wilkinson maintains that in such cases the entire estate, save for personal items of sentimental value, should be distributed equally among all consumers (Wilkinson, "A Theory of the Family," 37). Such a policy falsely assumes that equal opportunity cannot endure some testamentary freedom (as molded by such devices as inheritance taxation), as well as that such global distributions should be numerically equal, rather than graduated in accord with differences in income and wealth.

82. See Hegel, *Elements of the Philosophy of Right*, ¶80, p. 111; Hegel, *Vorlesungen über Rechtsphilosophie*, IV, 464–65, 467.

83. For this reason, Locke is not entirely correct in writing that "the right a son has to be maintained and provided with the necessaries and conveniences of Life out of his Fathers stock, gives him a Right to succeed to his Fathers Property for his own good" (Locke, *Second Treatise of Government*, section 93). The right to inheritance is qualified in two respects: it only applies if the son is still a minor, and a minor child is only entitled to that portion of parental property that covers the expenses of upbringing. Of course, the right in question applies not just to sons, but to minor children of any gender.

84. Glendon, *Transformation of Family Law*, 239.

85. Hegel, *Elements of the Philosophy of Right*, ¶180, p. 333; remark to ¶180, p. 334–35.

86. Glendon alludes to U.S. statutes prohibiting such *inter vivos* transfers (Glendon, *Transformation of Family Law*, 246). To the degree that such transfers involve malice, they warrant punishment, as well as compensation. The latter may be available only upon divorce, or, in cases where the malefactor is insolvent, may depend upon public subsidy.

87. Ibid., 239–40. As Glendon reports, variations still persist in inheritance law, with U.S. legislation strongly upholding the supremacy of the inheritance rights of spouses while French law still reserves a portion of marital property for children (240, 242–46, 247, 249).

88. Ibid., 239. In addition to discussing survivorship arrangements, Glendon mentions lifetime transfers, such as educational assistance to children (239). Only if such assistance took the form of a trust for future expenditure could it be said to fall outside the expense of upbringing.

89. Walzer argues that even in a welfare state, the sharing of family wealth is a crucial safeguard (Walzer, *Spheres of Justice*, 242). This is

certainly true of the domestic sharing that is part and parcel of conjugal and parental obligations. Beyond these relations, however, family aid has mixed implications for social and political life.

90. An irretrievably comatose individual can be called a human vegetable to the degree that life has dwindled to a purely nutritive, vegetative condition. By contrast, an individual who has never had the potential for or has permanently lost all rational faculties, but otherwise retains the self-moving, sentient capabilities of animal life, can be said to be a human animal.

91. Russell laments that any country, such as the England of his day, that refuses divorce for insanity places the spouse of the stricken person in as intolerable a position as prohibitions of divorce on grounds of venereal disease, habitual crime, and habitual drunkenness (Russell, *Marriage and Morals*, 154). Although Russell claims that all these factors warrant divorce because they make companionship impossible (154), even if this were true (which can be doubted of each of the latter problems), insanity's undermining of rational agency makes even divorce an untenable option, since the problem is not one of estrangement but of the destruction of the personhood of one spouse.

Chapter VIII. The Family in Relation to Civil Society and the State

1. Admittedly, it is debatable to what degree the disengagement of the family from society and state has actually been achieved. Christopher Lasch, for one, bemoans how in the modern world society intrudes into the privacy of the home. (Lasch, *Haven in a Heartless World*, xx–xxiii.) However, in order for social intrusion to even be an issue, the separation of household from social and political public domains must be presupposed.

2. See, for example, Plato, *Republic*, book V, 457B–466D, and Rawls, *Theory of Justice*, 74, 301, 511. In Rawls's scheme, where fair equality of opportunity has priority over all other principles except liberty, there would be little reason to retain the family unless family association could be tied to the latter principle of liberty, which is far from evident, given the monological character of liberty. Fishkin suggests these implications. See Fishkin, *Justice, Equal Opportunity, and the Family*, 3–4, 156.

3. The concept of ethical community must not be confused with its communitarian counterpart. As chapter I has argued, the communitarian notion of community involves two fundamental blunders: first, it renders community a formal notion, whose particular roles and ends are left matters of historical contingency; secondly, it absolutizes community as the exclusive framework of ethical validity. The former historicization ignores the foundation-free character of institutions of freedom, whereas the latter absolutization ignores how ethical community itself presupposes property right and moral accountability, which have nonarbitrary, nonatomistic determinations of their own without involving ethical community. Hegel

is the first thinker to have grasped these relations by conceiving right as falling into three divisions, Abstract Right, Morality, and Ethical Community.

4. For a discussion of the pitfalls of foundationalism in theory and practice, and of how self-determination overcomes them, see Winfield, *Reason and Justice*, and idem, *Overcoming Foundations*.

5. Such is the case in Plato's account in books VIII and IX of the *Republic* of the different forms of government as stages in the dissolution of the ideal polis as well as in Hegel's account of historical epochs as stages in the emergence of the institutions of freedom. Both accounts are thus prescriptive histories, predicated upon the concept of the just state, rather than descriptive a priori theories of what history must occur. For a discussion of how this is true of Hegel's concept of history, despite the contrary view of almost all secondary literature, see Winfield, *Overcoming Foundations*, chapter 12, "The Theory and Practice of the History of Freedom: The Right of History in Hegel's Philosophy of Right," 271–93.

6. Precisely because the determinations of nature and of the plurality of rational agents provide the preconditions for all forms of convention, good or bad, they cannot serve as *juridical* conditions from which valid conduct and institutions are *derived*. Unlike ill-fated foundational principles, they leave the content of right undetermined. For this reason, the institutions of freedom can have prior conditions on which their existence depends without compromising the self-grounding, foundation-free normativity that self-determination uniquely possesses.

7. For a comprehensive discussion of how civil society should be structured, see Winfield, *Just Economy*, part II, 87–232, and Winfield, *Law in Civil Society*, 33–173.

8. In this regard, Alex Shoumatoff cites Brigitte and Peter Berger's argument that the nuclear family is "a *precondition*, rather than a *consequence*, of modernization." See Shoumatoff, *Mountain of Names*, 119.

9. See Okin, *Justice, Gender, and the Family*, 17, 21–22.

10. Blustein falls prey to this problem in his attempt to justify the family by arguing for its indispensable role in forging the type of psychology allegedly required for justice. See Blustein, *Parents and Children*, 217–23.

11. Okin's psychological reductionism leads her to the unstated implication that, as Joshua Cohen observes in his review of *Justice, Gender, and the Family* (Joshua Cohen, "Okin on Justice, Gender, and Family," *Canadian Journal of Philosophy* 2, no. 2 [June 1992]: 281), neither single nor gay and lesbian parents can rear children capable of justice, since "only children who are equally mothered and fathered can develop fully the psychological and moral capacities that currently seem to be unequally distributed between the sexes"(Okin, *Justice, Gender, and the Family*, 107).

12. Horkheimer is another theorist who ignores the irreducibly intersubjective character of family, social and political relations in seeking to root totalitarian regimes in an authoritarian character psychologically derived from modern family structure. See Horkheimer, *Traditionelle und*

kritische Theorie, 229ff. Christopher Lasch follows in Horkheimer's Weberian/Freudian path by claiming that the family is the key instrument of socialization insofar as culture must be embedded in personality, which only the family can achieve as the cauldron of personality formation. See Lasch, *Haven in a Heartless World,* 4.

13. Significantly, Fishkin admits that his whole account of the "trilemma" of family freedom, equality of life chances, and meritocratic competition rests upon the assumption that economic disadvantage cannot be significantly eliminated without undermining social freedom (Fishkin, *Justice, Equal Opportunity, and the Family,* 49, 145). Yet, if that assumption is accepted, the problem of the family becomes moot, since social injustice is intractable irrespective of the existence of households. Similarly, Fishkin assumes that public intervention in child rearing automatically undermines family autonomy when the intervention aims at remedying parental conduct that impedes social opportunity but does not comprise a strictly defined child abuse endangering children's health, safety, and basic knowledge of social conventions. (See ibid., 35–36, 71.) Yet, as argued above, such intervention circumscribes, but does not cancel, the entitled prerogatives of parents to decide, within the limits of responsible guardianship, how to bring up their children to be independent members of civil society.

14. Blustein, like many other liberals who see little independent value in marriage, poses the question of the elimination of the family as if it revolved entirely around the effects of parenting on equal opportunity and the formation of the individual personality (see, for example, Blustein, *Parents and Children,* 218). Since marriage can be detached from parenting, the legitimacy of the family has a wider significance. Because liberalism is generally oblivious to ethical community and the different types of self-determination distinguishing family, civil society, and self-government from property right and morality, the positive normativity of the family remains a problem calling for psychological solutions. So Blustein declares, "Ultimately . . . our defense of the family will rest on values presupposed by statements ascribing psychological health to persons who have been raised in families" (218).

15. Fishkin claims that any such programs of "leveling up" are either inefficacious, prohibitively costly, or in conflict with the family autonomy of the affected children (see Fishkin, *Justice, Equal Opportunity, and the Family,* 66, 78). All three objections are questionable, especially in light of the efforts civil society is obliged to make in behalf of equal economic opportunity.

16. As Walzer observes, inequalities in parental love and expectations cannot be eliminated (Walzer, *Spheres of Justice,* 242), but this hardly means that these nonredistributable goods automatically undermine the exercise of social or political rights.

17. Blustein considers the view that "the use of common upbringings to *equalize opportunities* for children is incoherent" because common upbringing instills collectivist values that conflict with "the competitive pur-

suit of private satisfactions" that equal opportunity retains (Blustein, *Parents and Children*, 212–13). As Blustein observes, however, collective child rearing "does not in itself entail the propagation of any particular set of moral and social values" (213). The same indeterminacy applies to upbringing in the family. Both what values parents attempt to inculcate and how successful they may be in preventing children from choosing alternate values of their own are matters left open by the mere fact of child rearing in the family. Hence there is reason to doubt Blustein's claim that a common upbringing would be difficult to justify since "it is largely through the diversity of upbringings in the family system that diversity in values and ideals is preserved" (222). The toleration of diversity is itself a value, tied to respect for freedom, which not all ideologies or cultures respect. On a somewhat different plane, Blustein maintains that "a comprehensive system of collective childrearing . . . conflicts with the structural prerequisites of healthy psychological development" (215). Yet just as the difference between collective and parental upbringing leaves indeterminate with what values children come to identify, so the difference leaves undecided what psychological structure they will receive through the emotional crucible of each upbringing. After all, the products of public orphanages hardly need be more dysfunctional than the children of custodial parents, especially if differences in education and opportunity are factored out.

18. Shoumatoff observes how the Industrial Revolution subverted traditional kinship relations, undermining traditional gerontocracy and the demands of extended kinship groups by compelling individuals to be mobile in face of market opportunities that offered the young independent earning power and enabled newlyweds to live apart in separate households. See Shoumatoff, *Mountain of Names*, 128–29, 132.

19. In this connection, de Tocqueville observes how under conditions of aristocratic society, governed by primogeniture, the age and sex of family members irrevocably fixes each with a certain household rank and corresponding prerogatives, whereas differences of birth prevent romance from ending in marriage, encouraging a proliferation of fleeting and clandestine affairs. By contrast, he notes, under democracy (and one could add, within civil society), children enjoy equal prerogatives and independence, fathers are no longer masters and magistrates of tradition, but simply parents, and marriage and love can freely join. See de Tocqueville, *De la démocratie en Amérique*, I.242–44, 256–57. Walzer similarly observes that romantic love can be reintegrated into the family once the exclusion of nepotism, the abolition of aristocratic title, and the curtailing of inheritance allow marriage to be based upon free romantic attraction rather than economic or political alliance (Walzer, *Spheres of Justice*, 235). This possibility of marrying out of love, however, can become an available reality only if a social space exists in which individuals can meet and romance. As Walzer notes, the need for public intervention to create such a space is anticipated in the *Letter to d'Alembert on the Theater,* where Rousseau proposes a civic ball to facilitate free choice in marriage (236).

20. Shoumatoff describes how Soviet policy in the 1920s provides an extreme example of this in its efforts to encourage the family to wither away by simplifying unilateral divorce procedures and moving more and more of socialization and child rearing outside the home. See Shoumatoff, *Mountain of Names*, 138.

21. For an account of how law in civil society must stipulate family rights, see Winfield, *Law in Civil Society*, 108–11.

22. For a discussion of why negligence calls for punishment, and not just compensation, see ibid., 48–49.

23. Contrary to current U.S. practice, malicious failures to share household duties and resources are not merely "civil," e.g., nonmalicious wrongs calling for compensation, but "criminal," e.g., malicious wrongs calling for punishment. To protect the victims from further harm, the meting out of punishment must include provision for compensating families for the losses they suffer due to the punishment of a spouse or parent. In this vein, Joshua Cohen calls for mandatory shared-responsibility clauses in marriage contracts and for legally enforcing them against domestic shirking, combining tax incentives for domestic sharing with civil remedies as well as fines and penalties for infractions. See Cohen, "Okin on Justice, Gender, and Family," 267.

24. The U.S. legal system is triply at fault in this regard, failing to guarantee all members of civil society legal expertise in situations not involving litigation, failing to provide equivalent legal counsel to the needy in criminal cases, and failing to guarantee any legal resources to the disadvantaged in "civil" cases of nonmalicious wrong.

25. Accordingly, as Joshua Cohen points out in his review of Okin's *Justice, Gender, and the Family*, labor market discrimination, and not just male chauvinism in the division of household roles, significantly impedes family justice. See Cohen, "Okin on Justice, Gender, and Family," 283ff.

26. William Julius Wilson documents how the drastically deteriorating economic situation of urban blacks, resting upon industrial transformations most detrimentally affecting the victims of historical discrimination, produces just such an outcome in ghetto households. See William Julius Wilson, *The Truly Disadvantaged: The Inner City, the Underclass, and Public Policy* (Chicago: University of Chicago Press, 1987).

27. Although part-time employment of minors may be compatible with the requirements of upbringing, the demands of education and physical and psychological development mandate that children should be freed from full-time earning responsibilities to which adults are subject. Hence, with the exceptions of lucrative part-time child labor (e.g., models, performers, etc.), children will ordinarily contribute less than spouses to family income.

28. Engels, *Origin of the Family, Private Property and the State*, 102,113.

29. As Glendon points out, because social assistance programs concentrate on needs and resources, they tend to treat clients as individuals

rather than as family members. In so doing, modern legal systems here approach the ideal of the French revolutionaries: a state to which citizens stand in a direct relation, without intermediaries (Glendon, *Transformation of Family Law,* 287, 295, 298–99). Hegel would describe that ideal as the reign of absolute freedom and terror (see G. W. F. Hegel, *Phenomenology of Spirit,* trans. A. V. Miller [New York: Oxford University Press, 1977], 355ff). Nevertheless, the reality of family life has limited this extreme, as exhibited in how most social welfare programs assume that individuals will need public assistance only when their families cannot provide care and in how families still take a principal share of tending children, the aged, the disabled, and the indigent in even the most generous welfare states (Glendon, *Transformation of Family Law,* 306).

30. Lasch, on the other hand, deplores the socialization of reproduction, whereby the family is invaded by social authorities who therapeutically supervise domestic life as if the family were an asylum for prolonged treatment aimed at molding character (Lasch, *Haven in a Heartless World,* 189). Whether this picture accurately portrays contemporary American family reality, it is hardly necessitated by nor consistent with civil society's obligatory interventions in domestic affairs.

31. In 1968 the French Court of Cassation duly ruled that both the right to marry and the right to work were unreasonably restricted by a no-marriage clause in an employment contract (Glendon, *Transformation of Family Law,* 78). No-marriage clauses, have, of course, been used to prevent married women from achieving economic independence.

32. Walzer points out how nineteenth-century social legislation restricting child labor and women's employment and limiting the length of the working day represents an effort to protect the family from the market. See Walzer, *Spheres of Justice,* 233. As Okin observes, the part of such legislation restricting women's economic opportunities for the sake of the family served as bulwarks of gender inequality both within and without the home. See Okin, *Justice, Gender, and the Family,* 130.

33. This is an important example of how quality subsidized day care can play a role in preventing unequal family circumstances from undermining equal opportunity. See Okin, *Justice, Gender, and the Family,* 115, for a further discussion of the importance of publicly assured day care for child development.

34. Okin shows how the absence of such accommodations encourages spouses to agree to gendered inequalities in the division of household roles. See ibid., 102–3.

35. This is one more area of family right in which the United States falls well behind other nations. Not only is there no federal guarantee of paid maternity leave, let alone paid leave for any other guardians of the newborn child, but those maternity leaves provided by state law and private employers are generally far briefer and less inclusive than what most European countries guarantee every inhabitant. In Europe, maternity benefits typically pay for all related medical care and provide at least six months of paid leave, as well as up to an additional year of unpaid leave,

with complete protection of employment and fringe benefits. See Mary Ann Glendon, *Abortion and Divorce in Western Law: American Failures, European Challenges* (Cambridge: Harvard University Press, 1987), 53–54.

36. Such allowances could partly take the form of a wage from the state for those who care for children or needy spouses at home, avoiding the alternative of affordable child care centers and public welfare facilities. Russell suggests the former approach, with the restriction that payment be made exclusively to the mother, a restriction following from Russell's assumption of heterosexual monogamous marriage and gendered family roles. See Russell, *Marriage and Morals*, 143.

37. Wilson makes these points, adding how universal entitlements are more likely to garner political support. See Wilson, *Truly Disadvantaged*, 152–53. Until such entitlements become universal, rather than based upon a means test, the public and administrative law affecting families will continue to be, as Glendon observes, primarily significant for the poor (Glendon, *Transformation of Family Law*, 295). In this respect, tax deductions for children are doubly deficient: as Glendon observes, not only do they not take account of inflation, but they provide no help to the poor who pay little or no taxes. See Glendon, *Abortion and Divorce*, 135.

38. As Walzer observes, Plato's abolition of the family among the Guardians demonstrates how kinship made universal eliminates itself, becoming a political friendship instead. See Walzer, *Spheres of Justice*, 229.

39. As Engels notes in regard to the political organization resulting from the German conquest of the Roman Empire, territorial rule can be the outcome of a conquest of foreign peoples by a tribal community, which no longer can employ a gentile constitution to govern. See Engels, *Origin of the Family, Private Property and the State*, 206.

40. Ibid., 143–44.

41. For an extended treatment of this stipulation and enforcement, see Winfield, *Law in Civil Society*.

42. Although liberal theorists tend to differentiate government into legislative, judicial and executive branches, this division of powers is erroneous in two respects. First, it fails to recognize how judicial activity subsuming cases under the law is a part of the executive function of government. Secondly, it ignores how constitutionality requires that the legislature be limited by a separate authorizing power charged with certifying that adopted bills are constitutional, a certification that properly first allows legislation to count as the law of the state. See Winfield, *Reason and Justice*, 276–80.

43. See Winfield, *Law in Civil Society*, 86–88, 90–91.

44. This constitutional neglect reflects how, as Poster observes, Western Europe and the United States have never made family structure itself the object of intentional reform (Poster, *Critical Theory of the Family*, 203). Government has instead tended to address household matters solely when they relate to social and political concerns, as in the case of legiti-

macy, inheritance, and population control. See Tannahill, *Sex in History*, 425. Although Article 16-1 of the Universal Declaration of Human Rights affirms the right to marry, no such right is expressly mandated by the French, German, or U.S. constitutions, or in any British statute (see Glendon, *Transformation of Family Law*, 75–76).

45. Sandel distinguishes between an old and new notion of privacy, the former involving a substantive commitment to the ends of the family and the latter embracing the ethical neutrality of the liberal unencumbered self (Sandel, *Democracy's Discontent*, 94–100). In both cases, however, the emphasis on privacy involves a negative conception of family right in which what is at stake is protecting the household from external encroachments.

46. For the text of these conventions, see *Basic Documents on Human Rights*, ed. Ian Brownlie, 3d ed. (Oxford: Oxford University Press, 1994), 21–27, 169–202.

Works Cited

Archard, David. *Children: Rights and Childhood.* New York: Routledge, 1993.

Arendt, Hannah. *The Human Condition.* Chicago: University of Chicago Press, 1958.

Aristotle. *Nicomachean Ethics.* Translated by Terence Irwin. Indianapolis: Hackett, 1985.

————. *The Politics.* Translated by Ernest Barker. New York: Oxford University Press, 1982.

Becker, Gary Stanley. *A Treatise on the Family.* Cambridge: Harvard University Press, 1991.

Bellah, Robert N., Richard Madsen, William M. Sullivan, Ann Swidler, and Steven M. Tipton. *Habits of the Heart: Individualism and Commitment in American Life.* New York: Harper and Row, 1986.

Belliotti, Raymond A. *Good Sex: Perspectives on Sexual Ethics.* Lawrence: University Press of Kansas, 1993.

Blustein, Jeffrey. *Parents and Children: The Ethics of the Family.* New York: Oxford University Press, 1982.

Bradley, F. H. *Ethical Studies.* Oxford: Oxford University Press, 1988.

Brownlie, Ian, ed. *Basic Documents on Human Rights.* 3d ed. Oxford: Oxford University Press, 1994.

Cohen, Joshua. "Okin on Justice, Gender, and Family." *Canadian Journal of Philosophy* 2, no. 2 (June 1992): 263–86.

Derrida, Jacques. *Glas.* Translated by John P. Leavey Jr. and Richard Rand. Lincoln: University of Nebraska Press, 1986.

Dove, Kenley R. "Phenomenology and Systematic Philosophy." In *Method and Speculation in Hegel's "Phenomenology,"* edited by Merold Westphal. Atlantic Highlands, N.J.: Humanities Press, 1982.

Engels, Friedrich. *The Origin of the Family, Private Property and the State.* London: Penguin Books, 1986.

English, Jane. "What Do Grown Parents Owe Their Parents?" In *Having Children: Philosophical and Legal Reflections on Parenthood,* edited by Onora O'Neill and William Ruddick, 351–56. New York: Oxford University Press, 1989.

Fishkin, James S. *Justice, Equal Opportunity, and the Family.* New Haven: Yale University Press, 1983.

Gilligan, Carol. *In a Different Voice: Psychological Theory and Women's Development.* Cambridge: Harvard University Press, 1982.

Glendon, Mary Ann. *Abortion and Divorce in Western Law: American Failures, European Challenges.* Cambridge: Harvard University Press, 1987.

———. *The Transformation of Family Law: State, Law, and Family in the United States and Western Europe.* Chicago: University of Chicago Press, 1989.

Halper, Edward. *Form and Reason: Essays in Metaphysics.* Albany: State University of New York Press, 1993.

Hegel, G. W. F. *Elements of the Philosophy of Right.* Edited by Allen W. Wood. Translated by H. B. Nisbet. Cambridge: Cambridge University Press, 1991.

———. *Enzyklopädie der philosophischen Wissenschaften III.* Vol. 10 in *Werke in zwanzig Bänden.* Frankfurt am Main: Suhrkamp Verlag, 1970.

———. *Grundlinien der Philosophie des Rechts.* Vol. 7 in *Werke in zwanzig Bänden.* Frankfurt am Main: Suhrkamp Verlag, 1970.

———. *Phenomenology of Spirit.* Translated by A. V. Miller. New York: Oxford University Press, 1977.

———. *Science of Logic.* Translated by A. V. Miller. New York: Humanities, 1969.

———. *Vorlesungen über Rechtsphilosophie.* Edition and commentary by Karl-Heinz Ilting. Stuttgart-Ban Cannstatt: Frommann-Holzboog, 1974.

Herman, Barbara. "Could It Be Worth Thinking About Kant on Sex and Marriage?" In *A Mind of One's Own: Feminist Essays on Reason and Objectivity,* edited by Louise M. Antony and Charlotte Witt. Boulder, Col.: Westview Press, 1993.

Hobbes, Thomas. *Leviathan.* Edited with an introduction by C. B. Macpherson. Harmondsworth, U.K.: Penguin Books, 1986.

Holt, John. *Escape from Childhood.* New York: Ballantine, 1974.

Horkheimer, Max. *Traditionelle und kritische Theorie: Vier Aufsätze.* Frankfurt am Main: Fischer Taschenbuch Verlag, 1972.

Hume, David. *Essays: Moral, Political, and Literary.* Edited with a foreword, notes, and glossary by Eugene F. Miller. Rev. ed. Indianapolis: Liberty Classics, 1987.

Kant, Immanuel. *Lectures on Ethics.* Translated by Louis Infield. New York: Harper Torchbooks, 1963.

———. *The Metaphysics of Morals.* Translated by Mary Gregor. New York: Cambridge University Press, 1991.

Kierkegaard, Søren. *Either / Or,* Part II. Edited and translated by Howard V. Hong and Edna H. Hong. Princeton: Princeton University Press, 1990.

————. *Stages on Life's Way*. Edited and translated by Howard V. Hong and Edna H. Hong. Princeton: Princeton University Press, 1988.

Kojève, Alexandre. *Esquisse d'une phénoménologie du droit*. Paris: Éditions Gallimard, 1981.

Lasch, Christopher. *Haven in a Heartless World: The Family Besieged*. New York: W. W. Norton, 1995.

Locke, John. *The Second Treatise on Government*. Indianapolis: Bobbs-Merrill, 1952.

MacIntyre, Alasdair. *After Virtue*. Notre Dame, Ind.: University of Notre Dame Press, 1981.

Maker, William. *Philosophy Without Foundations: Rethinking Hegel*. Albany: State University of New York Press, 1994.

Martin, Mike W. *Love's Virtues*. Lawrence: University Press of Kansas, 1996.

Meyers, Diana Tietjens, Kenneth Kipnis, and Cornelius F. Murphy Jr., eds. *Kindred Matters: Rethinking the Philosophy of the Family*. Ithaca, N.Y.: Cornell University Press, 1993.

Nozick, Robert. *Anarchy, State, and Utopia*. New York: Basic Books, 1974.

Okin, Susan Moller. *Justice, Gender, and the Family*. New York: Basic Books, 1989.

Pateman, Carole. *Participation and Democratic Theory*. New York: Cambridge University Press, 1970.

Plato. *The Collected Dialogues*. Edited by Edith Hamilton and Huntington Cairns. Princeton: Princeton University Press, 1961.

Posner, Richard A. *Sex and Reason*. Cambridge: Harvard University Press, 1992.

Poster, Mark. *Critical Theory of the Family*. New York: Continuum, 1988.

Rawls, John. *A Theory of Justice*. Cambridge: Harvard University Press, 1971.

Rorty, Richard. *Contingency, Irony, and Solidarity*. New York: Cambridge University Press, 1989.

Rousseau, Jean-Jacques. *Emile or On Education*. Translated by Allan Bloom. New York: Basic Books, 1979.

————. *The Social Contract and Discourse on the Origin of Inequality*. Edited with an introduction by Lester G. Crocker. New York: Washington Square Press, 1967.

Russell, Bertrand. *Marriage and Morals*. New York: Bantam Books, 1959.

Rybczynski, Witold. *Home: A Short History of an Idea*. New York: Penguin Books, 1987.

Sandel, Michael J. *Democracy's Discontent: America in Search of a Public Philosophy*. Cambridge: Harvard University Press, 1996.

————. *Liberalism and the Limits of Justice*. New York: Cambridge University Press, 1982.

Shoumatoff, Alex. *The Mountain of Names: A History of the Human Family*. New York: Simon and Schuster, 1985.

Tannahill, Reay. *Sex in History*. New York: Stein and Day, 1982.

Taylor, Charles. *Sources of the Self: The Making of the Modern Identity.* Cambridge: Harvard University Press, 1989.

Toqueville, Alexis de. *De la démocratie en Amérique.* Vols. I and II. Paris: Garnier-Flammarion, 1981.

Walzer, Michael. *Spheres of Justice.* New York: Basic Books, 1983.

Wasserstrom, Richard. "Is Adultery Immoral?" *The Philosophical Forum* 5, no. 4 (summer 1974): 513–28.

Wilkinson, James H. "A Theory of the Family: Critical Appropriations of Hegel and Aristotle." *The Owl of Minerva* 24, no. 1 (fall 1992): 19–40.

Wilson, William Julius. *The Truly Disadvantaged: The Inner City, the Underclass, and Public Policy.* Chicago: University of Chicago Press, 1987.

Winfield, Richard Dien. *Freedom and Modernity.* Albany: State University of New York Press, 1991.

———. *The Just Economy.* New York: Routledge, 1988.

———. *Law in Civil Society.* Lawrence: University Press of Kansas, 1995.

———. *Overcoming Foundations: Studies in Systematic Philosophy.* New York: Columbia University Press, 1989.

———. *Reason and Justice.* Albany: State University of New York Press, 1988.

Wittgenstein, Ludwig. *Philosophical Investigations.* Translated by G. E. M. Anscombe. 3d ed. New York: Macmillan, 1968.

Index